"Few people have the comprehensive book that co _____ for an industry that I would ____ . Danielle Davenport has done that. She is able to take the reader on a trip through history and into the highly volatile dynamics of today's cannabis movement. Ms. Davenport has written a must-read book for anyone interested in the cannabis industry."

—Linda Strause, PhD G. Randall & Sons, Inc./
Randy's Club Co-Founder & Vice President

"I've been in the Cannabis industry for over 8 years and couldn't put Cannabis Inc. down. Danielle's book delves deep into the rich history and culture of Cannabis. Her book is an invaluable tool for anyone looking to understand the complexities and navigate the chaos of this industry. Danielle answers the top questions and provides invaluable predictions for the future of this controversial but healing plant. There is some seriously good stuff in here!"

—Terry Sardinas, Bird Valley Organics Co-Founder & CEO

CANNABIS, INC.

The Journey from Compassion to Industry Consolidation

DANIELLE DAVENPORT

Contents

Cannabis, Inc.

Our intimate past with cannabis and our billion-dollar future

•

1

Introduction

Why This *Book,* Now?

There were never so many able, active minds at work on the problems of disease as now, and all their discoveries are tending toward the simple truth that you can't improve on nature.

—Thomas Edison, 1902

I'm writing this book on the threshold of 2019; and Thomas Edison's words are as appropriate to today as they were to *his* world over a century ago. Indeed, sometimes it feels to me as though Edison was predicting our moment in these lines. The story you're about to read concerns two aspects of the "natural" world that Edison rightly claimed "can't [be] improve[d] on": the plant we call cannabis and an ancient system, hard-wired into our bodies, that responds to it. It's also, in part, a story that *hasn't* been told— because it hasn't yet been lived. And that's the narrative of how cannabis became a bigger, more complex, and more compassionate industry than most of us could have imagined.

In true Edisonian fashion, I hope my predictions in this book will prepare us for that moment.

As its subtitle suggests, this book offers a primer on the history of cannabis and an examination of the value the plant offers us—a value we're just beginning to comprehend. I discuss the work of pro-cannabis grassroots organizations and pioneers in the cannabusiness space and chart the way the industry has transformed in light of—and sometimes *despite*—the interests of big business and political factions. The fundamental question this book asks is: How do we continue both to honor the plant and all it has come to symbolize *and* position ourselves fiercely enough to ensure that big business doesn't own 100 percent of the market share when federal legalization finally occurs? The answer to this question is imperative, because as far as I see it, legalization is imminent.

But let's begin with some recent history.

In 1988, a team of scientists at the Saint Louis University Medical School discovered a receptor, embedded in cell membranes in the brain and central nervous system, that responded to tetrahydrocannabinol (THC)—the chemical compound in cannabis recognized for its psychoactive properties. Prior to this finding, it had been unclear exactly *how* both the cannabis plant and synthetic THC (drugs such as dronabinol and nabilone, produced by pharmaceutical companies and approved by the FDA for the treatment of severe nausea and wasting syndrome) worked on the body. The marijuana plant contains more than a hundred—indeed, perhaps *hundreds* of—different phytocannabinoids (THC and cannabidiol (CBD) are only the two most well known); and the fact that these newly-discovered receptors in the human body responded *specifically* to one of them was no small discovery.

Allyn Howlett and her team at SLU called this new receptor CB1; but naming it didn't answer either of the fundamental questions its discovery conjured: Why in the world do our bodies contain receptors apparently *explicitly* for accepting the THC compound in cannabis? And wouldn't the presence of these receptors suggest that our bodies are also *naturally* producing the very chemicals those receptors were ready to receive? In other words, is it possible that *we* naturally produce chemicals similar to the ones produced in the cannabis plant?

Those questions were answered in 1992—the latter in the affirmative. That year in Israel, Dr. Raphael Mechoulam, along with doctors William Devane and Lumir Hanus, identified and isolated the first endogenous cannabinoid (or endocannabinoid), which they named after the plant—*cannabis sativa*—that led to its discovery. It turned out that the human body *does* make its own neurotransmitters, a "human version" of THC. (Endogenous means "produced or synthesized within.") And while these neurotransmitters don't have the *same* chemical structure as THC—it's similar, but not identical—they bind to the same receptors and exhibit the same effects in the human body as the compound found in the cannabis plant.

A compound, mind you, that was stigmatized long before it was understood.

In other words, the human body—and in fact, the bodies of *all* mammals and *all* vertebrates—contains a system that is *uniquely equipped* to respond to the cannabis plant. We're hard-wired for it—which not only explains why cannabis exhibits such a vast range of healing properties; it also explains why cannabis *doesn't* produce the same toxic effects on our bodies that pharmaceutical drugs produce.

Dr. Mechoulam and his colleagues called their newly-discovered endocannabinoid "anandamide." (The Sanskrit word *ananda* means "eternal bliss" or "divine joy.") Three years later, in 1995, scientists in the same lab discovered a *second* endocannabinoid, which they called "2-arachidonylglycerol" (2-AG). When synthesized and released, both naturally-produced compounds activate the endocannabinoid receptors (CB1 and a later-discovered CB2) that we now know are some of the most abundant neuroreceptors in the brain. These same receptors, when activated by *phyto*cannabinoids (the cannabinoids in the plant, as opposed to the *endo*cannabinoids we naturally generate) produce both the psychoactive and therapeutic effects humans have observed in marijuana over millennia.

Literally, millennia.

So it came as a rather unsurprising revelation to many of us that our own endocannabinoid system produces similar therapeutic effects to the ones humans have been observing in cannabis since the ancient world.

Indeed, these two discoveries—of the cannabinoid receptors CB1 and CB2, and of the endocannabinoids *themselves*—opened the doors of possibility that cannabis could become our new modern medicine—possibly even something of a panacea. While they're among the most underreported developments in modern science, they're also among the most exhilarating: in terms of our understanding of the human body, its healing mechanisms, and the medical potential of an all-natural, non-synthetic, un-trademark-able plant.

After all, all the cannabis plant is doing is triggering *an entire internal system pre-adapted to receive it.* And now that this relationship has been clarified, a whole new realm of research has been similarly triggered. According to Antonio Waldo Zuardi of the Department of Neurology, Psychiatry, and Medical Psychology at the University of São Paulo, Brazil, in the 15 years after the first cloning of the CB1 receptor, 5,935 cannabis-related studies were published. (Compare that to the 273 studies published in the 15-year period between 1955–1969.)

Zuardi's review was submitted in 2005. Ten years later, renowned integrative medicine physician Dr. Dustin Sulak wrote, "At the time of this writing (February 2015), a PubMed search for scientific journal articles published in the last 20 years containing the word 'cannabis' revealed 8,637 results. Add the word 'cannabinoid,' and the results increase to 20,991 articles. That's an average of more than two scientific publications per day over the last 20 years! These numbers not only illustrate the present scientific interest and financial investment in understanding more about cannabis and its components ... they also emphasize the need for high quality reviews and summaries."

These publication numbers alone suggest the degree to which the discovery of the human endocannabinoid system has caused a stir in the medical world.

Frustratingly, the "high quality reviews and summaries" Dr. Sulak called for are hampered by the fact that cannabis remains classified by the U.S. government as a Schedule I drug. Drugs classified under this schedule are considered to have a high potential for abuse and addiction and to have no valid medical use—a wholly ironic description of cannabis in light of the fact that the government maintains a *patent* on the plant, even as it claims it's both medically useless and potentially harmful. (I'll say more about this patent later.) The Schedule I classification is one that individual, cannabis-legal states are doing their best to work around. Lawmakers in many of these states recognize the need for further study. Indeed, that this series of discoveries about our endocannabinoid system is so recent means there's still a great deal of research to be done in order to fully comprehend it.

What we *do* know is that the endocannabinoid system is a remarkably rich system—and not only *rich*, but *ancient*. Scientists now estimate that it evolved in the most primitive animals over 600 million years ago.

We also know—and this is paramount—that *the endocannabinoid system plays a key role in homeostasis*. Indeed, cannabinoids support and promote homeostasis at virtually every level of bio-logical life. And I think it's worth summarizing *how*, exactly, that system works in this introduction—because understanding the powerful degree to which cannabis (whether used recreationally or medically) can positively impact our health will give us a better understanding of the ways in which this industry is set to explode once enough studies have confirmed what *initial* studies have already shown.

If you remember anything about your high school biology class, you probably remember that homeostasis is one of the most fundamental biological concepts. Homeostasis refers to the body's maintenance of a stable, steady *internal* environment, regardless of fluctuations in its *external* environment. It's how we adapt to environmental changes and respond to stress in increasingly hostile external conditions, from embryonic implantation on our mothers' uteri, to childhood and adolescent growth, to injury-response as adults. In fact, endocannabinoids are naturally present in breast milk to encourage homeostasis from the beginning, promoting regular sleep patterns, healthy metabolisms, and strong immune systems, among other things. It's our body's tendency toward homeostasis, across systems—because only when they're in balance can each of our systems, and every one of our functions, perform at maximum capacity.

The set of exquisite mechanisms that homeostasis utilizes allows us to maintain what we might think of as "the Goldilocks zone" of "*just* right": responding to stressful conditions in a low-impact, sustainable manner; defending ourselves from disease; healing more quickly; and ensuring our overall survival. In the Goldilocks zone, our body temperatures and blood sugar levels are neither too high nor too low; infections are warded off and toxins are released; the acids and bases in our bodies are properly regulated; calcium levels in the blood are maintained (neither "too much" nor "too little"), as are water percentages in our individual cells. And so on.

So which systems in the human body are homeostatically regulated? The *long* answer is the cardiovascular, digestive, endocrine, excretory, immunological, nervous, musculoskeletal, integumentary, reproductive, circulatory, and respiratory systems. The *short* answer? All of them.

Now here's the thing: Endocannabinoids and their receptors have been discovered *in all of these systems*. They're spread throughout the nervous system. They're in our brains, our internal organs, our glands, our nerves, our connective tissues, our blood stream, our immune cells. They can be found along the entire axis of our spinal cords. There are even cannabinoid receptors located in our skin.

In fact, scientists believe that cannabinoid receptors represent *the most widespread* receptor system in our bodies.

So what does this all mean for the medical (or health-and-wellness) possibilities of cannabis ... and for the future of the cannabis industry as a whole?

Well, for one, it means that the very system receptive to the compounds in the cannabis plant is responsible for maintaining optimum performance in just about every biological process and physiologic system in the human body: pain, metabolic regulation, appetite, bone growth, immune functions, cardiovascular functions, energy metabolism, sleep. But the system doesn't only regulate us *physiologically*; it also regulates our mood—mediating emotions like aggression, for example, or inhibiting the kind of excessive excitation that produces stress, anxiety, and depression.

What's more, because endocannabinoid receptors are located at the *intersection* of our bodies' various systems, they allow different cell types to biochemically communicate and coordinate with one another to ensure proper maintenance of the whole, integrated body. And while the endocannabinoid system performs different *tasks* in every tissue, the goal is always the same: homeostasis—drawing our systems gently back into the Goldilocks zone of "just right," recalibrating us whenever we shift out of balance.

Given all this, you may be wondering if the phytocannabinoids in the cannabis plant have the potential to alleviate—if not cure—the vast majority of ailments, illnesses, and diseases out there.

I wonder it often. And the studies, so far, spell promise.

The endocannabinoid system is made up of three key components, two of which I've already mentioned:

- **Cannabinoid receptors**, which are located on the surface of our cells. CB1 is predominantly expressed in the brain, central nervous system, connective tissues, gonads, glands, and organs; CB2 is predominantly expressed in the immune system. These aren't the only receptors; but they *are* the best-studied ones.
- **Endocannabinoids** (anandamide and 2-AG, though there are others), the fat-like molecular neurotransmitters the body produces within cell membranes to *activate* cannabinoid receptors.
- **Metabolic enzymes**, which break down the endocannabinoids after they've done the work of homeostatic regulation.

When something is out of balance in our bodies—and *only* then—the system kicks in. Endocannabinoids are synthesized and released, locally and on demand, from fat cells when the body's neurons are activated by changing conditions. They then act as chemical messengers, traveling to the receptors, which sit on the surface of our cells and "listen" to conditions outside of it. When the endocannabinoids arrive and bind to the receptors, the appropriate cellular response is kick-started. Once the work is done, and homeostasis is achieved, the metabolic enzymes—the third components of the system—break the endocannabinoids down.

(The two biggest enzymes, fatty acid amide hydrolase (FAAH) and monoacylglycerol lipase (MAGL), break down anandamide and 2-AG, respectively.)

In other words, the enzymes ensure that the endocannabinoids are used *only* when they're needed, and for no longer than necessary. This makes endocannabinoids different from other biological molecules, which get stored in the body for later use. We're talking a *literally* on-demand system—temporarily activated in response to homeostatic deviations and arrested when the body's balance is once again achieved.

Interestingly enough, the cannabis plant has its own analogous "endocannabinoid system" that—like *our* system—serves to promote the plant's health and prevent disease. Phytocannabinoids such as THC have antioxidant properties that protect the plant's leaves and flowers from excessive ultraviolet radiation. These phytocannabinoids neutralize the harmful free radicals that the sun's UV rays might otherwise generate in the plant. And if you know anything about the effects free radicals have on *human* bodies, you know they damage cells, cause illnesses such as cancer, accelerate the aging process, and impair healing.

Indeed, one of the most exciting possibilities for medical cannabis—and an example of how homeostatic regulation is essential to the body's well-being—is in the field of cancer. Autophagy ("self-eating") is the process by which our cells create membranes that hunt out diseased or dead cells, digest and recycle them, and use the resulting molecules either for energy, or to make new cell parts. It's the body's internal recycling program ... and unsurprisingly, it's mediated by the endocannabinoid system. When it's working correctly, the autophagic process keeps normal, *healthy* cells alive; but, as Dr. Sulak writes, "it has a deadly effect on malignant tumor cells, causing them to consume themselves in a programmed cellular suicide. The death of cancer cells, of course, promotes homeostasis and survival at the level of the entire organism."

Or take the case of inflammation—the natural protective reactions our immune systems create in response to injury or bacterial infection. In such cases, pro-inflammatory fluid and immune cells move into the site of injury or infection to remove damaged tissue or pathogens (germs). If our immune systems get activated for *too long*, this can result in chronic inflammation; and if our systems inappropriately direct themselves toward *healthy* cells, we run the risk of autoimmune disorders. That's why the body releases endocannabinoids *along with* those pro-inflammatory molecules— to limit the immune system's signals and ensure the inflammatory response isn't excessive. This is yet another example of how our endocannabinoid systems support homeostatic regulation.

As Doctor Prakash Nagarkatti, Vice President of Research and Distinguished Professor of Pathology, Microbiology, and Immunology at the University of South Carolina, writes: "Most of our research demonstrates that endocannabinoids are produced upon activation of immune cells and may help regulate the immune response by acting as anti-inflammatory agents. Thus, interventions that manipulate the metabolism or production of endocannabinoids may serve as a novel treatment modality against a wide range of inflammatory disease."

One final example of the importance of endocannabinoids in homeostasis concerns pain regulation. As you'll soon hear, cannabis has been used by botanists and physicians as a pain reliever for millennia. We know *now* that when THC makes its way into our endocannabinoid system and connects with CB1, it "relieves" pain by modulating and reducing the pain signals being sent to the brain from the site of stress or injury.

It turns out that our *human* cannabinoids perform the same function. In an injury, for example, cannabinoids are produced on demand to moderate the release of sensitizers and activators from the injured tissue. This not only stabilizes the nerve cells to ensure they're not excessively firing; it also calms *nearby* immune cells (the ones I just discussed) to prevent the excessive release of pro-inflammatory substances. In short, it dials the pain down, reduces nerve stimulation, and keeps our systems from overreacting in response to injury (and from feeling more physical pain than we otherwise would).

Studies and clinical trials even suggest that the calming affect the cannabinoid system produces is crucial to preventing the uncontrolled electrical activity in the neurons which leads to seizures in epilepsy. Our CB1 and CB2 receptors detect when the cells are overstimulated, and endocannabinoids are synthesized on demand to modulate neuronal activity, so the receiving nerve cells can quiet down.

As I'll discuss in the next chapter, ancient texts from cultures such as China and Greece suggest that preparations containing *cannabis indica* were often prescribed by physicians and botanists to ameliorate pain. And now that we've got a better understanding of how our own cannabinoid systems *respond* to pain, we can not only justify these early cultures' empirically-founded hypotheses about the plant, we also possess a greater awareness—call it a hope, coupled with expectation—of the ways cannabis may be the very grounds for significant breakthroughs in the medical arena of pain treatment.

Why is the need for new pain treatments so pressing at this historical juncture? Because overdoses from narcotic painkillers— the opioids we call "conventional medical care"—*are presently the leading cause of death among Americans under the age of 50.*

Now here's the thing: You can't overdose on cannabis. And *not only* can you not overdose on it, but medical marijuana has been shown to be more effective in treating pain than the pharmaceutical painkillers being pushed by the medical industry—the ones that are effectively killing Americans at the rate of *one person every 19 minutes.* (I'll let you sit with that number for a minute. The vast majority of those prescription overdoses are accidental.) Indeed, in an article handily titled "Prescription Painkiller Deaths Fall in Medical Marijuana States," Kathryn Doyle writes, "In states with a medical marijuana law, overdose deaths from opioids like morphine, oxycodone and heroin decreased by an average of 20 percent after one year, 25 percent by two years and up to 33 percent by years five and six."

The opioid addiction crisis has reached such an alarming state that even the American Society for Addiction Medicine—an organization that has by no means been an advocate for cannabis decriminalization—has recently been willing to acknowledge that opioid overdose death rates are radically lower in states that have legalized marijuana.

Doctor Joseph Mercola writes:

> Research clearly confirms that cannabis is safer and less toxic than many prescription drugs. This includes liver and kidney toxicity, gastrointestinal damage, nerve damage and death. Moreover, cannabinoids often work when pharmaceutical drugs fail, so not only is cannabis safer but it's typically more effective. Besides treating intractable seizures, one of the strongest areas of research regarding marijuana's health benefits is pain control. In 2010, the Center for Medical Cannabis Research released a report on 14 clinical studies about the use of marijuana for pain, most of which were FDA-approved, double-blind and placebo-controlled. The report revealed that marijuana not only controls pain but in many cases, it does so better than pharmaceutical alternatives. If you compare opioids to marijuana, marijuana is unquestionably

safer. Contrary to opioids, a cannabis overdose cannot kill you because there are no cannabinoid receptors in your brain stem, the region of your brain that controls your heartbeat and respiration.

Dr. Margaret Gedde, a Stanford-trained pathologist, founder of the Clinicians' Institute of Cannabis Medicine, and award-winning researcher, described medical cannabis' superiority to pharmaceutical pain medications in an interview:

> So many pain medications are damaging to the stomach, to the gut. The cannabis doesn't hurt the gut. It helps heal the gut. People are so relieved. They say 'Oh. This isn't going to hurt me. It's actually going to help my stomach.' There's nothing else that does that. It won't hurt the organs. It won't hurt the liver. It won't hurt the kidneys. The Ibuprofen, for months and years... people can't stay on that. They can stay on the cannabis. As we know as well, there is no known lethal dose for cannabis, whether it's THC or CBD. A person couldn't die from it even if they were trying really, really hard.

I'm writing this book—and you're probably reading it—in the midst of our American opioid crisis. But my hope—and my prediction—is that we're currently at its height; and as decriminalization, legalization, and standardization become the norm, cannabis will become the antidote to our current emergency. Because while our bodies are clearly *not*—and never *have been*—equipped to respond to the chemicals prescribed to us by the pharmaceutical industry, we now know we *are* uniquely equipped to respond to the phytocannabinoids in cannabis. Surely this is the reason the plant has been touted as a kind of "cure-all" by so many in the industry. As Dr. Sulak writes, "This one herb and its variety of therapeutic compounds seem to affect every aspect of our bodies and minds. How is this possible? [...] How can one herb help so many different conditions? How can it provide both palliative and curative actions? How can it be so safe while offering such powerful effects?" Dr. Sulak straddles the medical and cannabis industries, so he knows the answer to his own questions. *All* diseases, after all, are consequences of a biochemical imbalance of some kind. And those biochemical imbalances are precisely what cannabinoids restore. (Remember: homeostasis.)

If you can even *begin* to imagine all the ways the human body needs to regulate itself over the course of a single day—in a perpetual life-or-death game of restoring balance—you can also begin to imagine the range of conditions it might be tending to. Some of them I've mentioned above. In his "Introduction to the Endocannabinoid System," Dr. Sulak writes:

> In one day I might see cancer, Crohn's disease, epilepsy, chronic pain, multiple sclerosis, insomnia, Tourette syndrome and eczema, just to name a few. All of these conditions have different causes, different physiologic states, and vastly different symptoms. The patients are old and young. Some are undergoing conventional therapy. Others are on a decidedly alternative path. Yet despite their differences, almost all of my patients would agree on one point: cannabis helps their condition.

Indeed, if I *were* writing a book on cannabis remedies, preclinical and clinical trials, affirmative initial findings, and apparent cures, it would be a lengthy one. Despite the fact that research on medical cannabis has been so limited by its Schedule I classification, the studies that *have* been done—and continue to be done—repeatedly confirm that medical marijuana provides support, alleviation, or functions as a remedy for a vast range of conditions and diseases.

Both phytocannabinoids and human cannabinoids are analgesics (pain relievers) and antispasmodic agents. Cannabis has been used as antiemetic for millennia—indeed, a synthetic form of THC, dronabinol (trade name Marinol) was approved by the FDA in 1985 for the nausea and vomiting experienced by cancer patients undergoing chemotherapy. It was then approved by the FDA in 1992 for the treatment of "wasting syndrome"— the unwanted weight loss experienced by patients with AIDS. (As anyone who smoked weed in high school might remember, THC is an appetite stimulant.) Extensive preclinical research—much of which has been sponsored by the U.S. government and resulted in that government patent I mentioned—offers evidence for CBD's antioxidant, anti-tumoral, anticonvulsant, anxiolytic (anxiety-reducing), anti-angiogenic (cutting off a tumor's blood supply), and neuroprotective properties.

Schizophrenia. PTSD. Tourette syndrome. Unbalanced sleep cycles and out-of-whack circadian rhythms. Intestinal motility disorders. Rheumatoid arthritis. Depression. Panic attacks. Spasticity. Heart disease. Amyotrophic lateral sclerosis (ALS). Autism. Asthma. High blood pressure. Glaucoma. Epilepsy. Chronic fatigue syndrome. Withdrawal symptoms in those attempting to wean themselves off alcohol and opioids.

Cannabis has been found useful in the treatment of all these things. And believe it or not, this is only a shortlist.

What's more, *deficiencies* in our own endocannabinoid systems have been implicated in migraines, fibromyalgia, irritable bowel syndrome (IBS), schizophrenia, depression, anorexia, multiple sclerosis (MS), Parkinson's disease, Huntington's disease, and more. The fact that there are naturally-occurring *phyto*cannabinoids that could potentially supplement for these deficiencies may vastly change the course of the medical industry.

I've opened this book by describing our own physiological capacities to respond specifically to the cannabis plant because these revelations about our bodies seemed to me to be a turning point in the cannabis industry. At least, I believe that we'll look back on it as such. Granted, there's been pushback against the federal government's classification of cannabis as a Schedule I drug since the 60's counterculture took up the fight; and the series of statewide decriminalization measures (I'm writing this after the 2018 midterms: Medical marijuana is now legal in 33 states and Washington, D.C.; recreational marijuana is legal in 10 states and D.C.) has kept the debate at the forefront of our political and cultural conversations for years. But my sense is that the strides being made in our knowledge of the human body is one of the primary factors that will speed along the growth of an industry that has already managed to grow to robust proportions—*despite* the fact that its object is illegal at the federal level.

After all, we now know the mechanisms cannabis drives in the body. The two largest physicians' associations in America—the American Medical Association (AMA) and the American College of Physicians (ACP)—are calling loudly for more research. They're backed by a 6,000-year history of cannabis' safe therapeutic use and strong proof and promising results in early scientific studies. The public is *also* demanding it, even in the face of the DEA's best efforts to discourage such research. We are living, working, and raising families in increasingly toxic, carcinogenic environments; and we'll need all the adaptive support we can get from our homeostatic mechanisms—which will mean additional, external support from phytocannabinoids.

Our world is only getting more difficult to remain healthy in. And we want both treatments and *preventative* options that are natural, safe, and inexpensive.

These are the driving forces moving us toward a rescheduling of the plant, or a *de*scheduling altogether (cannabis *is*, after all, the *only* plant on the DEA's schedule), and a new set of physiologically-grounded initiatives and inquiries into cannabis-based interventions.

In other words, the stage is set. *That's* why this book, now.

In the following pages, I'll be telling a story about cannabis that's hardly complete. I'm offering four stages here—four "chapters" of the story of cannabis, rolled up into three *book* chapters—and we're just now somewhere in the second stage. Those stages are: compassion, chaos, competitive advantage, and consolidation … though my hope is that the *first* stage—the compassion component—will persist through the remaining stages.

I see those final two stages playing out within the next ten years—an accelerated pace based on "the merger endgames curve" (also known as "the consolidation curve"; I'll discuss this at length in the final chapter). My prediction is based on several decades of business in mergers and acquisitions, and 10 years advising agribusiness and cannabusinesses.

If I'm correct—based on the breakneck pace at which the industry is moving—we're talking mass consolidation within a decade. If you plan to get in the game—or to *stay* in it—a deep understanding of market direction and the industry's biggest players will be paramount to success. This includes paying attention to Big Tobacco and Big Alcohol (which will likely subsume the recreational market) and Big Pharma (which will absorb the medical-grade players). *That* will be the endgame. Cannabusinesses who are aware of this cycle, and either prepare as a target in the endgame, or are willing to step up their business savvy, play the game with every ounce of energy they have, and likely take a few beatings in-between, will survive.

Beyond the predictions, the "compassion" element of this industry is one I feel very strongly about. It's the compassion component—the desire to heal others—that prompted the earliest physicians and botanists to look to the natural world for its healing properties. It's the compassion component that drove nearly 5.4 million Californians to vote "Yes" on Proposition 215—the Compassionate Use Act—in 1996, allowing their fellow Californians access to medical cannabis *despite* the FDA's refusal to test cannabis-based products for safety and efficacy. It's the compassion component that keeps people who don't even *need* medical cannabis for *themselves* making their voices heard—in the streets, on the ballots, in conversations with others—for the sake of those who *do* need it.

"Compassion" literally means "to suffer together with." It carries with it a sense of empathy, the desire to relieve the suffering of others because we're somehow able to put ourselves in their shoes. But we can also think of compassion as a more general *feeling-with*. The recent discoveries of our own personal cannabinoid systems—those internal regulators we carry with us—can hopefully prompt us to "feel *into*" and "feel *with*" our bodies—to understand that there *are*, indeed, compounds found in the natural world that mirror our own, to *feel* into the fact that we naturally produce substances with astonishing analogues in nature, that our systems are preconditioned, as it were, to interact with a plant.

It's a wonderful realization. Now, let's see what kind of business it will make.

2

The Compassion Component

Cannabis' Long Medicinal History

"Marijuana" is, of course, among the most hotly-debated issues in the United States today. Indeed, it's been a controversial topic in this country for decades—often in a front-page-news kind of way. As a result of years of misrepresentation about its psychological and physiological effects—not to mention the outright vilification of its users—many of us probably grew up under the impression that it was an evil, destructive (or, at the very least, a highly *suspect*) drug.

But this perception of cannabis (which didn't come to be called "marijuana" until the twentieth century—a story I'll tell shortly) is actually a very recent one. Dr. Barney Warf, a professor at the University of Kansas, has called it an "historical anomaly." If we can step back and broaden our lens to look at the big picture of mankind's relationship with cannabis—a picture whose timeline spans at least 12,000 years—we'll notice that the pattern of acceptance, appreciation, and even *reverence* for the drug was only disrupted in this last century.

In other words, while California's 1996 Compassionate Use Act may have been the first initiative to *use* the word "compassion" in acknowledging cannabis' therapeutic value, much of the plant's use across history has been compassion-based. For millennia prior to the twentieth century, cannabis was not only *legal* worldwide, it was also recognized by botanists, physicians, priests, shamans, and spiritual seekers for its medicinal properties. Almost every ancient handbook on plant medicine discusses it. Indeed, the therapeutic potential that many cultures attributed to it is only beginning to be fully understood today.

I think it's helpful to put recent social and legal developments regarding cannabis into a broader historical perspective—if only because it asks us to reexamine any preconceptions we might have about the drug. So let's take a survey of the role cannabis has played in humanity's development—particularly in its medical practices.

Cannabis in the Ancient and Medieval Worlds

The cannabis plant (which is typically called "hemp" in industrial and agrarian contexts: Cannabis plants are called "hemp" when they contain less than 0.3 percent THC, and "marijuana" when they contain more) is believed to have first flourished on the steppes of Central Asia, in the regions we know as Mongolia and Southern Siberia. Historians estimate that humans began tending cannabis crops about 12,000 years ago, which effectively makes it one of the oldest-cultivated crops. (In fact, recent discoveries of cultural artifacts have suggested the cultivation and use of the plant occurred *much* earlier than this. For instance, a rope discovered in 1997 at an archaeological site in what was then Czechoslovakia dates back to 26,900 BC.)

Ancient Chinese pots made with hemp cord and decorated with cannabis fibers have been dated to 10,000 BC. The economy of the Yangshao, the oldest-known Neolithic culture in China, appears to have been cannabis-driven. Archaeological evidence shows that the Yangshao, who lived in the Yellow River valley from 5,000 to 3,000 BC, wore clothing and produced pottery made of hemp.

Most early cultures who had access to hemp used the plant to make objects such as paper, rope, fishing nets, bowstrings, clothing, and other textiles; they also used its high-protein seeds for food (it was a staple grain) and oil. In fact, in my research on cannabis, I've come to believe that early humans were homeostatically healthy precisely *because* they absorbed CBD through their clothes and ingested trace amounts from pots and baskets ... not to mention outright consumption of seeds and oil. And while the earliest hemp plants contained very low levels of tetrahydrocannabinol (THC)—the chemical we now know is responsible for cannabis' mind-altering effects—there *is* some evidence that early cultures knew about the plant's psychoactive properties.

For example, in his *Histories* (c. 440 BC), the ancient Greek historian Herodotus, who is often called "The Father of History," described the Scythians—Central Asian nomads—as throwing cannabis seeds and flowers on heated rocks and inhaling the smoke to get high. For the Scythians, cannabis was used for both recreational and spiritual purposes: The scene Herodotus describes above was common in their funeral ceremonies. Wonderfully, Herodotus' description in the *Histories* has been corroborated by modern archeologists. Burned cannabis seeds have been discovered in the graves of shamans—as well as a Scythian couple—buried in China and Siberia around 500 BC. Burned seeds have also been found in much earlier Siberian burial sites: the Kurgan burial mounds, which date back to 3000 BC, and the tombs of the nobility in the Xinjiang region, which date back to 2500 BC.

Of course, while archeological evidence suggests that the plant was used for both spiritual and recreational purposes in the prehistoric and ancient worlds, by Tantric Buddhists to facilitate meditation in the Himalayas; or by Taoist monks, who consumed it with ginseng to open their psychic centers, what's *most* interesting about the plant in light of our contemporary debates around marijuana is the variety of ways cannabis has been used for medicinal purposes.

The "compassion component" of cannabis begins, it appears, in 2737 BC. At least, that's the earliest reference to the value of cannabis *as a medicine*. The Chinese emperor Shen Nung, considered "the first pharmacologist" and the father of Chinese medicine, and credited with discoveries such as the healing properties of ginseng, discovered the healing potential of cannabis, as well. He found these healing properties in the root, leaves, flowers, and seeds.

The *Pen Ts'ao Ching*, the world's oldest pharmacopoeia, written in the first century AD but based on oral traditions from Shen Nung, includes these indications for cannabis (called *ma* in Chinese): gout, rheumatism, constipation, malaria, menstrual problems, and absent-mindedness. This is a short list; Shen Nung recognized cannabis' ability to treat *over 100 ailments*. He also recognized its psychoactive side-effects ... but clearly believed its medicinal properties outweighed them.

While probably modified from the original first-century text, the *Pen Ts'ao Ching* is still used by practitioners of Traditional Chinese Medicine today. Chinese physicians still use cannabis seeds as laxatives, to aid digestion, and lower cholesterol. The fatty acids in the seeds are used topically for conditions such as psoriasis and eczema, and oral use is recommended for conditions such as rheumatoid arthritis and osteoporosis. Cannabis actually remained one of the 50 essential plants in Traditional Chinese Medicine for thousands of years; it only stopped being recommended in such a widespread fashion in the last century, due to the plant's controversial legal status.

What I find so compelling about the plant's remedial and curative origins in Traditional Chinese Medicine is the insistence on *compassion* in the classical Chinese medicine oath—the foundation, as it were, for medical ethics. The oath was written in the sixth century by the physician Sun Simiao, though the ideals he drew on were as old as Shen Nung himself. Sun Simiao called his oath "On the Absolute Sincerity of Great Physicians," though it's often referred to as "the Chinese Hippocratic Oath." Practitioners of TCM still study and adhere to it today—indeed, it's required reading for any student of the practice: "I will not give way to personal wishes and desires, but above all else hold and nurture a deep feeling of compassion," the oath reads. "Above all, I will keep an open heart. As I move on the right path, I will receive great happiness as a reward without asking for anything in return." And later: "People all too often look with contempt on those who suffer from abominable things ... however I shall maintain an attitude of compassion, sympathy and care. Never in a great physician should there arise an attitude of rejection."

Sun Simiao's writings may have drawn on the much earlier writings of Hua Tuo (c. 140-208), who *also* wrote a physician's oath of sorts: "Treat people equally, irrespective of their high or low status, of their poverty or wealth, of their distinction or obscurity ... do not run after riches, fear no hardships and toils, and take it as your first duty to take pity on the old and help the young."

In other words, compassion was the driving force, the physician's primary motivation, in classical Chinese medicine practice. One could not be a proper physician without *this* sensitivity, first and foremost. And *this* is the tradition that first discovered cannabis' healing properties. Talk about benevolent origins.

The medical use of cannabis was virtually inextricable from its spiritual use in India. The earliest reference to cannabis in Indian literature is found in the Hindu sacred texts called the Vedas. The fourth book of the Vedas, the *Atharvaveda*, lists cannabis (or *bhang*, which an edible preparation) as one of five sacred plants, or one of "five kingdoms of herbs ... which release us from anxiety." As a "joy-giver" and "bringer of freedom," cannabis was smoked at devotional services and in religious rituals, with the purpose of bringing the devotee closer to god and leading him to spiritual liberation. Indeed, the Hindu god Shiva is referred to as the "Lord of Bhang," and bhang was (and *is*) offered to the god in religious ceremonies. In this sense, the cannabis plant was nothing short of sacred.

Bhang, a drink made of dried cannabis buds and leaves, milk, ghee, and spices, was not limited to religious rituals and spiritual use. Bhang was used as an anesthetic and an anti-phlegmatic. The *Sushruta Samhita* (c. 600 BC), the first major Indian work to describe the use of cannabis in Ayurvedic medicine, cites cannabis as a cure for leprosy and dysentery, as well as insomnia, epilepsy, skin issues, physical aches and pains, depression, and gastrointestinal disorders. (A later Persian religious text influenced by the Vedas, the *Venidad*, purportedly written by Zarathustra, mentions *bhang*, the "good narcotic," and claims cannabis is the most important medicinal plant of a list of 10,000 plants.)

Indeed, in his review of the history of cannabis as a medicine, Antonio Waldo Zuardi writes of the plant's use in India as spanning a wide range of physical ailments: It was an "analgesic (neuralgia, headache, toothache), anticonvulsant (epilepsy, tetanus, rabies), hypnotic, tranquilizer (anxiety, mania, hysteria), anesthetic, anti-inflammatory (rheumatism and other inflammatory diseases), antibiotic (topical use on skin infections, erysipelas, tuberculosis), antiparasite (internal and external worms), antispasmodic (colic, diarrhea), digestive, appetite stimulant, diuretic, aphrodisiac or anaphrodisiac, antitussive and expectorant (bronchitis, asthma)."

The plant's use in India was in fact *so* pervasive for so many centuries that an Indo-British study of the usage of cannabis in India, prompted by questions from the British Parliament, was finally conducted in 1893–1894. The *Report of the Indian Hemp Drugs Commission* concluded that restricting the use of cannabis would be unjustifiable. Not only was its religious use among Hindus ancient and sacred, but the report also confirmed cannabis' medicinal value: "Besides as a cure for fever, bhang has many medicinal virtues … It cures dysentery and sunstroke, clears phlegm, quickens digestion, sharpens appetite, makes the tongue of the lisper plain, freshens the intellect, and gives alertness to the body and gaiety to the mind."

In ancient Egypt, cannabis was used to treat general inflammation and "sore eyes" (what we call glaucoma today): "A treatment for the eyes: celery; hemp; is ground and left in the dew overnight. Both eyes of the patient are to be washed with it early in the morning," recommends the 3700-year-old *Papyrus Ramesseum III*. (Glaucoma is a condition that cannabis is often prescribed for today. Remember what I said about cannabinoids and homeostasis in the introduction? In this instance, cannabinoids help alleviate the symptoms of glaucoma because they lower intraocular pressure, restoring eye pressure to that "Goldilocks zone.")

Indeed, if you were to walk into the Cathedral of the Assumption in Monreale, Sicily, today, you'd see a mosaic dating from the twelfth century called "Jesus Healing the Blind." Behind two blind men, growing out of the side of a hill, is an enormous cannabis leaf, a detail many biblical scholars refer to in their arguments that cannabis (קְנֵה-בֹשֶׂם or *kaneh bosm*) was one of the ingredients named in the holy anointing oil described in Exodus 25-30:22. Contemporary clinical studies have proven that cannabis delays retinal generation … so if Jesus was, indeed, using it to heal the blind, it appears he chose the right plant for the job.

Collections of medical knowledge such as the *Ebers Papyrus*, among the oldest and perhaps the most important medical papyrus of ancient Egypt, prescribed cannabis for hemorrhoids, administering enemas, and as an aid to childbirth: the latter apparently to help with contractions. (The first recorded woman to make use of medical marijuana during childbirth did so in Jerusalem in 300 AD.) Cannabis pollen has been discovered in the tombs of Egyptian pharaohs, such as Ramesses II and Akhenaten.

Perhaps the most interesting indication in these Egyptian papyri comes from the *Fayyum Medical Papyrus*, which appears to contain the earliest record of cannabis used as an ingredient in cancer medicine. In its discussion of terminal illnesses and their treatments, the papyrus suggests that cannabis was used to treat *both* early- and late-stage cancerous tumors (One method for "paralys[ing the tu]mours" required "extract of herbs, papyrus, sap of the hur-tree, lotus leaf, cannabis ... heated ... sweet clover ..."). If you've been following studies and trials on medical cannabis in cancer treatment, you now have a sense of how old the origins of these studies *are*.

The Sicilian Greek historian Diodorus Siculus would write that Egyptian women used cannabis to relieve sorrow and other "bad humours" (i.e. depression). And of course, cannabis played a role in the Greco-Roman world as well. Dioscorides (c. 40-90 AD)—the Greek botanist, physician, pharmacologist, and army medic who authored the five-volume *De Materia Medica*, which was read widely for more than 1500 years—prescribed cannabis for earaches, toothaches, inflammation, and edema. Pliny the Elder (23-79 AD), the Roman scientist and naturalist, wrote in *The Natural History* that the roots of the cannabis plant, when "boiled in water[,] ease cramped joints, gout too, and similar violent pain." Other indications for the plant were arthritis and labor pains—the latter for women of the Roman elite.

By around 200 AD, the Chinese surgeon Hua Tuo—the first recorded physician to use cannabis as an anesthetic, and the same Hua Tuo who advised physicians to "treat people equally, irrespective of their high or low status ... and take it as your first duty to take pity on the old and help the young"—was mixing cannabis powder with wine for his patients to drink before surgery. (The Chinese word for anesthesia, *mázui*, literally translates as "cannabis intoxication.") Chinese physicians were also, at this time, using nearly the whole plant (root, leaves, and oil) to treat other conditions, such as tapeworms, blood clots, and constipation.

By 800 AD, cannabis was used in the Arabic world for, as Martin Booth writes, "a wide variety of ailments (from migraines to syphilis) and as an analgesic and anaesthetic." Indeed, "the great ninth-century Islamic physician Rhazès ... prescribed it widely." In 1100, the Arabic scholar al-Mayusi was the first to make a written record of cannabis' use in epilepsy. A few centuries later, Ibn al-Badri (c. 1464) would record a "case study" concerning the epileptic son of the caliph's chamberlain. The boy was given hashish; and, al-Badri writes, "it cured him completely." Once again, the ancients were way ahead of us: It wasn't until January of this year, 2018, that the FDA finally approved an oral cannabidiol (CBD) solution, called Epidiolex, for the treatment of two rare and severe forms of epilepsy (Lennox-Gastaut syndrome and Dravet syndrome) in patients aged two and older.

Other Arabic texts refer to cannabis as a diuretic, a digestive aid, and a drug for "cleaning the brain" and relieving pain in the ears. In 1025, the Persian medical writer Avicenna, often called "the father of early modern medicine," completed his five-volume *Canon of Medicine*. In this opus, cannabis is named as a treatment for edema, gout, migraines, and infectious wounds. And as cannabis continued to be transported via invasions and trade routes over the centuries, it was eventually brought into Eastern Africa around 1300, where it was used to treat asthma, snake bites, malaria, fever, and dysentery, as well as to facilitate childbirth.

The first wave of European colonialism began in the 1400s, and the high demand to both build and maintain ships meant that hemp became an imperative *commercial* product. Ship builders realized that sails made of flax began rotting in a matter of months from the salty spray of the sea. They soon discovered that sails and rope made from hemp would last much longer; and this discovery, along with the new lateen (the triangular sail), allowed explorers to leave the "comfort" of the Mediterranean and head into the Atlantic for much longer journeys.

In 1533, King Henry VIII compelled all landlords to set aside a quarter acre for every 60 acres of land they tilled to cultivate hemp; this way, England would have the necessary fibres for rope and sailcloth for its navy. Those who failed to do so paid the penalty with a fine. Henry's daughter, Queen Elizabeth, would reintroduce the edict to expand her *own* navy in 1563.

But England wasn't the only European country that was realizing its need for hemp had outgrown the amount of land needed to cultivate the plant. The Spanish *also* realized they needed to escalate cultivation of the plant that would be so useful for their colonizing ships. (Conversely, some historians have argued that European exploration and colonization was spurred by the *need* for hemp, this remarkable raw material with so many uses, rather than the other way around.)

Either way, what this meant was that, even as physicians, pharmacologists, medical doctors, and others in Europe and the East were experimenting with what we now call "medical marijuana," cannabis was making its way to the New World. The physician and first English botanist William Turner praised the plant in his *New Herball* (1551); the herbalist and physician Nicholas Culpeper wrote in *The English Physitian* that hemp was good for "hot dry cough," jaundice, colic, and "troublesome humors in the bowels." It also "allayeth inflammations of the head ... easeth pains of the gout, the hard humours of knots in the joints ... and the pains of the hips" (1562). The Oxford scholar and clergyman Robert Burton recommended cannabis as a treatment for depression in his enormously popular *The Anatomy of Melancholy* (1621).

And as the "compassionate" aspect of the plant continued to be cultivated on *that* side of the Atlantic, the Americas were "discovering" it—while *they* were being discovered—for the first time.

Cannabis in Colonial America

Both English and Spanish explorers introduced hemp to the Americas upon arrival. The plant came to Brazil in the early-to-mid sixteenth century as a consequence of the slave trade from Africa. The Angolan slaves who brought the plant with them to the sugar plantations were apparently given permission to sow cannabis seeds between the rows of sugarcane and to smoke it in the time between harvests. Indeed, most of the words used for "marijuana" in Brazil (*maconha, diamba, limbo*) have their origins in the Angolan language.

In Brazil, cannabis was quickly incorporated into folk medicine and used to treat conditions such as rheumatism and toothache. In other Spanish colonies, such as Chile, its fibers were also used for rope and clothing.

While the plant was introduced to South America by way of the Spanish in the 1500s, the English first introduced it to *North* America when they carried it with them to the Jamestown colony in 1611. It appears that, while in colonial South America, it was used as much for its intoxicating properties as for its medicinal and practical purposes, in North America, cannabis was initially introduced as the common hemp plant and was not known, or used, as a psychoactive drug until the mid-nineteenth century. Nor were cannabis' medicinal properties widely recognized and accepted until that time … though as we'll see, the first president of the United States seems to have been experimenting with it as a pain reliever.

Hemp became as popular a crop as tobacco was in the colonies, acknowledged more for its commercial value than for anything else. The fibers were used for paper, clothing, textiles, ropes, and thick, durable sails for the maritime industry; hemp seed oil was used in the production of paints, varnishes, and soaps. And while the colonies initially grew hemp in order to export it back to England, it became the most strategically important plant for the colonies during the War of Independence *from* England, perhaps one of the great quiet ironies of history.

But to say that growing hemp was "encouraged" by the American colonies is an understatement. Indeed, because the crop was seen as so essential to the manufacture of such a wide range of commodities, 1619 saw what we might call America's first bit of marijuana legislation, when a new Jamestown colony law, passed by the Virginia Assembly, required all settlers to grow "Indian hemp." Implementation of other cannabis laws in the New World eventually followed, when laws mandating the cultivation of hemp were passed in the Massachusetts (1631) and Connecticut (1632) colonies. As late as 1732, Virginia was awarding bounties for the manufacture of hemp and imposing penalties on settlers who did not produce it. Until 1769, one could be jailed in the Colony of Virginia for refusing to grow hemp.

In Pennsylvania, Virginia, and Maryland, hemp was even used as legal tender: Until the early 1800s, farmers were allowed to pay their taxes with hemp.

Even the founding fathers grew their own cannabis. Thomas Jefferson grew it on his plantation at Monticello from 1774 to 1824; both his planting calendar and his directives are documented in his farming diaries, as in this entry from December 1811: "An acre of the best ground for hemp, is to be selected, & sown in hemp & to be kept for a permanent hemp patch ... Hemp should be immediately prepared to set them [the spinners] at work, & a supply be kept up."

George Washington grew hemp at his Virginia plantation, Mount Vernon, for three decades (c. 1745-1775). While he grew the plant for industrial and commercial purposes, Washington appears to have taken a keen interest in the medicinal use of cannabis—arguably for the treatment of his chronic toothaches. Author and activist Robert Deitch observes that "several of [Washington's] diary entries indicate that he indeed was growing cannabis with a high Tetrahydrocannabinol (THC) content—marijuana." For instance, these two entries from August 1765 and August 1766, respectively: "Began to separate the male from female plants ... rather too late"; "Pulling up the (male) hemp. Was too late for the blossom hemp by three weeks or a month."

In other words, while the chemical responsible for the psychoactive effects of cannabis is thought to have been too low in the founding fathers' hemp plants for mind-altering experiences (if colonial Americans were smoking *anything*, it was tobacco), it appears Washington was trying to grow female plants—which produce a high THC content—here. Either way, it's a compelling theory. For whatever reason, Washington's tooth decay, chronic tooth and jaw pain, and dentures have made history along *with* him; and if he was, indeed, looking for the most potent form of the cannabis plant—a form that would have made no difference to its *industrial* use—it's highly probable that pain relief was the driving force of this search.

By 1800, hemp plantations were flourishing in New York, Mississippi, Georgia, South Carolina, Kentucky, and Nebraska. Henry Clay—the speaker of the House from 1811–1825—grew hemp on his Kentucky plantation. How strange to think that the very federal government that today so resolutely insists that cannabis remain a Schedule I drug was *founded* by men who resolutely grew it.

All this is to say that the negative stigma cannabis carries in America today simply did not exist in the early years of the United States. And this wasn't only true of eighteenth-century America. At around the same time the House Speaker was growing his own hemp, Napoleon's forces were bringing cannabis back from Egypt to France (c. 1799) and were investigating it for its sedative and pain-relieving effects. Medical cannabis had already appeared in both *The New England Dispensatory* and *The Edinburgh New Dispensatory* (1764 and 1794, respectively) in Britain.

Medical Cannabis in the Nineteenth-Century U.S.

In the late 1830s, an Irish physician named William O'Shaughnessy accelerated the course of medical cannabis research in Europe, and eventually, in America, reinvigorating studies of the drug with the compassion element we saw in its earliest uses. O'Shaughnessy was serving in the East India Trading Company in Calcutta, where, as I discussed earlier, the use of cannabis for medicinal purposes was widespread. After studying the extensive literature on the plant, including its popular folk preparations, O'Shaughnessy began applying the scientific method to evaluate its effects in animals. He then conducted the first clinical trials of cannabis by giving tinctures and extracts to human patients with a variety of pathologies. These preparations were of his own devising, though they were based on native Indian recipes.

O'Shaughnessy gave cannabis tinctures to victims of a cholera outbreak, and discovered that ten drops of the solution every 30 minutes would typically lessen the stomach pain and stop the diarrhea and vomiting that often made the disease fatal. As Mary Lynn Mathre writes, "This seems to be the first mention in European clinical literature of cannabis as an antiemetic."

O'Shaughnessy also experimented with extracts and tinctures on sufferers of rheumatism, hydrophobia, rabies, and tetanus (which eventually led to its use as an antispasmodic and muscle relaxant), as well as on a one-and-a-half month old baby who suffered from convulsions. The child apparently responded well to the drug, and in less than three weeks, rebounded to "the enjoyment of robust health," according to the Irish doctor.

O'Shaughnessy's case studies were careful and concise; and when he returned to London, he began publishing his research in English medical journals—including an 1843 article called "On the Preparations of the Indian Hemp, or Gunjah," printed in the *Provincial Medical Journal*. Through these publications, O'Shaughnessy officially introduced cannabis' therapeutic uses— from a *clinical* perspective—to Western medicine. His findings caused a sensation: O'Shaughnessy appeared to have discovered a drug that was able to cure some of the most dreadful medical conditions of the era.

Word caught quickly, and this watershed research spurred further medical experiments in both Europe and the United States. As Harvard Professor Lester Grinspoon writes, "Between 1839 and 1900 more than one hundred articles appeared in scientific journals describing the medicinal properties of the plant." In 1973, Dr. Tod H. Mikuriya collected and summarized these documents (as well as later ones) in his *Marijuana: Medical Papers, 1839–1972*. They include the following therapeutic uses of cannabis: analgesic-hypnotic, appetite stimulant, antiepileptic and antispasmodic, prophylactic, treatment of the neuralgias, migraine treatment, antidepressant, antiasthmatic, childbirth analgesic, antitussive, topical anesthetic, withdrawal agent for opiate and alcohol addiction, and antibiotic.

It's one of the grand about-faces in the history of cannabis that the vast majority of studies produced on the plant *today* are written with the apparent intent of uncovering the negative attributes of the drug, while most of the hundred-plus journal articles published in the 19th and early 20th centuries discovered and documented its benefits. Federal regulation is to blame for this shift. If an organization wants to conduct clinical research on marijuana, it needs to have its study approved by the FDA and get licensed by the DEA. And in order to obtain research-grade marijuana, grown and harvested at the University of Mississippi, it needs permission from the National Institute on Drug Abuse (NIDA).

The problem with this? NIDA's mission—mandated by Congress—is specifically to research the *harmful* effects of controlled substances and to prevent drug abuse. NIDA's mission underscores this focus: "Our mission is to advance science on the causes and consequences of drug use and addiction and to apply that knowledge to improve individual and public health." So the only federally-approved source of research-grade marijuana in the U.S. *today* has no vested interest in establishing the plant as a medicine.

Luckily for O'Shaughnessy, he wasn't working under any of those restrictions.

Almost immediately after O'Shaughnessy began publishing his findings, cannabis extracts began selling in doctors' offices and pharmacies throughout both Europe and the United States for virtually all of the above ailments—and more. Within a decade (in 1850), cannabis was added to *The U.S Pharmacopeia*, the official medical compendium and standard-setting reference for all over-the-counter and prescription medicines. (It would be removed in 1942.) Its inclusion officially acknowledged what had quickly become a widely-accepted therapeutic drug in mainstream medicine.

In the United States, as demand for cannabis-based medications grew, an array of over-the-counter products, such as "Piso's Cure" and "One Day Cough Cure," became readily available to consumers in pharmacies and general stores. At the height of the drug's popularity, over 30 different medical preparations with cannabis as their active ingredient were available. American pharmaceutical companies were suddenly racing to produce and patent cannabis-based medications: Eli Lilly produced Dr. Brown's Sedative Tablets, the One Day Cough Cure (a concoction of cannabis and balsam), and a drug called Neurosine, which, according to Volume 16 of *The Clinical Reporter* (1888), was "most efficient in the treatment of Neurasthenia, Insomnia, Hysteria, Neuralgia, Chorea, Epilepsy, Mania, Migraine, Convulsive and Reflex Neuroses, Restlessness of fevers, etc."

Parke-Davis (now owned by Pfizer) created and marketed their own cannabis formulations, including Casadein, Utroval, and a veterinary colic cure. (Meanwhile, Merck was creating cannabis-based cures in Germany, as was Burroughs-Wellcome in England.) Pills of sugar-coated cannabis were sold widely as painkillers. Even as an 1862 issue of *Vanity Fair* advertised hashish candy, "a pleasurable and harmless stimulant" that allows its users to "gather new inspiration and energy," cure nervousness and melancholy, cannabis' *medicinal* use, rather than its recreational use, appears to have been the priority for both businesses and consumers in this century.

The year 1860 saw the first American clinical conference on medical cannabis, organized by the Ohio State Medical Society. The conference reported favorable treatments of stomach pain, chronic cough, and childbirth psychosis. Four pages were devoted to *Extractum Cannabis* in the Civil War edition of the *U.S. Dispensatory* (1868), the properties of which included the ability "to cause sleep, to allay spasm, to compose nervous inquietude, and to relieve pain."

So there was medical cannabis, at the height of its popularity—readily available, investigated, studied, researched, and reviewed, with neither stigma nor legal ramifications. It's been estimated that six percent of all drugs manufactured at the time contained some form of cannabis—whether tinctures, fluid extracts, powders, or tablets. Indeed, the years from the turn of the century to 1937— the year that saw the Marihuana Tax Act—are called by some "the Golden Age of Medical Cannabis."

And yet, between 1914 and 1931, 29 states passed laws prohibiting the plant. These anti-marijuana laws (because "marijuana" had quickly become the new term for cannabis) were virtually uncontroversial: They passed without legislative debate or public outcry.

How is it possible that, just decades after the formal introduction of the cannabis plant to American medicine, states across the country began prohibiting it? It's worth asking what happened in these years—because the answer may be useful to our moment.

The Beginnings of "Marihuana" Prohibition

As I see it, there were two primary forces at work in the cannabis prohibitions that appeared across the United States in the first half of the twentieth century; but all of them had their origins in the greed and political clout of big businesses. The first was the difficulty of standardizing cannabis medications to prepare reliable formulations—a difficulty that the 1906 Pure Food and Drug Act—enacted to enforce truthful labeling—shone a blinding light on. This, alongside the fact that people could grow cannabis themselves, meant that big pharmaceutical companies simply couldn't profit off of the plant.

The second was the ways the media racialized and demonized the drug when it came into popular recreational use through migrants fleeing the Mexican Revolution. Mexicans became one of a few natural scapegoats for business tycoons, such as the media mogul William Randolph Hearst, who stood to lose a lot from the ongoing popularization of cannabis. (For Hearst, whose financial investments were in the timber industry, it was because hemp presented an enticing alternative raw material for paper. But Hearst was hardly the only businessman under threat.) Because of its myriad uses, the plant was a fierce adversary to capitalists; and the only way to eliminate this adversary was to illegalize it.

Let's begin with the problem of standardization. It's worth remembering that it wasn't until 1964 that the active constituent in cannabis (D9-tetrahydrocannabinol, more commonly known as THC) was finally isolated and described. What's more, the human endocannabinoid system—which I discussed at length in the introduction—wasn't discovered until 1992. In other words, it wasn't until very recently that physicians began to understand the mechanisms of action in the body when it came to cannabis. They only knew *that* it worked; they didn't know *how*.

To make matters thornier, there was no establishing and codifying "correct" dosages in the notoriously finicky plant. The Dutch Association for Legal Cannabis and its Constituents as Medicine (NCSM) explains it well: "Difficulties with the supply from overseas (tropical regions), and varying quality of the plant material made it difficult to prepare a reliable formulation of cannabis. Because no tools existed for quality control it was impossible to prepare a standardized medicine, so patients often received a dose that was either too low, having no effect, or too high, resulting in serious side effects." Moreover, because cannabis extract is not water-soluble, it couldn't be injected; and the effects of oral administration were unreliable because bodily absorption was slow, erratic, and dependent upon individual physiology.

Aside from the plant's origin and the patient's physiology, the drug's efficacy also varied depending on the plant's age and its mode of preparation; taken together, this meant that replicable effects couldn't be obtained across batches. These problems necessarily

made accurate titration and dosage standardization impractical—
an Achilles heel for physicians and pharmaceutical companies alike.
As the writers at NCSM note, it meant that patients perpetually
ran the risk of receiving doses that were too high … and while, as
I've noted, there's no *over*dosing on cannabis, it can certainly have
unsavory, though temporary, side effects when over-consumed.

Thus, there was something naturally suspect about any tincture
or medicine containing the drug; and one could see how it *could*,
under these circumstances, be classified as a substance to be vigilant
with, if not a potentially "dangerous" one.

As early as the 1860s, states undertook to provide consumer
protection by passing new regulatory measures for a medical
marketplace in which "mislabeling" became a common byproduct
of such an unpredictable, variable plant. These measures were
supported by reformers, pharmacists, and physicians, the latter of
whom understandably hoped to underscore their professionalism
and authority by recommending accurate dosages and offering
their patients reliable, expert knowledge on the drug. In 1886,
lawmakers in New Jersey passed "An Act to Regulate the Practice
of Pharmacy," which outlined acceptable pharmaceutical practices
and itemized a list of "poisons" under the designation of "Schedule
A." Because of its irregularity, "Indian hemp" was included on the
list, alongside drugs such as opium and arsenic.

New Jersey's act required that all Schedule A substances be
"label[ed] with a red label [on] the bottle, box, vessel, or wrapper"
that contained the drug, along "with the name of the article" and
"the word 'poison.'" One can imagine why pharmacists in New
Jersey would suddenly be hard-pressed to sell a cannabis-based
drug: It's tough to come up with a selling point for a product whose
label appears to virtually guarantee harm.

While the earliest regulations were passed at the state level,
the first *federal* attempt at cannabis regulation occurred in 1906,

with the passage of the Pure Food and Drug Act, signed by President Roosevelt on June 30. The act required *all* products that contained alcohol, cocaine, opiates, and cannabis to be labeled. Whereas patent medicine companies had, until now, been largely unregulated, they now had to conform to proper packaging and precise labeling.

The passage of the Pure Food and Drug Act didn't mean that cannabis was no longer legal; indeed, it would continue to be available to consumers without prescription so long as it was precisely labeled. But "precise labeling" was precisely the sticking point. It's been estimated that sales of patent medicines containing opiates dropped by 33 percent after labeling was federally mandated. As for *cannabis*-based medicines, their inclusion in the Pure Food and Drug Act meant an essentially un-labelable drug was *also* unsellable.

This, alongside cannabis' classification with drugs such as arsenic, opium, chloroform, and other "poisons" in broad, state-level regulation efforts, California's Poison Act of 1913, for instance, helped ring the early-twentieth-century death knell for medical cannabis. By 1930, most states had poison laws in place; and while some didn't *explicitly* include cannabis in the language of the legislation, the drug's accessibility (and desirability) was certainly hindered by virtue of new labeling practices, now enforced at both state and federal levels. These measures were acts of *caution*; but they *registered* as warnings, and cannabis as the threat. As Dale H. Gieringer writes, "as in California, these laws were passed not due to any widespread use or concern about cannabis, but as regulatory initiatives to discourage future use."

But there was a secondary "discouraging" force at work. The Mexican Revolution, which had begun in 1910, generated an influx of immigrants to the U.S. who, while fleeing political upheaval, simultaneously introduced the recreational use of the plant into U.S. culture. (As I've noted, the vast majority of pre-1910 references to cannabis in North American literature concern either its medicinal use or its value as an industrial textile.)

This nascent-but-quickly-spreading recreational use coincided with two other historical circumstances. The first was 1920s Prohibition, during which cannabis became a common alternative to alcohol. As such, it was smoked in marijuana clubs, called "tea pads," that resembled speakeasy dens and appeared in every major city. (Such "hashish parlors" had already been in business; but historians argue that they multiplied considerably with Prohibition.) Authorities tolerated these establishments because cannabis was still legal—and because their patrons, who were high rather than drunk, neither made trouble nor caused public disturbances.

The second was the Great Depression. Even as cannabis was quickly becoming *the* subculture drug, popular among jazz musicians and poets, as well as Mexican immigrants, the massive economic downturn spurred a less welcoming reaction to the drug. The massive unemployment rates and social unrest of this era made Mexican immigrants an easy target for stigmatization, as Americans feared—indeed, were *made* to fear by the press—that these foreign newcomers were the origin of their hardships. (It should be noted that Indians were also often the objects of xenophobic anti-cannabis speech. In 1911, Henry J. Finger, a member of California's State Board of Pharmacy, wrote: "Within the last year we in California have been getting a large influx of Hindoos and they have in turn started quite a demand for cannabis indica; they are a very undesirable lot and the habit is growing in California very fast; the fear is now that it is not being confined to the Hindoos alone but that they are initiating our whites into this habit.")

Still, journalists found it easiest to build upon the unrest around an influx of brown immigrants at the southern border. They were charged to sensationalize the drug in their stories, a charge that many appear to have viewed as a green light for their own outlandish creative impulses. Newspaper articles from this era repeatedly make pronounced associations between cannabis and murder, cannabis and torture, cannabis and senseless violence—associations based less on actual occurrences than on the lively imaginations of their writers.

Take this *New York Times* headline from February 21, 1925: "KILLS SIX IN A HOSPITAL: Mexican, Crazed by Marihuana, Runs Amuck With Butcher Knife." Or *this* article from the February 27, 1930 issue of the *S.F. Examiner*, which claims marijuana produces "Murder Smoke": "The first 'Murder Smoke' cigarette brings strange and weirdly beautiful dreams, but after the first few cigarettes it takes more and more smoking to produce the dream, and suddenly the tortured nerves give way and the 'Murder Smoker' must cut and stab, and beat and shoot, to satisfy the tortured hunger created by the drug."

Among those who charged journalists with sensationalizing the drug was the newspaper tycoon William Randolph Hearst, who owned 28 newspapers by the mid-1920s. Hearst also had significant financial interests in the timber industry (his own Hearst Paper Manufacturing Division of Kimberly-Clark possessed an immense acreage of timberland), and owned the paper factories on which his dailies were printed. As Richard Sharp notes, thanks to new machines that could produce hemp pulp, "newsprint could now be produced far more cheaply than any other method, and one acre of hemp could produce as much newsprint as four acres of forest trees." Given hemp's unequivocal advantages, Hearst stood to lose no small portion of his empire if he didn't promote the lurid stories that linked cannabis-smoking Mexicans to violent acts like kidnapping, rape, and murder. The only way to encourage suppression of the hemp industry was to merge industrial hemp and psychoactive "marihuana" in the public consciousness.

To strengthen the apparent affinity between cannabis and immigrants, Hearst's papers dropped the "c" word and began using the "m" word, foreignizing the plant by accentuating the drug's "Mexican-ness." This was a strategy meant to play off the anti-immigrant sentiments, such as fear and vigilance, that were already brewing. As Matt Thompson writes: "Th[e] disparity between 'cannabis' mentions pre-1900 and 'marihuana' references post-1900 is wildly jarring. It's almost as though the papers are describing two different drugs." Under its new nomenclature, "marihuana" was stripped of any connection to cannabis; and few readers recognized that this murder-inducing drug was the *very same* plant that had, until recently, been so widely present and available in patented, legal American medicine.

It's worth noting that the sensationalized stories were as prevalent in Mexican newspapers as they were in U.S. papers. Indeed, Mexico beat the U.S. to the marijuana ban when they made the drug illegal in 1920. But the "marijuana crime stories" took on specifically anti-Mexican tones in U.S. media outlets. Recreational marijuana (the "Mexican Menace") came to be seen as a byproduct of undesired immigration—and therefore *itself* undesirable. As Eric Schlosser writes, "Police officers in Texas claimed that marijuana incited violent crimes, aroused a 'lust for blood,' and gave its users 'super-human strength.' Rumors spread that Mexicans were distributing this 'killer weed' to unsuspecting American schoolchildren."

By 1931, 29 states had moved beyond poison laws and outlawed "marijuana" outright. Meanwhile, Harry Anslinger, who was appointed commissioner of the Federal Bureau of Narcotics (now the Bureau of Narcotics and Dangerous Drugs) in 1930, had begun his own campaign to criminalize marijuana at the federal level. Some have argued that Anslinger, whose organization was suddenly underemployed when the prohibition of alcohol was lifted in 1933, managed to keep his team active by simply switching the terms of the battle: from demonizing alcohol to demonizing marijuana.

Certainly that could have played a part in it. The more probable reason for Anslinger's campaign, however, had to do with his direct (and significant) ties to the petrochemical industry—another industry that could easily have been handicapped by hemp. Anslinger was appointed to his office as Narcotics Commissioner by President Hoover's Secretary of the Treasury, Andrew Mellon. By all accounts, it was an act of nepotism: Anslinger was Andrew Mellon's future nephew-in-law.

Mellon's bank, the Mellon Bank of Pittsburgh, was the chief financial backer of the DuPont chemical company. In 1933, Pierre Samuel du Pont patented the process of making plastics such as nylon, rayon, and cellophane from coal and petrochemical oils. Two years earlier, Du Pont had *invented* nylon, a synthetic fiber that served as a viable competitor for hemp rope. Like Hearst, Du Pont had a substantial motive for wanting hemp removed—not only as competition for nylon, but also as competition for the synthetic petrochemical oils he hoped would replace the hemp seed oil found in paints, inks, lubricants, and other products.

And so, Harry Anslinger began his crusade for what would eventually result in the Marihuana Tax Act with the forceful "encouragement" of both Andrew Mellon and Pierre du Pont. The legislation would, after all, treat hemp just like other forms of cannabis (i.e. marijuana), eliminating the DuPont company's competition nearly altogether. It's been estimated that, if hemp hadn't been virtually outlawed by the Marihuana Tax Act, DuPont would have lost 80 percent of his business; as his primary investor, Andrew Mellon stood to lose much as well. Given this urgency, and given his familial ties, one can see why Anslinger's ultimate ambition as commissioner was to pass the Marihuana Tax Act.

The four men, Hearst, Du Pont, Mellon, and Anslinger, were, naturally, supported by a variety of pharmaceutical companies. Because marijuana doses couldn't be standardized, they couldn't be sold under the terms of the Pure Food and Drug Act. And even if they *could* be standardized and sold, it wouldn't have done Big Pharma much financial good: Neither plants nor their naturally occurring compounds are patentable. Consumers could grow their own backyard medicine, rather than having to succumb to the pharmaceutical industry for their medical needs. As such, cannabis *had* to be criminalized in order to leave consumers no choice but to hand over their money.

In the meantime, Big Pharma had been creating new drugs and medicines, in some cases, synthetic versions *of the very plant* and its compounds that they wanted to outlaw. (I'll have more to say more these synthetic cannabinoids later.) In other words, Big Pharma *recognized* that cannabis was an effective treatment for an array of conditions: Why try to replicate it otherwise? But Big Pharma *wasn't* going to lose billions of dollars to a common, unpatentable, naturally-occurring plant.

So, a crusade to criminalize marijuana began, against what would have been devastating competition for just about *everyone*—aided, conveniently, by Hearst's yellow journalism. Anslinger even took up the pen himself: "How many murders, suicides, robberies, criminal assaults, holdups, burglaries and deeds of maniacal insanity [marijuana] causes each year can only be conjectured," he wrote in a 1937 article titled "Marijuana, Assassin of Youth" and published in Hearst's own *American Magazine*. But Anslinger did more than take up the pen to reorganize the public consciousness around cannabis. He also, of course, had direct access to the nation's legislative body.

And the racial dimension of Anslinger's anti-cannabis animus remained deafeningly loud, even when presenting "witness" testimony before Congress. In a 1937 Senate hearing, the nation's top anti-narcotics official said,

> There are 100,000 total marijuana smokers in the US, and most are Negroes, Hispanics, Filipinos, and entertainers. Their Satanic music, jazz, and swing result from marijuana use. This marijuana causes white women to seek sexual relations with Negroes, entertainers, and any others. The primary reason to outlaw marijuana is its effect on degenerative races. Marijuana is an addictive drug which produces in its users insanity, criminality, and death. You smoke a joint and you're likely to kill your brother.

This same testimony, during which he urged forceful, and uniform, anti-narcotics legislation across all 48 states, included a letter from the editor of the *Daily Courier* in Alamosa, Colorado. In it, Floyd Baskette writes, "I wish I could show you what a small marihuana cigaret can do to one of our degenerate Spanish-speaking residents. That's why our problem is so great; the greatest percentage of our population is composed of Spanish-speaking persons, most of whom are low mentally, because of social and racial conditions."

Throughout his Congressional testimony, Anslinger drew again and again from what is now infamously known as his "gore file": an archive of heinous crimes allegedly committed by people under the influence of marijuana. His case rested—as it had all along—on two baseless assertions: that marijuana caused insanity and that it compelled its users to commit atrocious criminal acts. Though baseless, his argument was sufficiently persuasive. The hearing would result in the establishment of the first federal restriction on marijuana: The Marihuana Tax Act (1937).

Anslinger's testimony was bolstered by more than sensationalized newspaper coverage from the likes of Hearst; it also came on the heels of the 1936 propaganda film *Reefer Madness*—a film that has since become a cult classic. Originally financed by a small church group—and initially called *Tell Your Children*—the film was conceived to arouse marijuana-inspired terror in America's youth. Soon after it was shot, however, the footage was purchased by Dwain Esper, a producer and director of low-budget exploitation films. Esper cut in salacious shots and gave the film a more sensational title before distributing it. The adaptation offered the same narrative intended by the church group: a morality tale in which marijuana addiction destroys the lives of its ultimately-psychotic protagonists and gets others physically and sexually compromised, killed, and committed to asylums in the meantime.

The Marihuana Tax Act passed in the House after less than 30 minutes of debate and received only cursory coverage in the press. Stephen Siff writes, "House members seem not to have known a great deal about the drug. In response to a question from another member, Speaker of the House Sam Rayburn (D-Tex.) explained that marijuana was 'a narcotic of some kind,' while another Representative John D. Dingle (D-Mich.) appeared to confuse it with locoweed, a different plant" altogether.

Indeed, the only witness to speak *against* the bill was a delegate from the American Medical Association, Dr. William C. Woodward, Legislative Counsel. In his testimony, Dr. Woodward declared his own opposition to the bill and endeavored to clear up any impression that the AMA, or *anyone* in the medical field, for that matter—supported the legislation. (Anslinger had taken earlier AMA statements that had nothing to do with marijuana out of context and presented them as distorted evidence for his anti-cannabis legislation.) "The American Medical Association knows of no evidence that marijuana is a dangerous drug," Woodward emphatically stated.

Woodward also problematized the newly-popularized nomenclature for the drug—reproaching the Bureau of Narcotics for using it in the language of their testimony—and reminded the court of the likelihood of cannabis' vast medical uses:

> There is nothing in the medicinal use of Cannabis that has any relation to Cannabis addiction. I use the word 'Cannabis' in preference to the word 'marihuana,' because Cannabis is the correct term for describing the plant and its products. The term 'marihuana' is a mongrel word that has crept into this country over the Mexican border and has no general meaning … To say, however, as has been proposed here, that the use of the drug should be prevented by a prohibitive tax, loses sight of the fact that future investigation may show that there are substantial medical uses for Cannabis.

Congress ignored Dr. Woodward's arguments—though they certainly paid attention to the sensational stories presented as "testimony." Riding the waves of misinformation campaigns and growing national anti-marijuana sentiment, Congress passed the act. The first person prosecuted under the Marihuana Tax Act was arrested the day after the legislation went into effect. Samuel Caldwell, a 58-year-old farmer, was arrested for selling cannabis and ultimately sentenced to four years of hard labor.

While it didn't *criminalize* the possession or sale of cannabis (the states were already doing *that* themselves), the federal tax act essentially had the same effect. The law, as Rosalie Pacula et al. describe it, "maintained the right to use marijuana for medicinal purposes but required physicians and pharmacists who prescribed or dispensed marijuana to register with federal authorities and pay an annual tax or license fee." The fees were so heavy—and so prohibitive—that they ultimately rendered any commerce in the drug unprofitable. It was Congress' way of "prohibiting" marijuana in a roundabout manner: by bankrupting the industry, rather than outlawing its product.

A year after the passage of the Marihuana Tax Act, New York Mayor Fiorello La Guardia (after whom the LaGuardia Airport is named) commissioned the New York Academy of Medicine to research marijuana, in effect, to investigate the justificatory grounds of Anslinger's bill. The Academy's 1944 report, "The Marihuana Problem in the City of New York" (commonly known as the La Guardia Report) wholly debunked Anslinger's myth of the psychotic, licentious, and murderous marijuana fiend. The report concluded that marijuana was, *at worst*, a mild intoxicant: The smoker "readily engages in conversation with strangers, discussing freely his pleasant reactions to the drug and philosophizing on subjects pertaining to life in a manner which, at times, appears to be out of keeping with his intellectual level." (To this day, that last phrase makes me laugh every time I read it.)

The La Guardia Report's summary includes these points: "The practice of smoking marihuana does not lead to addiction in the medical sense of the word"; "The use of marihuana does not lead to morphine or heroin or cocaine addiction and no effort is made to create a market for these narcotics by stimulating the practice of marihuana smoking"; "Marihuana is not the determining factor in the commission of major crimes"; "The publicity concerning the catastrophic effects of marihuana smoking in New York City is unfounded."

For *his* part, Anslinger attacked the New York Academy of Medicine's report—before it was even released—in a solicited article for the *American Journal of Psychiatry*. This was only one of Anslinger's many attempts, in the coming years, to either defund cannabis research or discredit publications that contradicted his views on prohibition. Over a decade later, Anslinger would attempt to prevent the publication of a joint study by the American Medical

Association and the American Bar Association that proposed the penalties for marijuana possession were too harsh. (I'll discuss these penalties in a moment.)

The La Guardia Report was ultimately ineffectual—at least from a legal standpoint. By 1942—after a century of being acknowledged as a medicine in the U.S.—marijuana was removed from the *U.S. Pharmacopeia* and stripped of its medicinal status and therapeutic legitimacy. Despite being published by medical authorities, the report did nothing to reverse that course. This medical silencing, of course, is an all-too-common theme in the plant's recent history.

Increased Punishments and Mandatory Sentencing

Anslinger's apparently boundless support—in the form of the Hearst, Dupont, and Mellon empires, as well as an increasingly invigorated pharmaceutical industry—meant the political power to double down as he wished on stricter and stricter penalties against marijuana users. This legislation came in three consecutive waves: in 1951, 1956, and 1970.

The year 1951 saw the passage of the Boggs Act, which instituted strict mandatory minimum prison sentences for drug crimes, including possession. For purposes of sentencing, the act made no distinction between drug *traffickers* and drug *users* ... nor did it distinguish between marijuana and other narcotics. Cannabis was lumped together with drugs like heroin, for the first time in legislative history—under a series of uniform penalties: A first offense (again, even of simple possession) carried a minimum prison sentence of 2–10 years and a minimum *fine* of $2,000 (maximum $20,000). Second offenses increased the mandatory minimum sentence to 5 years; third offenses to a minimum of 10 years.

The 1956 Narcotic Control Act instituted even stricter penalties by increasing the mandatory minimum prison sentences the Boggs Act had outlined for first, second, and third offenses. It also instituted the death penalty for some drug offenses. With the passage of these two acts, cannabis was effectively demonized—as were its traffickers and users.

However, the 1969 Supreme Court case *Leary v. United* States determined that the Marihuana Tax Act was, in fact, a violation of the 5th Amendment. Four years prior, the Harvard professor and psychedelic activist Timothy Leary had been arrested at the U.S.-Mexico border when a U.S. Customs official found marijuana in his car and charged him under Anslinger's 1937 act. Leary and his legal team successfully argued that Anslinger's legislation was fundamentally unconstitutional because it required that he incriminate himself. In other words, by paying the very tax that he was forced to pay *under the Tax Act* for transferring marijuana between countries, he would effectively be exposing himself to further criminal penalties (those imposed by the Boggs and Narcotic Control acts) under federal law. The Supreme Court recognized the catch-22 these three laws collectively presented, and the Marihuana Tax Act was ruled unconstitutional.

Lawmakers responded to this nullification with the 1970 Controlled Substances Act (Title II of the Comprehensive Drug Abuse Prevention and Control Act (DAPCA)), signed by President Richard Nixon as part of his nationwide "War on Drugs." The acts determined two things in particular worth noting. The first is that they repealed the mandatory minimum sentences set by the Boggs and Narcotic Control Acts. At the same time as DAPCA abolished minimum penalties, however, the Controlled Substance Act (CSA) classified cannabis as one of the most addictive and dangerous drugs. In this sense, DAPCA is a legislative measure that is strangely out of tune with itself.

The CSA established five "schedules" (categories) under which to classify substances, with the aim of controlling both narcotic and psychotropic drugs under a single system. Cannabis was placed in Schedule I, the most restrictive category, with "drugs, substances, or chemicals ... with no currently accepted medical use and a high potential for abuse," such as heroin and LSD. Assigning cannabis to this schedule effectively meant outlawing its sale, possession, and use—medical applications included. And of course, by *criminalizing* marijuana, the legislation also impeded medical *research* into cannabis, by restricting doctors' and scientists' legal procurement of the plant for purposes of medical inquiry.

It's worth noting the reason given for categorizing cannabis as a Schedule I drug. Dr. Roger O. Egeberg, Nixon's Assistant Secretary of Health, composed a letter on August 14, 1970, recommending the plant's scheduling as such. Egeberg chose his words carefully:

> Some question has been raised whether the use of the plant itself produces 'severe psychological or physical dependence' as required by a Schedule I or even Schedule II criterion. *Since there is still a considerable void in our knowledge* of the plant and effects of the active drug contained in it, our recommendation is that marihuana be retained within Schedule I at least until the completion of certain studies now underway to resolve the issue. If those studies make it appropriate for the Attorney General to change the placement of marihuana to a different schedule, he may do so in accordance with the authority provided under section 201 of the bill. (Italics mine).

As neurosurgeon and medical correspondent Sanjay Gupta observed in an important 2013 article titled "Why I Changed My Mind on Weed," "Not because of sound science, but because of its absence, marijuana was classified as a Schedule I substance." Many of the studies Egeberg's letter mentions were "underway" at the time were never completed—indeed, some because of the impasse created by making the plant unavailable to researchers by criminalizing it … and then saying it could be *de*criminalized once researchers (who could no longer access it) had proven it a viable therapeutic option. Nearly 50 years later, the plant is still listed a Schedule I drug because of this very catch-22.

One might be tempted to ask: Why place the plant in Schedule I, then? Why not Schedule II, where it could at least be available to medical researchers? (Schedule II is reserved for "drugs with a high potential for abuse," according to the DEA, but also with potential medical use.)

The answer seems to lie in Nixon's animus toward the counterculture movement of the '60s. In the years leading up to the Controlled Substances Act, the United States saw a pronounced increase in recreational marijuana use among youth. This was a generation experiencing an excess of material wealth and questioning and rebelling against the *previous* generation's values—including, most visibly, the war in Vietnam. Marijuana quickly became a symbol for this generation's shared suspicion of authority: As Stephen Siff writes, "the mild pleasures of the drug itself seemed to refute the logic of the laws against it."

In 1965, President Lyndon B. Johnson dramatically increased American military involvement in Vietnam—from 23,000 to 184,000 soldiers. By 1967—when 35,000 young men were being drafted every month—the antiwar movement was growing at pace. It wasn't long before these two grassroots movements became indissolubly linked: Marijuana activism was subsumed into the antiwar movement, and the drug was omnipresent at rallies and antiwar protests across the country. If it wasn't already, cannabis had *become* fiercely political. In response to the striking increase of recreational drug use during the late 1960s, Johnson created the Bureau of Narcotics and Dangerous Drugs by reorganizing the Federal Bureau of Narcotics and the Bureau of Drug Abuse Control under a single umbrella. This was in 1968, a year before Johnson left office. It was then up to Nixon to take up the baton.

Nixon couldn't stop the antiwar protests; but he *could* criminalize his opponents' behavior. Even after the passage of the Controlled Substances Act (which created its own set of difficulties for law enforcement), his obsession with the drug's *users*—as opposed to the drug itself—was unmistakable. In a taped Oval Office meeting with his Chief of Staff, H.R. Haldeman, in May of 1971, Nixon said, "I want a goddamn strong statement on marijuana. Can I get that out of this sonofabitching, uh, Domestic Council? I mean one on marijuana that just tears the ass out of them." "Them," of course, were the anti-war protesters (though Nixon's anti-Semitism emerges in the conversation as well. Moments later, he tells Haldeman: "Every one of the bastards that are out for legalizing marijuana is Jewish").

In a 1994 interview, John Ehrlichman, the Watergate co-conspirator who was serving as Domestic Policy Chief when Nixon's administration declared its war on drugs, conceded that the drug war was a stratagem to sabotage Nixon's political opposition: blacks and Vietnam War critics. The journalist Dan Baum writes:

> At the time, I was writing a book about the politics of drug prohibition. I started to ask Ehrlichman a series of earnest, wonky questions that he impatiently waved away. 'You want to know what this was really all about?' he asked with the bluntness of a man who, after public disgrace and a stretch in federal prison, had little left to protect. 'The Nixon campaign in 1968, and the Nixon White House after that, had two enemies: the antiwar left and black people. You understand what I'm saying? We knew we couldn't make it illegal to be either against the war or black, but by getting the public to associate the hippies with marijuana and blacks with heroin,

and then criminalizing both heavily, we could disrupt those communities. We could arrest their leaders, raid their homes, break up their meetings, and vilify them night after night on the evening news. Did we know we were lying about the drugs? Of course we did.'

It was a remarkable admission. Yet, even as Nixon was pushing his hateful agenda, it was becoming clear that the earlier laws (the 1951 and 1956 laws that set mandatory minimum sentences for marijuana possession) were becoming untenable. In the first place, by making marijuana possession a felony, legislators effectively put marijuana offenders in the costliest law enforcement category (alongside felonies such as arson and rape). The Schaffer Library of Drug Policy notes that, in the state of California alone, there were 214,809 drug arrests between 1960 and 1967. Over 40 percent of those arrests (91,529 of them) were marijuana arrests. "When arrests started doubling and tripling," they write, "it soon became evident that treating marijuana like heroin was going to be a very expensive proposition indeed."

The second problem concerned the *demographic* that was being arrested and held to minimum prison sentences. The dramatic increase in illegal drug use was occurring primarily among affluent white youth—on college campuses and in upscale suburbs. Matthew D. Lassiter uses California as an example of "the shifting racial and socioeconomic profile of the population arrested on drug charges" during the 1960s:

> Los Angeles County responded [to wide-scale recreational pot use in white suburbs] by declaring 'all-out war' against marijuana pushers, who turned out to be entrepreneurial suburban teenagers ... The police launched undercover operations in multiple suburban high schools, which prompted angry protests ... Marijuana arrests predominated

by 1967, with white Californians accounting for 68 percent of adults charged and 73 percent of juveniles, with the median drug criminal a 19-year-old white middle-class male busted for possession. Concentrated enforcement in the suburbs and on college campuses created a criminal class that judges and juries were unwilling to convict—successful prosecutions of marijuana defendants fell from 93 percent in 1960 to 48 percent by 1967. Given these realities, the California legislature revised the marijuana possession penalty in 1968, giving judges the discretion to sentence first-time offenders to probation. The police in many prosperous suburbs adopted a more informal policy of 'arresting young users to frighten them but not filing charges.'

The phenomena was hardly limited to California: Across states, marijuana arrests increased simultaneously with the increase of users on college campuses and in white neighborhoods. But neither judges nor legislators were enthusiastic about locking up America's young middle-class sweethearts—its "best and brightest"—for what seemed more and more like a minor offense. Suddenly the punishments of the Boggs and Narcotic Control Acts appeared out of proportion to the crime (or, at least, to the racial and sociopolitical status of the criminal). Lassiter continues:

> The founding of the National Organization for the Reform of Marijuana Laws (NORML), which defined its constituency as middle-class college students and professionals, enhanced the strategy of framing legalization as a mission to rescue white victims of the war on drugs. NORML's initial public relations campaign, titled Pot Luck, featured a forlorn white teenage girl locked inside a cell with an untouched plate of prison food on her lap. A 1969 CBS-TV special similarly asked if incarceration remained an appropriate punishment for 'laws broken so often by so many normally law-abiding

people,' contrasting drug use among Mexican immigrants and in black ghettos with a white 'career girl' who smoked pot to relax, a white suburban teenager who said 'the kids don't see any problem,' and a charming white bohemian facing a 20-year sentence.

Arguing that "the mandatory sentence can work extreme injustice," Senator Thomas Dodd introduced legislation in 1969 to allow judges more discretion in their sentencing, especially for those "college students and young people of middle and upper economic status" who are "not hardened criminals." Perhaps it's clear, now, why the 1970 Comprehensive Drug Abuse Prevention and Control Act, which passed, by the way, with only six dissenting votes, finally abolished minimum prison sentences.

In 1970, Nixon commissioned an investigative body, formally known as the National Commission on Marihuana and Drug Abuse, to "aid in determining the appropriate disposition of this question [how to treat cannabis at the federal level] in the future." The president appointed Republican Pennsylvania Governor Raymond P. Shafer—a former prosecutor with a reputation for strict enforcement—to lead the commission. Apparently, Nixon assumed Shafer would do his bidding and ultimately present a study that proved the danger of the substance and recommended permanent cannabis prohibition.

However, Nixon was already clear about what he was willing to hear. In a televised news conference held on May 1, 1971, the president claimed that he would *not* in fact legalize marijuana, regardless of what the report from the Shafer Commission (as it's informally known) recommended: "As you know, there is a Commission that is supposed to make recommendations to me about this subject; in this instance, however, I have such strong views that I will express them. I am against legalizing marijuana.

Even if the Commission does recommend that it be legalized, I will not follow that recommendation."

Nixon got his chance to fulfill that promise. In 1972, the National Commission on Marihuana and Drug Abuse released its report, tellingly titled "Marihuana: A Signal of Misunderstanding." Undoubtedly to Nixon's consternation, the report proposed decriminalizing the personal use of marijuana—which would have meant removing it from its Schedule I designation. Under the Shafer Commission's recommendation, "Possession of marihuana for personal use would no longer be an offense, but marihuana possessed in public would remain contraband subject to summary seizure and forfeiture. Casual distribution of small amounts of marihuana for no remuneration, or insignificant remuneration not involving profit would no longer be an offense."

Despite Nixon's rejection of the commission's recommendation—and despite the fact that its resolute Schedule I designation made procuring cannabis for research studies onerous at best—research on medical marijuana picked up pace. Remember, in the midst of all this—in 1964—the Israeli chemist Raphael Mechoulam, Professor of Medicinal Chemistry at the Hebrew University of Jerusalem, identified and synthesized the molecular structure of THC, the main psychoactive component in cannabis. He and his team also isolated the chemical structure of CBD. Even as debates about the plant raged at the political level, the properties of the plant were becoming understood at the biological level.

This new knowledge about the plant's chemical composition—knowledge that finally made it possible to extract its pure constituents—certainly contributed to renewed scientific and medical interest in cannabis. By 1972, NORML was petitioning the DEA to reschedule cannabis to Schedule II so that studies could commence, physicians could legally prescribe cannabis-based treatments, and citizens could benefit from its curative properties. Initially, federal authorities refused to accept NORML's petition. Even after the U.S. Court of Appeals *mandated* that they do so— in 1974—the DEA refused to properly process the petition for another eight years. (When they finally did, it was once again by a court order.)

In September of 1988, the DEA's own Administrative Law Judge, Francis Young, formally recommended that cannabis be placed in Schedule II in response to NORML's 16-year-old petition. According to Young, "marijuana, in its natural form, is one of the safest therapeutically active substances known to man." What's more, "the evidence in this record clearly shows that marijuana has been accepted as capable of relieving the distress of great numbers of very ill people, and doing so with safety under medical supervision. It would be unreasonable, arbitrary and capricious for the DEA to continue to stand between those sufferers and the benefits of this substance in light of the evidence in this record."

The DEA Administrator, Jack Lawn, ultimately overruled Young and ordered that cannabis remain a Schedule I substance, unattainable by medical patients.

Legalization Becomes a State Fight

With such irrational obstinacy at the federal level, one can see why cannabis finally became a state issue. As states listened to popular demand (street-level activism and ballot initiatives) in the midst of increased understanding about the plant and its therapeutic properties, they began paving their own paths toward legalization. In 1973, even as the DEA was being formed to enforce the newly-created drug schedules of the CSA, Oregon became the first state to decriminalize possession of small amounts of marijuana. By the late 1970s, a dozen states, among them Alaska, Maine, Colorado,

Mississippi, New York, Nebraska, North Carolina, and Ohio, had followed suit. In the meantime, other states had reduced the penalties associated with possession.

As states decriminalized the drug, patients quickly began reporting its medical benefits: Those suffering from chronic pain, glaucoma, spinal injuries, multiple sclerosis, and other maladies were finally experiencing various forms of relief. Cancer patients observed that smoking marijuana reduced the extreme nausea caused by chemotherapy; researchers at Harvard in the 1970s scientifically bolstered their claims.

Indeed, Lester Grinspoon, Professor Emeritus at Harvard Medical School who has written several important books on marijuana, has discussed the ways marijuana helped his son, who died of leukemia at the age of 13 in 1973. The drug eliminated the nausea and vomiting Danny experienced after each round of chemotherapy. It's worth noting that Grinspoon undertook his first book, *Marijuana Reconsidered* (1971), with the conviction that marijuana was an extremely harmful drug; his intention was to articulate the nature of its dangers. But the more research he did, the more he realized that he, and the general public, had been completely misled. Hence the book's title.

In 1978, New Mexico passed the Controlled Substances Therapeutic Research Act. In doing so, it became the first state to pass legislation acknowledging the medical value of cannabis. The following year, Virginia passed legislation allowing doctors to recommend cannabis to patients suffering from glaucoma or the side effects of chemotherapy. In fact, by the end of 1982, 30 states had passed legislation addressing the medical use of cannabis, the majority of which sought to institute federally-approved therapeutic research programs. This included more conservative states such as Alabama, Georgia, Louisiana, and Texas. (Like Virginia, these states seem to have been particularly interested in treatments for both glaucoma and cancer, according to Steven C. Markoff's "State-by-State Medical Marijuana Laws.")

Eventually, these programs came to a halt during the Reagan Administration. Reagan's 1986 Anti-Drug Abuse Act reinstated the previously-repealed mandatory minimum sentences for a wide variety of drug offenses and raised penalties for possession and distribution. Indeed, just as medical cannabis was gaining great momentum at the state level, Reagan's inclusion of marijuana in his "War on Drugs" became the wall that every state's legislation ultimately crashed up against.

Reagan's eventual interference aside, it's *this* decade—the 1970s—in which, as I see it, humans circled back to the compassion component I discussed in the introduction and at the beginning of this chapter. And *those* cases of compassion were happening at both state and federal levels.

In November 1976, for example, in federal court case *United States v. Randall*, a Washington, D.C. man by the name of Robert Randall sought recourse in the little-used Common Law Doctrine of Necessity to defend himself against the criminal charges he was facing for marijuana cultivation. Randall had suffered from glaucoma since he was a teenager and was cultivating his own small supply of cannabis to alleviate his symptoms, which included vision loss and visual distortions. Randall's medical doctor helped him present the argument that, of all the drugs he had access to, marijuana had been the most effective in helping him avoid vision loss. (Randall had developed a tolerance to all the other drugs, rendering them useless.) The judge in that case, James Washington, determined that Randall's cultivation and use of marijuana constituted a "medical necessity" and dropped all criminal charges.

While the Supreme Court was handing down this ruling, federal agencies were responding to a petition Randall filed in May of that year, offering him FDA-approved, legal access to a government supply of medical marijuana. This was a landmark moment: In 1976, Robert Randall became the first American to lawfully receive marijuana to treat a medical disorder. (As an aside, Randall's ophthalmologist had told him, in the early '70s, that he would surely go blind within a few years. When Randall died, in 2001, he was still regularly using government-issued cannabis ... *and he had not lost his sight.*)

Randall's government-supplied marijuana was granted through a new FDA code called the Investigational New Drug (IND) Compassionate Use Program. He became one of a handful of patients to receive government cannabis, supplied by the National Institute on Drug Abuse (NIDA). IND patients' diagnoses ranged from multiple sclerosis, to multiple congenital cartilaginous exostoses, to glaucoma, to AIDS. In 1991, the government suspended the Compassionate Use Program; and in 1992, they officially terminated it. This was due to the surge in applicants during the AIDS epidemic. Michael Iskioff's write-up in the June 22, 1991 edition of the *Washington Post*, titled "HHS to Phase Out Marijuana Program," is worth citing in full:

> A federal program that has provided free marijuana to the seriously ill is being phased out by Health and Human Services officials who have concluded it undercuts official Bush administration policy against the use of illegal drugs, according to HHS officials. While a small number of patients already receiving marijuana will continue to do so, new applicants will be encouraged to try synthetic forms of delta-9-THC, the psychoactive ingredient in marijuana, rather than the weed itself, according to a new policy directive due to be signed by James O. Mason, chief of the Public Health Service.

Mason said Friday he was concerned about a surge in new applications in recent months, especially from AIDS patients, and the message it would send if HHS were to approve them.

While Mason didn't clarify *what* "message it would send" if HHS were to approve cannabis for AIDS patients, the stigmatizing—and homophobic—language here is unambiguous. What's more, the fact that IND patients were recommended, as alternatives, synthetic forms of the *very same drug* the administration deemed "illegal" is once again proof of the power of Big Pharma. Indeed, the same year the government closed the Compassionate Use Program, it approved the pharmaceutical medication dronabinol, a synthetic form of THC, as an appetite stimulant for AIDS wasting syndrome and anorexia. (The FDA had previously approved dronabinol in 1985 as an antiemetic for patients receiving chemotherapy.)

As the saying goes: Follow the money if you want to know where the corruption is.

While the thirteen patients receiving medical cannabis through IND would be "grandfathered in" and continue to be supplied, all pending applicants would be without access, indefinitely. Two years later, in 1994, the Assistant Secretary of Health, Dr. Philip Lee, announced his decision not to reopen the Compassionate Use Program. Dr. Rick Doblin's write-up of Dr. Lee's announcement in the *Newsletter of the Multidisciplinary Association for Psychedelic Studies* once again reveals a government-generated catch-22:

> Dr. Lee indicated that he has decided not to reopen the Compassionate Access Program. According to Dr. Lee, the fatal flaw of that program was that it did not generate data that could be submitted to the FDA to either support or reject the hypothesis that smoked marijuana had a safe and efficacious medical use. Dr. Lee did not offer any government funds for research, yet indicated that only FDA-approved research could resolve this controversy.

No money for research … and yet *only* research could reopen the program. Naturally, the pharmaceutical companies were delighted at this turn of events. Marinol, one of the trade names for Dronabinol, was originally placed in Schedule II when Unimed Pharmaceuticals was granted the patent for its synthetic THC. In July of 1999, however, the DEA agreed to move Marinol to Schedule III in response to a rescheduling petition from Unimed. As Mark Eddy writes, the DEA's decision to reschedule was "to make [Marinol] more widely available to patients. The rescheduling was granted after a review by the DEA and the Department of Health and Human Services found little evidence of illicit abuse of the drug. In Schedule III, Marinol is now subject to fewer regulatory controls and lesser criminal sanctions for illicit use."

Remember, the DEA placed cannabis in Schedule I because of its "high potential for abuse." Yet, wholly illogically, it placed its synthetic counterpart in Schedule III, because the drug is *not* illicitly abused. Yet the natural compound continues to prove more capable than its synthetic counterpart. As Kambiz Akhavan writes, state-sponsored studies have "revealed that thousands of patients found marijuana safer and more effective than synthetic THC." Paul Fassa points to Big Pharma's corruption before noting a critical difference between cannabis and Marinol: "Big Pharma researches natural items for only one reason: to find out how to create synthetic versions, patent them, and market them with FDA approval for big profits whether they are actually *effective and safe or not* … The FDA reported four deaths from synthetic Marinol, while raw cannabis's death toll remains at zero."

Other synthetic cannabinoids that have come on the market are Cesamet (Schedule II), used to treat neuropathic pain and nausea; Syndros (Schedule II), used to treat chemo-induced nausea and wasting syndrome; and Sativex (Schedule IV), used for persistent cancer-related pain.

But new access to these synthetic forms of cannabis had little effect on citizen initiatives to legalize the real thing. In 1991, San Francisco resident and marijuana activist Dennis Peron organized Proposition P, the San Francisco medical marijuana initiative, which passed in November of that year with 79 percent of the vote. Peron's activism was fueled by the memory of his partner, Jonathan West, who had used medical marijuana to treat his AIDS symptoms. Proposition P was not legally binding—it didn't have the force of law; but as a resolution that declared the city's support for medical cannabis, it was a significant formal step. And while it didn't *legalize* cannabis, it made the plant's possession, cultivation, and distribution the SFPD's lowest priority.

Peron went on to work with Dr. Tod H. Mikuriya to organize Proposition 215, the Compassionate Use Act, which would legalize marijuana for medical use at the state level. (Mikuriya, remember, had worked relentlessly to collect and summarize all the scientific literature on the therapeutic uses of cannabis in 1973. He remained devoted to the cause of decriminalization throughout the '80s and '90s.) On November 5, 1996, over 5 million California voters approved Peron's proposition, which passed with 55.6 percent of the vote. The Compassionate Use Act was the first legislation of its kind—indeed, it made California one of the first governments *in the world* to permit both patients and their primary caregivers to possess and cultivate cannabis as long as they had a physician's recommendation.

Moreover, physicians who approved or recommended the use of medical marijuana for a patient's relief could not lose their licenses under this act. As such, patients, primary caregivers, and physicians were all (at least in theory) protected from federal punishment. The Compassionate Use Act's list of qualifying conditions included AIDS, anorexia, arthritis, cancer, chronic pain, glaucoma, migraine, and spasticity; although the law also permitted physicians to recommend medical marijuana for "any other illness for which marijuana provides relief."

In this sense, the origins of our modern cannabis culture *do*, indeed, have their roots in compassion. Finally, Californians who were suffering from debilitating or terminal illness could find relief through one of the only drugs that appeared to provide it in a powerful, and sustained, way.

Even as President Clinton continued Reagan and Bush's "War on Drugs," the Compassionate Care Act set off a chain reaction of medical marijuana legalization across North America: Oregon, Alaska, and Washington followed suit in 1998; Maine in 1999; Hawaii, Nevada, and Colorado in 2000; Vermont and Montana in 2004 … and as the years went on, that list got longer. As of this writing, 33 states have legalized cannabis for medical use, as have Washington, D.C. and the US. territories of Guam and Puerto Rico.

The details, of course, vary by state: some limit medical cannabis to pills or oils and prohibit the smoked form; the lists of qualifying conditions vary between states, as well. The more common conditions include cancer (and the side effects associated with chemo), glaucoma, HIV/AIDS, multiple sclerosis, Parkinson's disease, Crohn's disease, ALS (Lou Gehrig's disease), chronic pain, hepatitis C, Alzheimer's disease, Tourette's syndrome, PTSD, epilepsy, Huntington's disease, fibromyalgia, arthritis, and dementia. Some states' lists are even longer than this.

But legalization didn't stop at medical use. On January 1, 2014, Colorado became the first state to legalize cannabis for *recreational* use ("adult use"), permitting dispensaries to sell marijuana to consumers with or *without* physician recommendation. Washington became the second state to legalize recreational marijuana later that year. Alaska, Oregon, Massachusetts, Nevada, Washington, D.C., California, Maine, and Vermont followed suit. Just last month—in the November 2018 midterms—voters in Michigan approved a ballot measure making their state the first in the Midwest to legalize adult-use. (November's mid-terms also saw both Missouri and Utah approving initiatives legalizing medical marijuana.) As of this writing, 10 states and Washington, D.C. have legalized marijuana for recreational use.

And public support for legalized marijuana—both medical *and* recreational—continues to grow at a sustained clip. In 2005, Gallup Poll Assistant Editor Joseph Carroll wrote: "In 1969, just 12 percent of Americans supported making marijuana legal, but by 1977, roughly one in four endorsed it. Support edged up to 31 percent in 2000, and now [in 2005], about a third of Americans say marijuana should be legal." Four years later (2009), support had grown to 44 percent; by October of 2017, support was at 61 percent. And according to a Quinnipiac poll from April of this year (2018), "American voters support 63 percent legalizing marijuana in the U.S., the highest level of support ever measured in a Quinnipiac University Poll. The previous high was 61 percent in an August 3, 2017 survey. Support for use of medical marijuana is 93 percent."

At this point, you can probably see why public support is as loud as it is—even (or perhaps *especially*) in the face of Big Pharma.

In a 2012 study titled "Prevalence of Medical Marijuana Use in California," Suzanne Ryan-Ibarra et al. reported that 92 percent of Californians who were prescribed cannabis confirmed that it had helped them treat a serious medical condition. Doctors and patients are finding—sometimes accidentally—that cannabis can treat more conditions than they'd ever imagined (sunburn, for example). Cancerous tumors are shrinking. And—as Dr. Margaret Gedde mentions in an interview with Joseph Mercola—perhaps one of the most exciting aspects of the quickly-burgeoning cannabis industry is that "because we have just these hundreds of different strains of marijuana and cannabis, each of which is slightly different, there is a huge potential to customize for each person."

After decades of demonizing "marijuana," the United States may finally be ready to treat cannabis with the same reverence the ancients did. And the compassion component seems, indeed, to be leading the way. Sanjay Gupta described this historical moment of reevaluation well (though he was speaking for himself):

> I mistakenly believed the Drug Enforcement Agency listed marijuana as a Schedule I substance because of sound scientific proof. Surely, they must have quality reasoning as to why marijuana is in the category of the most dangerous drugs that have 'no accepted medicinal use and a high potential for abuse.' They didn't have the science to support that claim, and I now know that when it comes to marijuana neither of those things are true. It doesn't have a high potential for abuse, and there are very legitimate medical applications. In fact, sometimes marijuana is the only thing that works … it is irresponsible not to provide the best care we can as a medical community, care that could involve marijuana. We have been terribly and systematically misled for nearly 70 years in the United States, and I apologize for my own role in that.

Along with Dr. Gupta, Americans, it appears, are wising up. We're starting to realize how a powerful pharmaceutical industry has helped shape the story of cannabis, demonizing a miracle plant for the sake of profits. As Dr. Gupta said in an interview with CNN earlier this year:

> When … I started looking at all the scientific literature … 94 percent … of the studies were designed to find harm: What is the risk of addiction, what is the risk of cancer, what are the side effects? And only about 6 percent were designed to find

any benefit. So if you're looking at that from a macro level, you'd say, well there's nothing here; this is mainly problematic. And I realized that was a problem upstream. Studies designed to find benefit were not getting funded; researchers could not conduct those studies; it was preordained as a substance that has no medicinal value ... that's when it started to change [for me].

It's changing for many of us, who are ready for the details about all the benefits cannabis has to offer us.

In the meantime, the industry that has grown up—and grown up *quickly*—in the wake of state-level ballot measures faces a number of obstacles, thanks to the plant's federally-illegal status and the financial and political clout of big business (among other things, such as a flooded market and a public that's uninformed about the differences between CBD, THC, and hemp). If you're *in* the industry, you understand these obstacles acutely. But for outsiders eyeing the industry and looking to get in, or simply curious about what it looks like on the inside, I'll cover these details in the next chapter.

3

The Current State of the Industry

Optimism Amidst the Chaos

The DEA has been "considering," and ultimately denying, petitions to reschedule cannabis for decades: from NORML's 1972 petition, to a 1981 bill co-sponsored by none other than the conservative future Speaker of the House Newt Gingrich, to citizens' petitions in 2001 and 2006. So the DEA's most *recent* refusal to reschedule cannabis, in August of 2016, in response to an appeal from a cohort of U.S. senators, including Elizabeth Warren, Cory Booker, Ron Wyden, and Kirsten Gillibrand, is only one instance in a decades-long pattern of brazen rejection in the face of medical evidence.

Indeed, amidst its most recent "considerations," DEA staff coordinator Russ Baer acknowledged that yes, "marijuana is important … but our efforts are mainly focused on the nation's growing opioid crisis." Baer's comment demonstrates an outrageous ignorance about the *actual* relationship between cannabis and "the nation's growing opioid crisis"—namely, that the *legalization* of the former would mean the *alleviation* of the latter. Studies have already begun to show that one consequence of marijuana legalization is lower rates of opioid overdose. One 2014 study, "Medical Cannabis Laws and Opioid Analgesic Overdose Mortality in the United States, 1999–2010," showed that opiate overdoses decreased *by nearly 25 percent* in states that had legalized marijuana. After all, patients in those states now have access to a natural alternative that is self-limiting and doesn't allow for overdose.

Given that one arm of the federal government (the DEA) continues so stubbornly—indeed, so perversely—to restrict cannabis to Schedule I, it may confound you to hear that in October of 2003, *another* arm of the U.S. government (the Department of Health and Human Services) *received a patent for cannabinoids.* Yes; you read that correctly. U.S. Patent No. 6,630,507 is for the therapeutic use of "cannabinoids as antioxidants and neuroprotectants." Its abstract reads:

> Cannabinoids have been found to have antioxidant properties. This new found property makes cannabinoids useful in the treatment and prophylaxis of wide [sic] variety of oxidation associated diseases, such as ischemic, age-related, inflammatory and autoimmune diseases. The cannabinoids are found to have particular application as neuroprotectants, for example in limiting neurological damage following ischemic insults, such as stroke and trauma, or in the treatment of neurodegenerative diseases, such as Alzheimer's disease, Parkinson's disease and HIV dementia. Nonpsychoactive cannabinoids, such as cannabidoil, are particularly advantageous to use because they avoid toxicity that is encountered with psychoactive cannabinoids at high doses useful in the method of the present invention.

Given what you now know about the centuries-long medical history of cannabis, you may be bewildered by the patent's claim that cannabis' antioxidant properties are "new found"—as though the HHS was the first to discover them. But here's the thing worth noting: When the Department of Health and Human Services refers to "non-psychoactive cannabinoids" in this patent, they're talking about both synthetic *and natural* cannabinoids. In other words, the patent is, in part, for compounds from the plant itself.

Now remember: Schedule I substances are categorized as such because they've been deemed to have *zero* medical value ("no currently accepted medical use and a high potential for abuse," according to the DEA). This means that, even as the government insists that cannabis *offers no therapeutic benefits whatsoever*, it holds a patent indicating that it *does* believe cannabis has a "useful" place in medicine. The word itself is in the patent's abstract … along with the word "advantageous."

What's more, the patent states that "no signs of toxicity or serious side effects have been observed following chronic administration of cannabidiol to healthy volunteers … *even in large acute doses*." (Again, compare the effect opioids have in "large acute doses.") It's a radical acknowledgement in the face of its own definition of a Schedule I drug. According to the patent, cannabis *has* medicinal properties, and the very compounds that demonstrate these properties are not unsafe for human consumption.

Patent 6,630,507 reveals a radical disconnect between government departments—and it's only one of many examples of such discord (a discord perhaps less gently called "hypocrisy"). After all, the patent concedes that, for as long as the DEA has been denying rescheduling petitions, it has *known* about cannabis' potential medical value: The patent, filed in 1999, references 12 other cannabis-related U.S. patents that date back as far as 1942.

This discord is the grounds of what I see as the "chaos stage" of the broader cannabis narrative: the realm in which the current industry is attempting to find its footing, define itself, and sustain itself.

Granted, the government's cannabinoid patent isn't for the whole cannabis plant. Because it only covers *some non-psychoactive* cannabinoids, for example, it has nothing to do with tetrahydrocannabinol (THC), though it *does* mention CBD quite often. And while the patent isn't for the compounds *themselves*, it *is* for 26 different *methods of use* (called "method claims"), some of which are very broad. Claim 1, for instance, covers "a method of treating diseases caused by oxidative stress, comprising administering a therapeutically effective amount of a cannabinoid that has substantially no binding to the NMDA receptor to a subject who has a disease caused by oxidative stress."

So while the government doesn't own patent rights to cannabis *per se*, it *could* prevent another entity from using cannabinoids to treat any *number* of "disease[s] caused by oxidative stress." Oxidative stress may be the cause of *a lot* of diseases, Alzheimer's, Parkinson's, and cirrhosis among them. Elizabeth Crozier at *Prøhbtd* writes: "The patent goes on to speculate about the benefits of these compounds in treating glaucoma, seizures and more. Think of these compounds like plastic wrap or a ziplock, which you would use to cover food you don't want getting old and dried out ... When they say CBD is an antioxidant, they mean it prevents your brain from oxidizing, better known as aging."

That's a wide range of uses the government has patented claims o, and for a very significant set of processes.

When the government gave this patent to itself, it ensured, of course, that it would see financial gains on the methods of use it encompasses. The New York-based company Kannalife Sciences Inc. is the sole licensee of patent 6,630,507. The company has exclusive rights to use the technology outlined in the patent to develop cannabinoid- and CBD-based drugs that treat hepatic encephalopathy, a form of brain damage that can result from a number of conditions, including cirrhosis.

Kannalife began raising $15 million in private investments in 2016—*after* the DEA's most recent decision not to reschedule. And that chronology is worth noting: Dean Petkanas, Kannalife's CEO, claimed that the DEA's ruling was "the best possible outcome" for his company. But it's *also* a great outcome for the National Institutes of Health—the specific agency of the Department of Health and

Human Services that received patent 6,630,507. The agreement between Kannalife and the National Institutes of Health (NIH) entitles the NIH, a governmental body, to a percentage of royalties once Kannalife starts seeing financial returns on their product. These royalty payments are expected to be in "the six figures," and will be accompanied by milestone payments.

So it's not just Kannalife that's set to make a fortune from patent 6,630,507. And you can imagine why neither Kannalife nor the NIH would be interested in approving marijuana at the federal level: Patents could then, in theory, come in from everywhere. Indeed, Petkanas has said that he anticipates Kannalife will eventually seek orphan drug status—an FDA designation for drugs that treat rare conditions. (Of course, orphan drug status typically involves financial incentives such as protracted periods of exclusivity. In other words, while patent 6,630,507 is set to expire on April 21, 2019, being granted orphan status would mean that *only* Kannalife could market the drug and *only* Kannalife and the NIH would see the financial returns.)

The (Other) Special Interests Keeping Cannabis Criminalized

I wanted to start with this baffling and duplicitous government patent because, for all the discussion of Big Pharma in the last chapter (and oh, there's more discussion on Big Pharma to come!), it's worth keeping in mind that the pharmaceutical industry isn't the *only* powerful industry that's doing all it can to keep cannabis criminalized at both federal and state levels. It's *these* special interests whose repudiation of research on cannabis' benefits—and whose disregard for citizens' petitions and public opinion—are co-creating and maintaining the chaos in the industry:

Big Government

We know, now, that the National Institutes of Health is set to make a potential fortune from Kannalife's work under patent 6,630,507 ... *assuming*, that is, that the DEA continues to hold cannabis in Schedule I. But the NIH (and, by extension, the HHS) are hardly the only government entities that benefit from the ongoing criminalization of cannabis.

In 2010, Jeffrey Miron, Senior Lecturer and Director of Undergraduate Studies in the Department of Economics at Harvard University, published a study called "The Budgetary Impact of Ending Drug Prohibition." What Miron found was that the legalization of marijuana would result in roughly $8.7 billion in savings by the federal government on law enforcement spending—that's over $10 billion today, if we account for inflation. What's more, according to Miron, another $8.7 billion in tax revenue would be generated ... indeed, we've already started to see this in states such as Colorado and California, who've legalized both medical and recreational marijuana.

But while those numbers are great for citizens (in 2017, $41 million of Colorado's marijuana tax fund went to education and public health, for example), what legalization would mean for government agencies whose role is drug *enforcement* is that they'd have to give up their budgets and their power—and no agency is going to be willing to do that voluntarily. (Remember, part of the impetus behind Harry Anslinger's anti-marijuana crusade in the 1930s was that Prohibition had ended. Once alcohol was a legal substance again, he needed to turn his animus elsewhere or risk losing funding for his Federal Bureau of Narcotics. Agencies such as the DEA face the same risk today that Anslinger faced back then.)

Marijuana prohibition is a $20 billion-a-year federal jobs project. To give you a sense of what that looks like at the state level, in the decade leading up to Miron's study, between 2000 and 2010, local governments in Washington *alone* spent $211 million to enforce marijuana laws, according to estimates by the American Civil Liberties Union. That's $211 million to arrest, jail, prosecute, defend, and convict adults for even the slightest of marijuana offenses, in *one* state. (Washington legalized recreational marijuana in 2012). More broadly, we're also talking over 10,800 DEA employees, as well as employees in agencies such as the CIA, the NSA, the DoD, and the State Department—all of whom have enforcement for the War on Drugs written into their budgets.

And if federal marijuana prohibition ends, it won't just mean scaled-down agency budgets. In a report issued in March of 2017 by the U.S. Department of Justice, the Inspector General found that the DEA seized approximately $3.2 billion in cash from drug-related suspects in the ten years leading up to the study—and that's just *cash*; it doesn't include seized assets. And the word "suspects" is the crucial word in that sentence: Many of those seizures resulted in neither civil nor criminal charges being brought against the property owners. Of course, whether or not there are charges makes no difference to the DEA, which keeps what it seizes regardless.

In the description of its Domestic Cannabis Eradication / Suppression Program, the DEA currently claims on its website that it has seized "in excess of 20.5 million dollars of cultivator assets." But in light of the Inspector General's report—as well as claims elsewhere that it "seized $27 Billion in assets in 2014 through its cannabis enforcement program"—there seems to be a lot the DEA isn't publicly accounting for. You can imagine why keeping cannabis illegal is a great boon not only for the DEA, but also for every other agency involved with drug enforcement. The financial boon, depending on the agency, can be dual: It keeps their agencies funded and their budgets strong, *and* gives them the legal authority to seize cash and assets from "suspects."

Big Alcohol

At every level imaginable, cannabis outrivals booze and the alcohol industry is fully aware of this, despite "studies" that claim otherwise. Cannabis is alcohol's zero-calorie, no-hangover competitor, with *vastly* fewer short- and long-term health risks. According to the National Institute on Alcohol Abuse and Alcoholism, "an estimated 88,000 people (approximately 62,000 men and 26,000 women) die from alcohol-related causes annually, making alcohol the third leading preventable cause of death in the United States." (Tobacco and "poor diet and physical in activity" are the first two.) Compare this to ProCon.org's study of "Deaths from Marijuana vs. 17 FDA-Approved Drugs," in which cannabis was found to be the primary suspect of death in *exactly zero* cases. (Those 17 FDA-Approved drugs didn't perform so well in the competition, either ... but I'll get to *that* shortly.)

Not only is there no "lethal dose" when it comes to cannabis, the drug carries centuries of documented health benefits with it. Alcohol, on the other hand, had been linked to liver disease, organ failure (such as heart damage and pancreatitis), and cancer. Even the NIH—the *same* NIH that's set to benefit from Kannalife—admits that "results of most epidemiologic studies ... have shown that alcohol intake is associated with increased breast cancer risk." According to the 2013 study "Alcohol-Attributable Cancer Deaths and Years of Potential Life Lost in the United States," "Alcohol consumption resulted in an estimated 18,200 to 21,300 cancer deaths." Contrast those dire numbers with research that shows cannabinoids trigger apoptosis (cell death) in cancerous cells ... and their anti-cancer efficacy could very well change the course of cancer research, if only further studies could be done.

In light of the obvious uphill battle it faces, the alcohol industry has doubled down on efforts to advertise and market its products as having inherent health benefits—despite the fact that alcohol can be harmful *even when* consumed in moderation ... and can be downright fatal otherwise. Granted, this isn't a new PR strategy: Big Alcohol has sought to portray "moderate drinking" as one element of a healthy, active lifestyle for some time. The most recent iteration of this misinformation campaign was the Moderate Alcohol and Cardiovascular Health trial: a study conducted by the National Institute on Alcohol Abuse and Alcoholism (NIAAA—a division of the NIH).

The title of the study alone suggests the "researchers'" motivations are suspect; but if you still weren't convinced of an inherent bias in the study, the fact that its donors are among the most powerful alcohol corporations in the world should seal the deal for you. A recent news release on the study from the NIH reads: "The trial is funded in part by NIAAA, which expected to commit $20 million to the overall project over 10 years, of which $4 million has been spent, and in part by private donations of $67.7 million ... Private-sector funders are Anheuser-Busch InBev, Carlsberg Breweries A/S, Diageo plc, Heineken, and Pernod Ricard USA LLC."

All five of those private-sector funders are alcohol companies.

And here's the thing: That excerpt is from a June 2018 news release titled "NIH to End Funding for Moderate Alcohol and Cardiovascular Health Trial." The decision to cut funding, the NIH claims, was "based on concerns about the study design that cast doubt on its ultimate credibility." Exactly how the NIH lacked the foresight to recognize that a study about alcohol's "health effects," funded by "donations" to the tune of $67 million from alcohol companies, would ultimately have credibility issues, is beyond me. But at least in *this* case, the NIH woke up to the truth of the matter.

It's not only the "scientific" studies that are in jeopardy. Alcohol has seen a drop in sales since the beginning of state-level cannabis legalization—particularly of recreational cannabis. A 2017 study co-authored by Alberto Chong, Professor of Economics at Georgia State University, found that in counties that have decriminalized medical marijuana, alcohol purchases had decreased by as much as 15 percent. What's more—according to the Georgia State University News Hub—"the study authors also looked at counties along state borders and found those with legal access to marijuana had 20 percent lower alcohol sales than those across the border in states without medical marijuana laws." This suggests, of course, that people are crossing state borders to get what is ultimately a healthier recreational substance.

In counties where both medical and recreational marijuana is legal, cannabis sales are eclipsing alcohol sales. In Colorado's biggest resort towns—Aspen and Boulder—for instance, tourists and residents alike help generate more profits and tax revenues through marijuana sales than through alcohol sales in bars. A February 2018 article in *The Aspen Times* reads: "Legal-pot purveyors hauled in $11.3 million in revenue last year compared with $10.5 million for liquor stores, marking the first time marijuana sales outpaced booze for the year in Aspen." Indeed, cannabis sales have seen sharp annual increases in Aspen since the town opened its first pot shop in 2014.

Alcohol sales have also begun underperforming in Oregon and Washington now that both states legalized recreational use and implemented a retail infrastructure. Right now in Washington, sales numbers for cannabis and alcohol are nearly identical.

Given the superiority of its competitor, one can see why the beer and alcohol industries have lobbied for years to ensure cannabis remains federally illegal. Their wars have been waged through subversion of medical research, backroom lobbying, and collusion with major government agencies. According to Alfonso Serrano at *The Guardian* (October 2016), "the Arizona Wine and Spirits Wholesale Association gave one of the largest donations to the state's anti-legalization campaign when it paid $10,000 to Arizonans for Responsible Drug Policy. And the Beer Distributors PAC recently donated $25,000 to the Campaign for a Safe and Healthy Massachusetts, making it the state's third-largest backer of the opposition to recreational cannabis."

In 2010, the California Beer & Beverage Distributors "donated" $10,000 to Public Safety First, a committee organized to obstruct the passage of Proposition 19, which would have legalized adult recreational use of marijuana 6 years earlier than it was ultimately legalized in the state. And these donations are only the tip of the iceberg: It's been estimated that Public Safety First *alone* has received $4 million in donations (read: investments) from various entities in the beer and alcohol industry. The National Association of Wine Retailers' 2018 "Report on Alcohol Wholesaler State Campaign Contributions" discloses alcohol wholesalers have donated more than $107 million to political campaigns over the past five election cycles. According to Steve Davis at *Big Buds Magazine*, many of the politicians receiving money from Big Alcohol belong to organizations that promote anti-marijuana messaging.

The grand irony, of course, is that the alcohol industry is helping stoke a misinformation campaign about the health and public safety risks posed by cannabis, when *their* product is actually the one posing those risks. And the U.S. Government doesn't exactly seem interested in following the money... because, once again, they're implicated.

One story in particular about government involvement in the misinformation campaign is worth sharing. In 2015, Michael Siegel, professor at the School of Public Health at Boston University, was invited to meet with George Koob, Director of the Institute on Alcohol Abuse and Alcoholism. The meeting was over research the NIAAA had requested from Siegel, and funded, on the association between alcohol marketing and underage drinking.

As we've seen before (remember Nixon?), the government's response to the truth was outright hostile. When Siegel presented evidence to support how showing alcohol in television shows impacted underage drinking, Koob responded by leaping out of his chair and screaming, "I don't fucking care!" Siegel was initially baffled by Koob's response (wouldn't the director of the NIAAA be *thankful* to learn about misconduct in the industry?); but he later learned that Koob was "quietly wooing the alcoholic beverage industry to contribute tens of millions of dollars for a study on whether drinking "moderate" amounts of alcohol was good for the heart"—the same Moderate Alcohol and Cardiovascular Health study I mentioned above, which the NIH eventually pulled out of.

As Sharon Begley, senior science writer at *STAT*, writes, "Koob, in a previously undisclosed email sent six months before the contentious 2015 meeting … had assured the alcohol industry's leading trade group that research like … Siegel's on alcohol advertising, which was published in respected journals, would never again be funded."

After these revelations came to light, the director of Public Citizen's Health Research Group, Dr. Michael Carome, released a public statement. It protested the appalling fact that "since Dr. Koob became NIAAA director, the institute has not funded any new alcohol advertising research." Carome continues: "Rather than acting in the best interest of the American public, Dr. Koob has been acting at the behest of the alcohol industry's interests. The only way to excise this corruption from within the NIAAA and begin to restore public trust in the institute is for Dr. Koob to resign or be fired."

Carome's statement is dated April 5, 2018. I am writing this in November, and Koob is still the NIAAA's director. This is the same man whose agency oversees studies that show—according to Koob himself—"that marijuana use can lead to harmful consequences for individuals and society." So you can place Big Alcohol, and *keep* Big Government, on your list of entities doing what they can to ensure marijuana remains illegal at the federal level.

Big Tobacco

The tobacco industry has had a rather ambivalent relationship to cannabis for decades now, perceiving it as both a potential *product* and a potential *competitor*. As Rachel Ann Barry, et al. write in their study "Waiting for the Opportune Moment: The Tobacco Industry and Marijuana Legalization":

"Documents reveal that since at least 1970, despite fervent denials, three multinational tobacco companies, Philip Morris (PM), British American Tobacco (BAT, including its US subsidiary Brown & Williamson [B&W]), and RJ Reynolds (RJR), all have considered manufacturing cigarettes containing cannabis. The documents demonstrate the tobacco industry's willingness and preparedness to enter legalized marijuana markets, which the companies believed to have a large sales potential. Although the tobacco industry has not visibly supported marijuana legalization, as policymakers discussed decriminalization and potential legalization, the tobacco industry's corporate planners took into consideration the shifting public opinion and future consumer demand."

Indeed, tobacco giants have been observing, and acting on, "shifting public opinion" since the 60s. You'll recall the explosion of recreational marijuana use during the Vietnam War that I discussed in the last chapter. (Maybe you'll also recall it from personal experience.) In 1970, at the height of this boom, Philip Morris, the maker of Marlboro, applied for, and was granted, a special permit from the government to grow and cultivate cannabis and make marijuana extracts. And in 2016, the company invested $20 million in the Israeli company Syqe, which has patented a cannabis inhaler not unlike those used in the treatment of asthma.

Despite an apparent readiness to enter the market—apparently because of the enormous financial gains at stake—Big Tobacco is, simultaneously, lobbying against the legalization of cannabis. Of course, we're talking immense lobbying power here. Take Florida, for example: A lobby group called Drug Free Florida campaigned relentlessly in 2014 to help beat the state's medical marijuana ballot that year. It turns out that the spokesperson for Drug Free Florida—Sarah Bascom—was also a long-time, prominent lobbyist for Dosal Tobacco Corporation, the third-largest cigarette company in Florida.

Naturally, the question arises: Why would tobacco companies, who would make both immediate and long-term enormous financial gains, lobby *against* cannabis if the ultimate goal was to profit from it? In part, I believe it's because cannabis has proven an effective treatment for smokers (as well as alcoholics) trying to kick their habits. But in part, Big Tobacco's relationship to marijuana legalization is much the same as Big Pharma's: What Big Tobacco is *really* lobbying against is the easing of restrictions that would make cannabis accessible to *everyone* to produce.

The authors of "Waiting for the Opportune Moment" recommend that:

> In the current favorable political climate for marijuana decriminalization, policymakers and public health authorities should develop and implement policies that would prevent the tobacco industry (or other comparable corporate interests with a penchant for marketing harmful products to children) from becoming directly involved in the burgeoning marijuana market, in a way that would replicate the smoking epidemic, which kills 480,000 Americans each year.

This is a wise recommendation—perhaps particularly in light of our recently-exited Attorney General. As I'll discuss at greater length later in this chapter, Jeff Sessions rescinded the Cole Memo this year—an Obama-era policy that essentially protected states that had legalized marijuana from federal scrutiny. Sessions' Anslinger-like animosity toward marijuana is well known. What's probably *less* well known is that, in 1996, the tobacco industry *literally helped get Jeff Sessions elected to the Senate.* Indeed, the campaign "donations" he received from the tobacco company R.J. Reynolds (the makers of Camel cigarettes) were so excessive that, in October of 1997, Sessions had to send money back to the company for having exceeded legal donation limits.

In this way, Big Tobacco is yet another industry fighting tooth and nail, with help from the federal government, for the ongoing criminalization of cannabis, so that they can invest in the singular opportunities left to them alone.

The Prison Industrial Complex

This is an industry that's easy to forget about, because, unlike the pharmaceutical, alcohol, and tobacco industries, it's not a direct competitor of cannabis. But that doesn't make it any less impacted by federal laws on the drug. Both private prisons and state institutions directly benefit from the ongoing illegality of marijuana—after all, it means a steady stream of new inmates for them. Indeed, Corrections Corporation of America (now CoreCivic), which owns and operates detention centers and private prisons across the country, has disclosed on a number of occasions that keeping drugs illegal at the federal level is imperative to their business success.

According to a 2014 *Washington Post* report titled "How For-Profit Prisons have Become the Biggest Lobby No One is Talking About," CCA wrote in its 2014 annual report:

> The demand for our facilities and services could be adversely affected by the relaxation of enforcement efforts, leniency

in conviction or parole standards and sentencing practices or through the decriminalization of certain activities that are currently proscribed by our criminal laws. For instance, any changes with respect to drugs and controlled substances ... could affect the number of persons arrested, convicted, and sentenced, thereby potentially reducing demand for correctional facilities to house them.

And of course, for-profit prisons like CCA's are in the business of filling beds: They contract with states for an occupancy rate and charge the state for whatever portion of the quota goes unmet. Another private prison company, the GEO Group, Inc., boasted in its 2015 annual report that "we maintained an average company-wide facility occupancy rate of 95.7 percent including 75,302 active beds and excluding 3,708 idle beds for the year." Last year alone (2017), the GEO Group spent $1,710,000 on lobbying, and the Corrections Corporation of America / CoreCivic spent $840,000. (This was hardly a high for CoreCivic, which spent $3,380,000 in 2005.)

While details about how much lobbying spend goes to *which* groups are notoriously vague, these corporations make millions through the incarceration of nonviolent drug offenders—, so it's doubtless that this is where their interests lie. According to the Prison Policy Initiative, 1 in 5 prison inmates are currently locked up for a nonviolent drug offense. And these aren't short stays. A special report from the U.S. Department of Justice titled "Drug Offenders in Federal Prison: Estimates of Characteristics Based on Linked Data" observes that "the average sentence" for marijuana offenders "was more than 7 years (88 months) and the median was 5 years (60 months)." However, as *High Times* notes, "25.8 percent of marijuana offenders had sentences of five to 10 years, 16.2 percent had sentences of 10 to 20 years and 5.8 percent had sentences of 20 years or more."

Marijuana offenders also happen to be the *kind of* inmates prison employees want to work with: nonviolent, young, healthier, and more capable of prison work. According to a 2017 report from the Department of Corrections, 98 percent of offenders incarcerated for marijuana-related crimes are male, and "the average age of offenders incarcerated for amphetamines or marijuana is… 34 years."

So naturally, prisons don't want to see lowered minimum sentences for certain non-violent crimes (like marijuana use and possession); and they *certainly* don't want to see cannabis legalized. More people have been arrested in recent years for marijuana than for all violent crimes (rape, robbery, assault, etc.) *combined*. The prison industrial complex wants to keep it this way—*those* are their ideal inmates—and wants to ensure that as many of those arrests as possible lead to incarceration.

Lee Fang, co-founder of RepublicReport.org, writes: "Prison guard unions have also played a part in defending lucrative drug war policies. In California, the prison guard union helped finance the 'three strikes' ballot measure in 1994 that deeply increased the state prison population. In 2008, the California prison union provided funds to help defeat Proposition 5, a measure to create prison diversion programs for nonviolent offenders with drug problems."

And that's the final point when it comes to the prison-industrial complex. Prison guard *unions* realize, of course, that legalizing cannabis would ultimately reduce the need for staff. Corrections jobs are an important source of rural employment: The Bureau of Labor Statistics shows 428,870 employees in its "Correctional Officers and Jailers" category. And there are over 40,000 employees in the federal prison system … many of whose jobs would be on the line if those "1 in 5" nonviolent drug offenders were abruptly released for an act that was suddenly deemed legal.

Police Unions

I've already discussed federal law enforcement; let's not overlook *local* law enforcement. Federal policy on cannabis means ongoing guaranteed revenue for agencies; it also means officers can fulfill their quotas with low-risk, nonviolent "offenders."

What's more, unions receive money any time property is seized from a (real or perceived) drug crime. Civil asset forfeiture, a holdover of the omnibus crime bill written during the 1984 drug war (think Nancy Reagan's "Just Say No" campaign), allows police departments to keep a percentage of property seized during raids on *suspected* (not confirmed) drug activity. As Randy Balko writes in *Rise of the Warrior Cop*:

> The most significant provision in the newest crime bill … dealt with asset forfeiture. The new proposal was to let law enforcement agencies involved with federal drug investigations share in any asset forfeiture proceeds that the case might produce. Previously, forfeiture revenues went toward general operations. Under the new law, the Justice Department would set up a fund with the cash and auction proceeds from its investigations. After the lead federal agency took its cut, any state or local police agencies that helped out would also get a share … With drug investigations now a potential source of revenue for police departments, everything would change … Now the raids could generate revenue for all of the police agencies involved.

Property stolen from ultimately innocent civilians in these raids (according to the *Washington Post's* article "Asset Seizures Fuel Police Spending," 81 percent of asset forfeiture victims are never even charged) includes homes, cars, and even land. These assets have paid for things like SWAT teams and military-grade equipment, and put cash directly in officers' pockets.

Naturally, law enforcement officers have a vested interest in maintaining the status quo. Here's Lee Fang again, who claims that about half the money raised for a 2016 anti-legalization campaign in California came from prison and law enforcement groups:

> Opposition to the marijuana legalization initiative [the ultimately successful Proposition 64] ... has been organized by John Lovell, a longtime Sacramento lobbyist for police chiefs and prison guard supervisors. Lovell's Coalition for Responsible Drug Policies, a committee he created to defeat the pot initiative, raised $60,000 during the first three months of the year ... The funds came from groups representing law enforcement, including the California Police Chiefs Association, the Riverside Sheriffs' Association, the Los Angeles Police Protective League's Issues PAC, and the California Correctional Supervisor's Organization.

Between Big Government, Big Alcohol, Big Tobacco, the prison industrial complex, and prison and police unions, there are a *lot* of special interests with big pockets working to ensure that cannabis remains *suspect* at the voter level and *illegal* at the federal level. And that's not to mention other, smaller interests: Prosecutors, drug court judges and lawyers, drug testing laboratories, drug counselors, rehab and treatment centers, and more will all continue to profit for as long as the government holds a strong stance on cannabis as a Schedule I substance.

A more extensive understanding of the powers at work behind the scenes might help us better understand the degree to which the chaos in the cannabis industry is a reflection of the conflicted interests that pull the puppet strings from above. But before I dive into the nature of that chaos—and what small cannabusinesses will have to do in the *midst* of that chaos to survive—let's dive a little deeper into the biggest special interest of them all.

Big Pharma: The Cannabis Competitor with the Most to Lose

Of course, Big Pharma is the biggest beneficiary of cannabis' Schedule I status ... and it's probably the plant's most insidious adversary. After all, consumers are in a position to make a 1:1 comparison between the pharmaceutical industry's products and medical marijuana. Cannabis and painkillers (for example) are mutually exclusive products: If a patient buys *one* to relieve their symptoms, it likely means they *won't* have bought the other. And with a growing number of studies showing that Big Pharma's products simply don't compete with the whole plant, Big Pharma is becoming increasingly threatened—and thus increasingly hostile. It's a bit like the David-and-Goliath of the modern medical world.

The most recent example of such a market advantage occurred in June of this year (2018), when the U.S. Food and Drug Administration did something it had never done before: It approved the first cannabis-derived drug. The drug, a twice-daily oral solution called Epidiolex, manufactured by GW Pharmaceuticals, contains the *plant-derived*, nonpsychoactive cannabinoid CBD.

And that modifier "plant-derived" is the history-making part. The FDA had previously approved drugs that contain *synthetic* cannabinoids: In the 1980s, it greenlit Marinol (dronabinol) and Cesamet (nabilone), both of which contain synthetic forms of THC, as anti-nausea and anti-vomiting medications. In July 2016, it approved Syndros, which contains synthetic THC, for "anorexia associated with AIDS and nausea and vomiting associated with cancer chemotherapy." As each of these drugs was approved, it was classified *separately* from the whole plant, and put on a schedule as a discrete substance: Cesamet and Syndros were classified as Schedule II substances; Marinol was listed as Schedule III. In other words, while the DEA kept *plant-based* THC in Schedule I, its synthetic counterparts were classified so as to be considered legal medical treatments under the Controlled Substances Act.

While Epidiolex isn't the first cannabis-based medicine that's garnered FDA approval, it *is* the first plant-derived one. What this means is that the gatekeepers to "safe and effective" medical treatments have, by virtue of their approval, conceded to the fact that parts of the *actual* (natural) cannabis plant have a legitimate place in mainstream medicine. It's a groundbreaking admission.

Epidiolex treats two rare and severe forms of childhood epilepsy in patients aged two and over: Lennox-Gastaut syndrome and Dravet syndrome. Both conditions begin in the first years of life, Dravet in year one, and Lennox-Gastaut between years three and five, and have proven otherwise baffling to treat (the medical term is "intractable"). They've been resistant to the majority of anti-seizure drugs and children who have either condition typically suffer from multiple (often in the hundreds) seizures a day.

With natural CBD, however, that resistance diminishes. In rigorous clinical trials published in the *New England Journal of Medicine* (May 2017) and the peer-reviewed general medical journal *The Lancet* (January 2018), Dravet patients experienced a 39 percent reduction in convulsive seizures in a randomized, double-blind, placebo-controlled trial; and patients with Lennox-Gastaut saw a 37-42 percent decrease in seizures in a Phase 3 placebo-controlled trial (the range depended on the dosage). Those are some significant—indeed, possibly life-changing—reductions in seizure frequency. And the studies that showed them were funded, of course, by GW Pharmaceuticals.

Of course, these studies—studies the medical industry and the public have been calling for decades—merely confirmed what many of us have long known: that CBD offers relief for a wide variety of conditions, epileptic seizures among them. Among those who've "known" are the families who've been forced to uproot their lives and move to states where CBD is medically or recreationally legal in order to find relief for their children's suffering. Indeed, parents have been fighting for access to this "miracle drug" since 2013, when Dr. Sanjay Gupta's documentary, *Weed*, first aired on CNN. The documentary narrated the story of Charlotte Figi, a 6-year-old with Dravet syndrome who was suffering up to 300 grand mal seizures every week ... until CBD oil eliminated 99 percent of them. (Charlotte now has only 2-3 seizures *a month*.) Following the airing of Dr. Gupta's documentary, hundreds of families moved to Colorado to make life more bearable for their epileptic children.

In theory, now that there's an approved, regulated, and nationally-available medication, those children can get legal treatment no matter *where* they happen to live. (Epidiolex will be available at their local Walgreens, or CVS, or Rite Aid ... but *not* in local dispensaries, since FDA-approved drugs can only be sold by entities with a pharmaceutical license.) But here's the catch—or rather, there are *two* catches:

The first catch is that Epidiolex is going to be *much* more expensive than the CBD treatments patients currently receive in state medical programs. These programs, which have successfully treated children's epilepsy for years, cost between $200 and $500 a month, according to New Frontier Data. GW Pharmaceuticals' price point, on the other hand? *Around $2,700 a month.* (That's $32,400 a year, for those of you who don't feel like doing the math.) And while that price *will* drop considerably for insured patients, both insurance companies and the federal agencies that determine Medicare and Medicaid reimbursements have yet to decide *whether* to cover it—coverage is not a surety. For patients who *aren't* covered, GW Pharmaceuticals will have made a drug with a price tag that puts it financially out of reach for precisely the patients it's intended to "help."

The second catch is that the approximately 40 percent decrease in seizures both studies funded by GW Pharmaceuticals show is only part of the story. As Dr. Joseph Mercola writes of the May 2017 study on Epidiolex published in the *New England Journal of Medicine*, "a whopping 93 percent of children in the CBD group—as well as 75 percent of those in the placebo group—suffered adverse events in this trial. Eighty-four percent of adverse events in the treatment group were deemed mild or moderate, and included vomiting, fatigue, fever, upper respiratory tract infection, decreased appetite, convulsions, lethargy, drowsiness and diarrhea. Eight patients in the treatment group withdrew from the study due to side effects." Medical cannabis, on the other hand, derived from the *whole* plant and sold by marijuana dispensaries, has been used by patients, with very few negative side effects, for years.

And here's where the difference lies. Epidiolex is processed (and therefore adulterated) in order to remove the plant's psychoactive compound, THC. Inevitably, chemicals get *added* in this procedure. As Thomas Ropp reminds us in "The CBD Takeover," "we do not know exactly what is in Epidiolex ... [but] other similar THC pharmaceutical brands use toxic ethanol and/or propylene glycol, which are toxic." What's more, *every other important compound gets removed in the process*. Epidiolex is "pure CBD," an extract of *one* cannabinoid. But as Sanjay Gupta writes, "evidence is mounting that these compounds work better together than in isolation: That is the 'entourage effect.'"

In the "whole plant" approach, which is what compassionate and state-sponsored medical programs have used for decades, patients respond to the *synergistic* effects of the various natural compounds in the plant. There are *over 480 known components* in botanical marijuana, but Big Pharma's drugs typically isolate a single cannabinoid (THC or CBD). These synergistic effects simply can't be replicated in a version of the drug that selectively chooses compounds—*even* when it's comprised of a cannabinoid as remarkable as CBD. Even the pharmaceutical giant Insys Therapeutics, which I'll have more to say about shortly, has conceded that whole-plant marijuana is superior to their own product (dronabinol, a synthetic THC), and has described cannabis as a "competitive threat."

Between the price point and the substantial differences in side effects and efficacy, cannabis remains the superior choice for medical patients. And this is where I think the hope ultimately lies for cannabusinesses in their ongoing battle with the pharmaceutical industry: that it will be *consumers* who ultimately recognize and fight for access to whole-plant approaches.

But for now, obstacles remain—because if it isn't winning at the *medical* level, Big Pharma is certainly winning the game at the *political* level. In great part, this is due to the fact that the industry has friends in very high places (indeed, the *highest* places) who can clear paths for it. Already, paths have been cleared for future medications. As Thomas Ropp writes:

> In addition to Epidiolex, GW Pharma, with the help of the U.S. Patent and Trademark Office, owns eight patents with another 22 pending for the treatment of conditions including epilepsy, cancer, constipation, general pain, and nausea, as well as for the methods of extraction, proprietary uses, and hybrid strains of cannabis. One of the big ones is patent No. 8,790,719, which makes an intellectual property claim for the use of plant-derived cannabinoids in the treatment of prostate cancer, breast cancer, and colon cancer. Another salient patent is No. 9,205,063, clearly, a play to claim ownership of cannabis as a drug in the prevention and treatment of Alzheimer's disease, Parkinson's disease, and multiple sclerosis.

In other words, GW is receiving patents for techniques and substances that have been widely used in the cannabis world for years.

But let's return to the FDA's remarkable decision to approve Epidiolex. In a statement released by the FDA Commissioner on the day of the drug's approval (June 25), Dr. Scott Gottlieb was cautious in his wording:

> This product approval demonstrates that advancing sound scientific research to investigate ingredients derived from marijuana can lead to important therapies ... This is an important medical advance. But it's also important to note that this is not an approval of marijuana or all of its components. *This is the approval of one specific CBD medication for a specific use.* And it was based on well-controlled clinical trials evaluating the use of this compound in the treatment of a specific condition ... It's a path that's available to other product developers who want to bring forth marijuana-derived products through appropriate drug development programs. That pathway includes a robust clinical development program, along with careful review through the FDA's drug approval process. This is the most appropriate way to bring these treatments to patients.

The italics, by the way, are mine.

Gottlieb's qualification that FDA approval is for "one specific CBD medication for a specific use" suggests that GW Pharmaceuticals may be the *only* ("specific") beneficiary of approval for a CBD-based drug... at least for a while. The pharmaceutical giant, after all, has resources that smaller companies simply *don't* including the money to fund the "well-controlled clinical trials" Gottlieb mentions in his statement. So while the commissioner *claims* that GW Pharmaceuticals has paved a "path that's [now] available to other product developers who want to bring forth marijuana-derived products," the fact is that only giants such as GW *have* the "robust clinical development programs" that the FDA's approval process necessitates.

Then there's what happened to federal "sentiment" around CBD after the FDA's approval. As might have occurred to you, FDA approval of Epidiolex put the government in a kind of self-inflicted bind. At the time, CBD, as a *component* of cannabis, was considered a Schedule I drug, which meant that it had "no currently accepted medical use and a high potential for abuse," according to the DEA. But as soon as the *FDA* approved GW Pharmaceuticals' CBD-based drug, both arguments for keeping the compound in Schedule I were obliterated: The approval itself meant that CBD *had* a viable medical use. What's more, just months prior, an expert advisory committee for the FDA's Epidiolex decision had unanimously concluded that "CBD has a negligible abuse potential."

Of course, GW Pharmaceuticals' drug couldn't go to market until the DEA was willing to change its tune on CBD or it would otherwise be selling a federally-illegal substance. Many of us expected that the DEA would do with Epidiolex what it has done with other cannabis-based drugs: Classify the drug *itself* in a schedule that suggested "medical value," but leave marijuana, the whole plant or any of its components, in Schedule I. Shawn Hauser, attorney and director of the law firm Hemp and Cannabinoid Group, based in Denver, said "there is misunderstanding that cannabis or CBD will be immediately rescheduled, but that is not the case; it will be Epidiolex itself." Jonathan Havens, former attorney at the FDA and currently an associate attorney with Saul Ewing Arnstein & Lehr, said "I don't think the DEA will take this opportunity to reschedule CBD broadly. I think that they will add Epidiolex as Schedule IV."

So what happened just months ago, as of this writing, was a *bit* of a surprise. (I'll explain why it was only a *bit* in a moment). The DEA's announcement, dated September 28, 2018, reads:

> With the issuance of this final order, the Acting Administrator of the Drug Enforcement Administration places certain drug products that have been approved by the Food and Drug Administration (FDA) and which contain cannabidiol (CBD) in schedule V of the Controlled Substances Act (CSA). Specifically, this order places FDA-approved drugs that contain CBD derived from cannabis and no more than 0.1 percent tetrahydrocannabinols in Schedule V.

A CBD "rescheduling" from Schedule I to Schedule V is no small jump (Schedule V is the classification used for the *least* dangerous drugs). While drugs in this schedule are still illegal without a prescription, they're believed by the DEA to have a low potential for abuse *and* to have a proven medical use. Schedule V drugs include pain relievers, cough medicines containing codeine (think prescription-strength Robitussin), and antidiarrheal medications.

Of course, it's not *all* CBD that's being descheduled here—and this is the part of the announcement that *wasn't* so astonishing. The key qualifier in the DEA's language is that its rescheduling covers "drug products that have been approved by the Food and Drug Administration" ... and of course, for now, Epidiolex is *the only CBD-containing drug product* for which that's the case. This one drug, with a potentially limiting price tag, is approved for two rare conditions (though with the potential for off-label uses). *All* other CBD-based drugs are still illegal under federal law.

Unsurprisingly, shares in GW Pharmaceuticals rose 7 percent following news of the "rescheduling."

While much remains to be seen, my sense is that the cannabis industry will see short-term drawbacks but long-term gains thanks to the (limited) rescheduling of CBD. In one sense, of course, it's a signal that opposition to cannabis, at least in terms of its medical value, is beginning to crumble. And while Big Pharma is *the* beneficiary at the moment, the move ultimately legitimizes a compound that for so long has been viewed as suspect, if not downright harmful.

The change opens up the long-term possibility of new CBD formulations on the market, new waves of interest around the medical applications of CBD and other cannabis compounds, and a lessening of restrictions for medical researchers who want to study those applications for CBD. My hope is that smaller cannabusinesses will get in the game *now*, and do it *right* (I'll talk more about this in the next chapter), so that it isn't only mega corporations like GW who get to revel and thrive in these changes.

But knowing what they're up against is the first step. For one, Epidiolex (and any future FDA-approved CBD drug) will be distributed strictly through pharmaceutical channels (from a doctor's prescription to the drug store), rather than through a dispensary or a designated medical marijuana caregiver, leaving small, independent distribution businesses out of the new CBD paradigm. Secondly, FDA approval of GW Pharmaceuticals' drug doesn't necessarily mean it *will* be easier for other companies to propose cannabis-based medicines for similar approval. Indeed, Epidiolex has received "orphan drug" status from the FDA, meaning GW Pharmaceuticals has exclusive rights to market the drug for seven years. The designation essentially opens the door for GW to bring lawsuits against other makers of CBD... and while the company *claims* it has no objection to other companies creating CBD-based drugs, we've seen powerful evidence to the contrary in recent years. (More on *that* in a moment.)

Finally, having chosen one pharmaceutical giant as its beneficiary, the *FDA itself* may try to block other formulations of the plant extract. Indeed, in the months before its Epidiolex approval (and likely in *preparation* for it), the FDA sent warning letters to four Colorado businesses for making "illegally unsubstantiated health claims" about their CBD products. This suggests that there may be increased FDA scrutiny of smaller businesses now that the FDA has chosen to back Big Pharma.

Big Pharma, of course, seems to have done just fine on its own—*with* or *without* increased FDA scrutiny of its competition. In early 2018, journalist Mitchell Colbert interviewed a number of hemp farmers in Oregon. While the FDA hadn't even *approved* GW's drug yet, Mitchell writes, "One farmer had already received a cease and desist letter from GW":

> Three years ago, Trey Willison, the breeder and owner of Eugenius [an eco-friendly cannabis production business], received a cease and desist letter from GW for a strain he was growing, and they went so far as to threaten lawsuits. A personal friend and patent attorney stressed the gravity of the situation to Willison and, after that interaction, he says that GW 'really frightens' him. He mentioned hearing rumors about GW employing lobbyists in 17 states, and 'pushing for FDA-approved CBD only.'

Less than a year later, *this*, of course, is what GW got.

As Mitchell notes, the company had been fighting its "FDA-approved-only" battle at the *state* level for some time. Its most notorious lobbying efforts occurred during South Dakota's great CBD battle of 2017, which concerned Bill SB 95. As originally written, the bill would have exempted CBD from the South Dakota's definition of cannabis, rescheduling the compound from Schedule I to Schedule IV, and opening the gates for CBD extracts and products to be legally sold. That summer, lobbyists for GW Pharmaceuticals and its American subsidiary, Greenwich BioSciences, fought aggressively for a limiting amendment to the bill. The amendment would narrow the products to which the scheduling changes would apply to … guess which drugs? (If you guessed *only* those CBD drugs that had FDA approval, you've caught on to GW's battle position.) Epidiolex was still in the pipeline at that point, and ready to go to market once approved.

The amendment didn't pass; but at least for now, that doesn't seem to have mattered. With the DEA's scheduling of Epidiolex, GW now has the virtual monopoly it wanted. What's more, it has it at the *federal* level rather than merely at the state level. All of this is to say that the DEA's recent decision was, in part, the result of a fight that GW first picked long ago—and has been fighting ever since.

I could linger on specific cases of Big Pharma's lobbying for long enough to write a second book; but I'll just mention one more recent case here. This one took place in Arizona, where Insys Therapeutics, the makers of the synthetic cannabinoid drugs Marinol and Syndros, as well as Subsys, a sublingual fentanyl spray, donated half a million dollars to help defeat the legalization of marijuana in Arizona. At the time, it marked one of the largest single contributions ever made to a marijuana-opposition campaign; and it made Insys the largest donor *ever* to *Arizona's* anti-legalization fight. (Insys gave the money to the prohibitionist group Arizonans for Responsible Drug Policy, which fought on their behalf. Insys' "donation" comprised 10 percent of all donations ARDP received in that election cycle.)

In *this* case, Big Pharma was successful; the measure, Proposition 205, which would have allowed Arizonans age 21 and older to grow up to six marijuana plants for recreational use and to possess up to one ounce of marijuana, failed to pass. And it's worth putting the marked effect of Insys' donation in context: Arizona's marijuana measure was *the only measure of its kind* that failed at the polls in 2016. California, Massachusetts, Nevada, Florida, North Dakota, and other states legalized either *recreational* marijuana or some form of *medical* marijuana that same year.

This gives you a sense of what half a million dollars can buy in the political arena. But it should *also* give you an idea of the range of insidious practices at play … because in the months before the election, Arizonans were subjected to a wave of television ads, "paid for" by ARDP (and, therefore, by Insys), that rolled out across the state, complete with ominous music and doomsday prophecies that argued the legalization of cannabis would be a danger to public health and unleash misery upon Arizona's children.

It was an effective strategy insofar as it made Insys appear to be taking the moral high road. Indeed, the company has proclaimed its good intentions all along, campaigning against a "dangerous substance" and championing children's safety: The very reason Insys cited for its opposition to Proposition 205 was that "it fails to protect the safety of Arizona's citizens, and particularly its children."

But the company's 2007 filing with the Securities and Exchange Commission (SEC) tells another story. In the disclosure statement, a spokesperson from Insys explained to potential investors:

> Legalization of marijuana or non-synthetic cannabinoids in the United States could significantly limit the commercial success of any dronabinol product candidate … If marijuana or non-synthetic cannabinoids were legalized in the United States, the market for dronabinol product sales would likely be significantly reduced and our ability to generate revenue and our business prospects would be materially adversely affected.

So there it was straight out of the mouth of Insys itself: Sales would be "significantly reduced" and the company would be "adversely affected" by marijuana legalization. The pharmaceutical company could talk *publicly* about responsible drug policy all it wanted; but what was going on behind closed doors was a different conversation entirely.

If its ulterior motives weren't clear by the company's sizeable contribution to ARDP, just five months after Proposition 205 was defeated in March of 2017, Insys announced that the DEA had greenlit Syndros, a synthetic cannabinoid spray to treat AIDS patients struggling with wasting syndrome and cancer patients struggling with nausea, for the market. As Katherine Pickle at the Emory University School of Law writes: "It is undoubtedly ironic that a company which said it 'firmly believes in the clinical benefits of cannabinoids' would so vigorously campaign against the cannabinoid rich plant on which its synthetic version is directly based."

Of course, we can all see where the hypocrisy lies: Drop half a million dollars to delegitimize "the real deal" in an election that has real consequences for sick patients, then receive approval for your own *synthetic* formulation that treats the *same* symptoms the natural plant does … except *not as well*. "It's a little bit disgusting when you think of the collateral damage for human beings," said Dr. Gina Berman, medical director at the Giving Tree Wellness Center, a cannabis dispensary in Phoenix.

I couldn't agree more.

That's *especially* the case when you consider Insys' legal history. In an article entitled "Big Pharma is Donating to Anti-Legalization to Gain a Head Start in the Weed Business," Miroslav Tomoski writes: "[Insys'] last attempt at a cancer-oriented medication landed the CEO and other top officials in court when it was discovered that the company faked the medical records of their patients in order to obtain insurance coverage. For four years the company worked with doctors to prescribe their medication to patients who didn't need it."

Indeed, in December of 2016, *six* company executives including Insys' CEO, Michael Babich, were arrested "on charges that they led a nationwide conspiracy to bribe medical practitioners to unnecessarily prescribe a fentanyl-based pain medication and defraud healthcare insurers," according to a news release from the United States Attorney's Office for the District of Massachusetts (dated December 8).

The document goes on: "The medication, called 'Subsys,' is a powerful narcotic intended to treat cancer patients suffering intense episodes of breakthrough pain. In exchange for bribes and kickbacks, the practitioners wrote large numbers of prescriptions for the patients, most of whom were not diagnosed with cancer."

Fentanyl is an opioid that is up to 50 times more powerful than heroin and 100 times more powerful than morphine. It may be most familiar to you as the opioid that caused Prince's accidental fatal overdose in 2016. The year after Prince's death Insys once again found itself in legal trouble, when its founder, John Kapoor (who'd been serving as CEO since Michael Babich was arrested) was *also* arrested for bribing doctors to prescribe the drug. According to *Fortune*, at least four doctors were jailed for taking bribe money from Insys. They included "Jerrold Rosenberg, who lost his medical license and was ousted from his post as a Brown University professor, [and who] pleaded guilty to taking more than $188,000 in kickbacks disguised as speaker fees and creating false patient records to dupe insurers into covering Insys's Subsys pain medication."

I've already discussed medical marijuana in light of America's opioid crisis. Between 1999 and 2016, the number of overdose deaths involving opioids has *quintupled* (that's multiplied *fivefold*). According to the National Institute on Drug Abuse, "Every day, more than 115 people in the United States die after overdosing on opioids." At least half of those 115 daily deaths are caused by prescription medications ... yet the prescriptions keep getting written, despite the corresponding raise in fatalities. Chronic pain is a *very* lucrative market for opioid makers—*none* of whom are planning to stop producing or pushing their drugs. And that includes Insys.

(It also includes Purdue Pharma and Abbott Laboratories, the makers of the narcotic painkillers OxyContin and Vicodin, respectively, and two of the largest contributors to the anti-cannabis group Partnership for Drug-Free Kids. Purdue, by the way, was sued early in 2018 by Montana Attorney General Tim Fox, who alleged the company "promote[d] opioids deceptively and illegally in order to significantly increase sales... As a direct consequence, the rampant use, overuse, and abuse of opioids is devastating Montana and its families.")

But if there's a silver lining, here it is: In states with established medical marijuana programs, physicians prescribe 1,826 fewer doses of painkillers annually, according to a study by Dr. W. David Bradford, professor at the University of Georgia. (That's not to mention an average of 562 fewer doses of anti-anxiety medications, 542 fewer doses of anti-nausea medications, 486 fewer doses of seizure medications, and 265 fewer doses of antidepressant medications. In other words, in the states where marijuana is legal, the number of overall prescriptions is down by 11 percent.) And of course, cannabis is treating chronic pain more effectively than opioids do and *without* the addictive qualities or accidental overdoses.

In 2017, a study from New Frontier Data used Dr. Bradford's 2016 findings (the 11 percent drop in prescriptions) to conclude that Big Pharma would stand to lose between $4.4 billion and $4.9 billion *per year* if cannabis was federally legalized. And that's not just from patients who would choose cannabis for pain management. That's from patients who would use it—indeed, who *are* using it—for PTSD, anxiety, nausea, Tourette syndrome, epilepsy, glaucoma ... the list goes on.

That's why Insys was willing to drop half a million dollars to defeat a bill in one state, and why GW Pharmaceuticals fought as long and hard as they did for a virtual monopoly on FDA-approved CBD. If studies aren't prohibited, they'll continue to show that whole-plant approaches far surpass the single-cannabinoid drugs on market (for instance, Epidiolex). But they'll *also* continue to show that natural cannabinoids far surpass synthetic cannabinoids (which is what Insys makes).

One 2013 study, "Acute Toxicity Due to the Confirmed Consumption of Synthetic Cannabinoids: Clinical and Laboratory Findings," published in *PubMed*, reads:

> Agitation, seizures, hypertension, emesis and hypokalaemia seem to be characteristic to the synthetic cannabinoids ... tachycardia, agitation, hallucination, hypertension, minor elevation of blood glucose, hypokalaemia and vomiting were reported most frequently [in synthetic cannabinoids]. Chest pain, seizures, myoclonia and acute psychosis were also noted.

These are symptoms that patients simply don't experience with natural cannabis use. Nor do they experience the price point. As Katherine Pickle notes, "drugs like Marinol are sold for $18 per 5 mg capsule, the equivalent of $3,600 per gram. In contrast, botanical marijuana can be obtained for $15 a gram, though potency and price of the plant can vary. For patients without insurance, legal botanical marijuana provides an affordable option to relieve their symptoms."

GW Pharmaceuticals' and Insys' actions in recent elections (as well as in recent executives' arrests and incarcerations) suggest that Big Pharma recognizes it's going to have to fight hard for its share of an industry that is quickly gaining public recognition, *especially* from medical patients, and that has been establishing itself *without* them for decades. That's why, on the whole, the industry has spent *over $880 million* in the last decade to fight cannabis reform. As long as pharmaceutical companies can keep marijuana off the market, patients will have no choice—which means more prescriptions, more negative side effects, and more deaths … none of which will matter to Big Pharma in the face of their steady profits.

Of course, the public has long seen through this charade. They recognize that any care or concern Big Pharma voices for patients is mere lip service. They also recognize that there's a large—indeed, a *growing*—community of compassionate medical professionals who are working and fighting to help the public live healthier lives. As the hypocrisy becomes clearer at the federal and corporate levels, the public sees the compassion component is still there.

But the business of compassion is fraught with difficulty due to that list of political powerhouses I've discussed above, all of whom are working (and spending) hard to create oligopolies of the rich, dishonest and politically-connected. That's not to say I don't have hope that small businesses *can*, and *will*, find ways to thrive in this industry—both as it finds its feet *and* over the long haul. Indeed, I'll have much more to say about this in the next chapter. In the meantime, as the industry is legalized across states, there are the complexities of new regulations to iron out—as well, of course, as the ongoing tension borne of state-legal businesses operating under a federally-illegal umbrella.

If you're already *in* the business, I don't have to tell you about the complexities around taxes, banking, regulatory frameworks, product testing, and the perpetually looming threat of the black market in the midst of it all. But if you're looking to get involved, either as a business that "touches" the plant or as a "no touch" company, you'll want to know the obstacles you'll likely be up against. Obstacles, by the way, whose features are likely to keep changing ... but obstacles that may be well worth putting the work in to overcome. It's a rewarding and gratifying industry to take part in; and the complexities of the moment can be as exciting as they are frustrating.

Chaos in the Current Industry

The word "chaos" may cause you to want to close this book and look for an industry that won't be as volatile or emotionally taxing. I'd understand that compulsion. But let me start by saying that the cannabis industry right now is chaotic *at worst*. If you know the codes; have a strong, professional, and knowledgeable support system; and are willing to jump through the regulatory hoops and take the hits *early on*, the industry will find its footing just like every other newly-regulated industry has (think alcohol); and *you'll* be established in it (think craft beers or artisanal scotches). It's certainly not an industry for the weak of heart; so gather it up as we dive into this next section together.

Internal Revenue Code (IRC) § 280E: Additional Tax Complexities for Cannabis Businesses

IRC § 280E was enacted in 1982 after a cocaine dealer named Jeffrey Edmondson brazenly deducted the operating costs of his illegal business on his federal income taxes. Edmondson had served a prison sentence for dealing; after he was released he was sent a Notice of Deficiency (NOD) by the IRS. Making use of the Cohan rule—which allows taxpayers to deduct expenses even if receipts don't exist, so long as the testimony is credible—Edmundson claimed that he bought the drugs he sold on consignment. He also claimed to have incurred many expenses over the course of running his business, some of which the Tax Court gave him credit for in the final ruling. The text of *Edmundson v. Commissioner* (1981) describes Edmundson as "self-employed in the trade or business of selling amphetamines, cocaine, and marijuana." The portion about the allowances reads:

> We hold that one-third of petitioner's rental expense of $2,360, or $787, constitutes an ordinary and necessary expense of petitioner's trade or business and is to be allowed as a deduction. Petitioner's remaining claimed business expenses consist of the purchase of a small scale, packaging expenses, telephone expenses, and automobile expenses. We hold that these expenses were made in connection with petitioner's trade or business and were both ordinary and necessary [and therefore allowed].

IRC 280E ("Expenditures in connection with the illegal sale of drugs") was essentially a policy response to *Edmundson v. Commissioner*. A convicted cocaine trafficker had managed to claim his right under federal tax law to deduct "ordinary and necessary" business expenses, and Congress had to make sure that other drug traffickers wouldn't attempt to follow suit in the future. (Remember, this was 1982; the Reagan Administration was nearly fanatic in its War on Drugs). IRC 280E reads:

> No deduction or credit shall be allowed for any amount paid or incurred during the taxable year in carrying on any trade or business if such trade or business (or the activities which comprise such trade or business) consists of trafficking in controlled substances (within the meaning of schedule I and II of the Controlled Substances Act) which is prohibited by Federal law or the law of any State in which such trade or business is conducted.

In other words, if your business involves a Schedule I or Schedule II substance, you *can't* claim deductions or take credits on your income taxes. (Congress excepted cost of goods sold (COGS), which I'll discuss shortly.)

Of course, when 280E was codified, there *were* no state-sponsored medical marijuana programs, nor was marijuana legal in any state. Reagan's Congress probably couldn't have predicted that, thirty-six years later, cannabis would be legal in 33 states. (Indeed, in many of those 33 states, cannabusinesses are treated like any other for-profit business when it comes to *state* income taxes—though this often adds confusion, as processes and required documents for both sets of tax returns is so dissimilar. State-legal cannabusinesses are often filing very different state and federal returns.)

The complexities hinge on a single two-letter word of 280E. The fact that the code covers substances "prohibited by Federal law *OR* the law of any State" means that *all* cannabis businesses are subject to 280E, since they're trafficking in a *federally*-illegal (Schedule I) substance. This is true regardless of whether cannabis is legal in their respective states. And it shouldn't surprise anyone that the IRS is enforcing 280E when it comes to state-legal cannabusinesses. After all, there's money in it for them … this time, in the form of tax dollars.

Section 280E applies to all businesses that "touch" the plant—in other words, any business involved in directly handling the cannabis, no matter at what stage in the plant's life (cultivation, processing, or sale). This includes producers, cultivators, marijuana retail stores, medical dispensaries, manufacturers of cannabis oil and concentrates, and manufacturers of infused products. Each of these businesses is held to a different set of standards than ordinary businesses are when it comes to taxation: None of them can take tax deductions or credits in their filings.

If you're not sure exactly what this means, think of it this way: When filing taxes, business entities are typically allowed to deduct expenses that arise during the normal course of doing business. (Remember the Tax Court's use of the modifiers "ordinary and necessary"). As complex as the individual *numbers* might be, the federal *formula* is simple: Begin with gross income, subtract ordinary business expenses to arrive at taxable income, and pay taxes on the *remaining* amount (the net income, which is always smaller), rather than on the *initial* amount (the gross income).

If you've ever run a small business, you have a sense of what these "ordinary expenses" entail ... and you know that there are many of them. They include rent, travel, phone bills, employee salaries, health insurance premiums, contractor expenses, repairs and maintenance, legal costs, accounting costs, marketing and advertising costs, utilities (internet, telephone, electricity, etc.), and more. Indeed, small businesses' ability to *deduct* these costs is often the only thing that allows them to continue to operate: Most businesses are able to derive profits from their credits and deductions—otherwise they're in the red at the end of any given year.

If you run a *cannabis* business, however, the process looks a lot different. It begins with having to classify your income as "illegal" on your federal tax return. (Yes, the IRS insists that illegal businesses pay their taxes, too; it's more than willing to "dirty its hands" by taking that money out of *yours*.) After this declaration of illegality comes the hard part: Cannabis businesses must dispense with *all* costs they incurred related to distribution, sale, management, administration, promotion, support, overhead, and advertising ... because *none* of those things are deductible as far as IRC 280E is concerned.

What cannabusinesses *can* deduct—indeed, the *only* thing they can deduct—is cost of goods sold (COGS). If you're a cannabis *producer*, that means any costs directly involved in producing the plant itself: soil, seeds, water, nutrients, and any expenses incurred in cultivation and harvest. If you're a cannabis *retailer*, you can claim even fewer COGS expenses: think purchase costs, inventory costs, and shipping costs.

COGS, of course, constitutes only a small percentage of a business entity's overall costs. (Consider the list of "ordinary expenses" I gave you above.) What this ultimately means is that many cannabusinesses are virtually paying taxes on their *gross* income rather than on their *net* income—on sales rather than on profits. Some dispensary owners are paying taxes on *80 percent or more* of their actual profits. I've seen effective income tax rates on some cannabis businesses as high as 90 percent.

In effect, 280E situates cannabusinesses directly between a rock and a hard place. Many of these businesses *want* to be legitimate and play by the rules of the game. But the rules of *this* game eliminate the foundation of small business success and economic equity in the United States. Even as states continue to legalize both cannabis and products *derived* from cannabis, section 280E makes it economically impractical (if not impossible) for an entity to do business in the substance—at least not without operating at a loss. As the National Cannabis Industry Association has written ("Internal Revenue Code Section 280E: Creating an Impossible Situation for Legitimate Businesses"):

> Maintaining a strong working relationship with the IRS legitimizes these businesses and, in turn, the entire cannabis industry. But the current taxation climate has convinced some cannabis entrepreneurs to either ignore 280E on their tax filings, or forego paying taxes altogether. These businesses would rather gamble on the IRS overlooking their filing than see their revenues evaporate due to 280E. As Henry Wykowski, a California attorney who works with marijuana clients on tax issues, states, 'Section 280E de-incentivizes people from filing tax returns. It penalizes people who are trying to be transparent and operate within the law.'

The financial reality of trying to function as a legitimate business in the *regulated* industry is indeed much harsher than running the same business on the black market would be.

280E is currently applied more often to state-regulated cannabis businesses than it is to the illegal drug dealers that the code was initially intended to penalize. As Grover Norquist, President of Americans for Tax Reform (and a Republican), has said, "The intent of the law was to go after criminals, not law-abiding job creators. Congress needs to step up and clarify that this provision has become a case study in unintended consequences."

In order for small cannabusinesses to be able to compete in the growing industry, tax reform will be necessary—otherwise, the burden may eventually be too heavy for *any* business in the industry to withstand.

Because the IRS has offered little guidance on how businesses are to *apply* IRC 280E when filing their taxes, it's been court cases that have both outlined the parameters and tested the limits of the code—and it's worth following future cases if you run a cannabis business, or are considering doing so. (It's also absolutely worth studying Section 280E, or hiring an accountant or tax preparer that is well-versed in this code.) Perhaps the most useful—and the most *hopeful*—case was fought in 2002, in *CHAMP v. Commissioner*. This is a case I particularly love because it forefronts the compassionate component I've been discussing all along.

Californians Helping to Alleviate Medical Problems ("CHAMP") was a caregiving facility based in San Francisco that served people with debilitating illnesses. Nearly half of its members were AIDS patients; others suffered from multiple sclerosis, cancer, and other diseases. Patients had to possess a valid medical marijuana card in order to receive access to CHAMPs' services. The monthly membership fee was just enough to allow the organization to break even.

Once they were members, however, patients had access to much more than medical-grade, California-compliant cannabis: CHAMP offered daily lunches, yoga classes, internet access, one-on-one counseling, and more. So when the IRS audited CHAMP's 2002 tax returns—determining a deficiency of around $355,000 and issuing a $70,000 penalty to the organization—the court had to determine whether CHAMP (which called upon the Tax Court) was operating a single business or two separate businesses. After all, if it was only running a single—and therefore wholly federally illegal—business, 280E would apply; and CHAMP would be penalized for deducting items such as rent, salaries, and maintenance. If it was running *two* businesses, on the other hand (one that was trafficking in a federally illegal substance, and another that offered compassionate care services to its members), some of its claimed deductions would indeed be allowable.

The IRS, of course, claimed that CHAMP was a single entity that had trafficked in a controlled substance, and therefore, *all* of its business deductions should be disallowed. *CHAMP* claimed that it was operating two different businesses, with diversified services, under one roof: Its primary trade was in providing caregiving services, while its secondary trade was in supplying medical marijuana. The Tax Court sided with CHAMP in this particular case:

> We do not believe it to have been artificial or unreasonable for petitioner to have characterized as separate activities its provision of caregiving services and its provision of medical marijuana. Petitioner was regularly and extensively involved in the provision of caregiving services, and those services are substantially different from petitioner's provision of medical marijuana. By conducting its recurring discussion groups, regularly distributing food and hygiene supplies, advertising and making available the services of personal counselors,

coordinating social events and field trips, hosting educational classes, and providing other social services, petitioner's caregiving business stood on its own, separate and apart from petitioner's provision of medical marijuana.

The court determined that 18 of CHAMP's 25 employees were employed in the *caregiving* side of the business; therefore, the organization could claim deductions—such as salaries—for these 18. (Because the remaining seven employees were involved with providing medical marijuana, CHAMP could not claim deductions for them.) The court also allocated certain expenses—rent paid on one of CHAMP's facilities *not* used to distribute cannabis, laundry and cleaning expenses, and auto expenses—to the caregiving side of the business.

CHAMP v. Commissioner was a big win for CHAMP; and I have since worked with several companies to help them optimize *their* structures for reduced tax obligations.

But cannabis businesses still have to be very careful when trying to work around Section 280E with the "two business" argument. Indeed, a later case—*Olive v. Commissioner*—didn't go nearly as well for the petitioner, Martin Olive. While Olive based his entire argument on the precedent laid down by CHAMP, the Tax Court ruled in favor of the IRS. They did so because even though Olive's business—The Vapor Room—*provided* other services, marijuana was its only source of revenue. (The Vapor Room provided those other services free of charge.)

Cannabusinesses who smartly structure their organizations to have a "trafficking" side and a "non-trafficking" side (or rather, a portion of the business that *touches* the plant and a portion of the business that *doesn't*) have to be *impeccable* in their record keeping. Even better, they should conduct their non-touch business through a separate legal entity, and file two separate income tax returns.

The part of the business that produces or distributes cannabis will file a return *without* the deductions that 280E bars. The part of the business involving activities that are *legal* under federal law (compassionate care services, paraphernalia, ancillary products, owning and managing the building that the cannabis business operates in, etc.) will file a return that claims all the ordinary business deductions.

Taken together, the two companies can maximize deductions and pay less in taxes than they would if they operated as a single entity. Craig Smalley, co-founder and CEO of both the Tax Crisis Center and the Cannabis Accounting Group, explains a typical process of organizational structuring:

> For instance, if [the business is] a dispensary, we section off about 25 percent of the dispensary and it holds the inventory. Then we make the owner of the business the inventory manager. All they do is deal with inventory. 25 percent of rent, and utilities are deductible, and the owner's salary is deductible as COGS ... [Now,] most dispensaries will get a discount from their producer if they buy in bulk. However, there is nowhere [sic] to store the excess inventory, so we start a management company, that stores the excess inventory. The dispensary pays the management company a fee, and that is added to COGS. Not to mention we have created a non-Sect 280E company.

The folks at The Weed Blog offer another example:

> For instance, under 280E, you cannot deduct wages that you pay to your retail employees. However, if you can demonstrate that your retail associate is a registered nurse or medical student and that you are taking a *consultation-related* employee expense, it may become an allowable expense. Clearly, this is a case-by-case analysis that will yield different results for each individual business.

Again, with immaculate record keeping and expert legal advisers to help you create a viable legal structure, the "two business" loophole is entirely legal. But "immaculate," "expert," and "viable" are the key modifiers in that sentence. (A lack of sufficient records has been the reason some cannabusinesses operating with a two-business structure have lost in Tax Court: Take a look at *Alterman v. Commissioner* if you want an extreme example of failed record-keeping.) So while IRC 280E can *certainly* be challenging to navigate—and while it's certainly slowing legal, responsible industry growth—businesses are finding ways to work around it, with much care.

Cannabusinesses will also need to determine whether to structure themselves as LLCs, S Corporations, or C Corporations. Both LLCs and S Corporations are "pass-through" entities, meaning the business itself is not subject to income tax. Rather, its *owners* are individually taxed on entity's income. This means that, in the case of bankruptcy, business owners can't be held personally liable: The *company* might have to go out of business, but the owner's personal finances and credit survive mostly intact. In C Corporations, on the other hand, the business has a separate legal life from its owners. This ultimately creates a double-taxation scenario: Rather than "passing through" to the owners, tax rates are charged *once* to the business, and then again to its shareholders.

Given the volatility of the industry, it might seem that an LLC or an S Corporation would be the best choice to make when structuring a cannabis business. But 280E complicates those structures' taxes. For example, S Corporations require that a "reasonable" salary be paid to the owners and operators of the business ... a requirement which doesn't present a problem in any other industry. But of course, in the *cannabis* industry, salaries are nondeductible thanks to IRC 280E. What this ultimately means is double-taxation in an entity that is only *supposed* to be taxed once:

Owners are taxed first as employees and then as shareholders. (See Loughman v. Commissioner).

IRC 280E—and its effects on business entities—isn't the only IRS-issued document you'll want to know well (or ensure your tax preparer knows well). In January 2015, the IRS Office of Chief Counsel issued Chief Counsel Advice (CCA) 201504011. The intention of this memo was to clarify *what* COGS deductions were available to cannabusinesses. The memo references two other IRC sections worth knowing: §1.471-3(c) and 1.471-11 (if you're a cannabis *producer*), and §1.471-3(b) (if you're a cannabis retailer). *Then* there's Form 8300, which all businesses (including cannabis businesses) are required to fill out any time they receive a cash payment of $10,000 or more.

There have been—and there *are* in the works—a number of bipartisan efforts to amend tax law as it pertains to cannabis businesses. Any *sensible* solution will ultimately bring the tax code *out of* 1982 and into the modern era, allowing cannabusinesses to operate in accordance with the wishes of both state voters and the legislators who are demanding that in-state business be done in the context of a legitimate environment. Over the long run, of course, amending 280E will let cannabis businesses invest in their local communities with the money earned back on deductions and credits: hiring more employees at competitive salaries, for example.

In the meantime, let's discuss what's happening with the cannabis industry in light of our current political administration.

Cannabusiness and Banks: FinCEN, The Cole Memo, and Jeff Sessions' Repeal

The struggle with tax law is only one of the risk factors unique to the cannabis industry because of continued federal insistence on the plant's Schedule I status. Federal illegality means that *other* federal institutions—such as the U.S. Patent and Trademark

Office, bankruptcy courts, and federally-regulated banks—are substantially restricted (or barred altogether) in their dealings with cannabis businesses. Businesses can't receive patents or trademarks for their cannabis-based goods. Plant-touching businesses can't file for federal bankruptcy protection. It's somewhere between very difficult and virtually impossible for a cannabis business to obtain a commercial loan, a mortgage, or insurance. And so on.

More specifically, cannabusinesses that touch the plant don't yet have a confident way to bank, since the majority of financial institutions are wary of doing business with organizations that traffic in federally-illegal substances. Thanks to the 1970 Bank Secrecy Act (more on this in a moment), traditional investors have typically steered clear of infusing capital into the industry for fear they'd be treated *themselves* like drug traffickers.

During the Obama Administration, however, certain regulations were put into place that protected cannabis businesses—albeit loosely—from federal interference in their operations. The Rohrabacher-Farr Amendment (later known as the Rohrabacher-Blumenauer Amendment) and the Cole Memo were two such regulations.

The Cole Memo was drafted by the U.S. Attorney General under Obama—James Cole—in 2013. It came on the heels of recreational legalization in Colorado and Washington, and the implementation of legal, regulated industries in those two states. The memo was published by the Department of Justice and addressed U.S. attorneys; it set expectations for negotiating states that had voted in, and legally implemented, adult-use cannabis programs. Cole modeled his memorandum on another memo issued four years earlier by Deputy Attorney General David Ogden, which instructed U.S. attorneys "not [to] focus federal resources in [their] states on individuals whose actions are in clear and unambiguous compliance with existing laws providing for the medical use of marijuana." Of course, Cole dealt with *recreational* marijuana as well.

James Cole's memo was, likewise, a directive concerning priority. (You'll note Ogden's use of the word "focus"). It enjoined law enforcement to *prioritize* prosecuting *only* those state-legal cannabusinesses that met one or more items in a list of eight criteria. *These*, the memo claimed, should be prioritized:

- "Preventing the distribution of marijuana to minors;
- Preventing revenue from the sale of marijuana from going to criminal enterprises, gangs, and cartels;
- Preventing the diversion of marijuana from states where it is legal under state law in some form to other states;
- Preventing state-authorized marijuana activity from being used as a cover or pretext for the trafficking of other illegal drugs or other illegal activity;
- Preventing violence and the use of firearms in the cultivation and distribution of marijuana;
- Preventing drugged driving and the exacerbation of other adverse public health consequences associated with marijuana use;
- Preventing the growing of marijuana on public lands and the attendant public safety and environmental dangers posed by marijuana production on public lands; and
- Preventing marijuana possession or use on federal property."

If you were a business (or an individual) engaging in *none* of these activities, law enforcement and state prosecutors were directed toward a more hands-off, laissez-faire approach: You'd be protected, in theory, from federal harassment. As such, cannabusinesses complying with robust state regulations could be fairly (if a little uneasily) assured of federal non-interference. Natasha Winkler sums up the stipulations well: "If you implement a strict regulatory framework and employ a seed-to-sale tracking system to monitor the growth, distribution, and sale, of regulated cannabis to prevent diversion and create a transparent, accountable market, the federal government will leave it alone."

Whereas the Cole Memorandum only *deprioritized* marijuana prosecutions in states where it was legal, the Rohrabacher-Farr Amendment—which was adopted by Congress the following year—went a step further: It *prohibited* the use of federal funds to inhibit state-legal medical marijuana programs and activities. (Note the qualifier: Rohrabacher-Farr only concerns medical marijuana.)

The amendment—named after the bill's co-sponsors, Dana Rohrabacher (R-CA) and Sam Farr (D-CA)—was proposed in response to an increasing number of raids on medical cannabis providers. Obama signed the bill into law on December 17, 2014, though the Justice Department ignored it and continued to prosecute state-legal businesses until the U.S. District Court ordered them to comply in October 2015. The amendment was renewed in May of 2018, and was set to expire at the end of September. (The bill is now stalled on the Congress floor. Rohrabacher spoke at the National Cannabis Industry Association this year, and was very confident that bills will be passed. For now we continue to watch and wait.)

Earlier that same year—on February 14, 2014—the Obama administration attempted to facilitate working relationships between cannabis businesses and banks. As I mentioned above, federally-insured banks had typically held marijuana businesses at arm's length because of early regulations issued by the Financial Crimes Enforcement Network (FinCEN) concerning money laundering. FinCEN's 1970 Currency and Foreign Transactions Reporting Act (commonly referred to as the "Bank Secrecy Act" or "BSA") requires all U.S. financial institutions to assist government agencies in detecting and preventing money laundering. The act requires banks to thoroughly investigate their customers and *not* do business (whether knowingly or negligently) with "bad actors." Processing money from such sales would put them at risk of drug racketeering charges.

This meant that the onus was on the *banks* to ensure that their customers (and those customers' deposits) were legal. Of course, by virtue of their federal status, cannabusinesses had *always* fallen into the "bad actor" category as far as banks were concerned; so even *with* federal guidance, they tended to avoid potential trouble by simply refusing to do business with them. Keep in mind that this meant more than preventing cannabusinesses from having a safe haven for their cash: It meant difficulty obtaining credit, receiving loans, and purchasing real estate. It was a common narrative for a cannabusiness to open a bank account and have that account subsequently shut down once the bank realized the source of the revenue.

The administration's February 14 guidance, entitled "BSA Expectations Regarding Marijuana-Related Businesses," reads:

> The Financial Crimes Enforcement Network ('FinCEN') is issuing guidance to clarify Bank Secrecy Act ('BSA') expectations for financial institutions seeking to provide services to marijuana-related businesses. FinCEN is issuing this guidance in light of recent state initiatives to legalize certain marijuana-related activity and related guidance by the U.S. Department of Justice ('DOJ') concerning marijuana-related enforcement priorities. This FinCEN guidance clarifies how financial institutions can provide services to marijuana-related businesses consistent with their BSA obligations, and aligns the information provided by financial institutions in BSA reports with federal and state law enforcement priorities. This FinCEN guidance should enhance the availability of financial services for, and the financial transparency of, marijuana-related businesses.

Now here's the thing: FinCEN's new guidance *hinged on the Cole Memo*. It allowed banks to legally provide financial services to cannabis businesses *as long as those businesses abided by the same eight criteria the Cole Memo prioritized*. At the same time, the guidance provided financial institutions with nearly two dozen "red flags" that might indicate a client's violation of federal law (for example, if "the business receives substantially more revenue than its local competitors," if there is a "rapid movement of funds, such as cash deposits followed by immediate cash withdrawals," or if there are "deposits by third parties with no apparent connection to the account holder").

While FinCEN's 2014 clarifications essentially gave financial institutions a roadmap for conducting business transactions with legal marijuana sellers (finally allowing cannabusinesses to safely stash savings and more easily make payroll and pay taxes, like any other business), you'll note that the onus remained on the banks to determine whether or not their clients were acting within legal limits. FinCEN's guidance also required banks to perform due diligence in other realms: verifying with the state that the cannabis business was licensed and registered, reviewing the license application and relevant documentation, monitoring public sources for information about the business, and more.

As Robert McVay writes: "Most of these guidelines are common sense, but they do have cost [sic]. A bank with 200 cannabis business clients will have a lot of work on its plate monitoring publicly available sources for adverse information about the business and related parties." Once again, ensuring their clients' legitimacy often proved too onerous a task to make doing business worth it.

Indeed, by 2016, only 301 of the roughly 12,000 banks and credit unions in the United States were working with cannabis companies. (For those of you who don't feel like doing the math, that's about 3 percent of financial institutions.) And in many cases, the cost of doing business with those banks was—and continues to be—predatory: fees upwards of $10,000 just to open an account, and exorbitant fees on each transaction afterward. Some businesses have no choice but to concede. The other option is to shuttle millions of dollars in revenue back and forth in the form of cash: Using cash payments from customers to pay employees, suppliers, vendors, and even tax authorities. The security risks are tremendous; businesses who choose not to use a financial institution are susceptible to theft by both employees and outsiders.

So that already-shaky ground was shaken up a bit more on January 4 of this year, when Jeff Sessions, Donald Trump's recently-resigned Attorney General and the former head of the DoJ, rescinded the Cole Memorandum. (Note that this was just days after the first recreational pot shops opened in California, inaugurating what will likely be the world's largest market for recreational marijuana. It was also after the Task Force on Crime Reduction and Public Safety—a task force Sessions *himself* directed to review the Obama administration's memo and recommend changes to—found that existing policy was sensible enough that it required no changes. But at this point in marijuana's history, we've become quite used to political bodies appointing tasks forces and scientific studies, then ignoring their findings to prioritize predisposed beliefs.)

In rescinding Cole, Sessions simultaneously jeopardized the FinCEN guidance that listed the criteria for which banks could legally do business with cannabis businesses. The rescission once again gave state-level attorneys the right to exercise their own discretion in bringing marijuana charges against both individuals and businesses—even in the 29 states in which cannabis was, at that point, legal (it's now 33); and even if those businesses were acting in compliance with state laws. In other words, the general policy of non-interference that Cole had established no longer took precedent; if U.S. attorneys in cannabis-legal states wanted to enforce the Controlled Substances Act, they were free to do so.

There are 93 U.S. attorneys, by the way—which means Sessions' rescission could have had (and may, in theory, *still* have) 93 different interpretations in respective jurisdictions. In *theory*, each of those 93 will choose how to prioritize their resources: Some will remain hands-off; others may decide to aggressively enforce federal marijuana laws. As Hilary Bricken wrote on the day of the rescission: "It, therefore, behooves you—now more than ever—to familiarize yourself with the stances your particular U.S. Attorney has regarding cannabis." That remains an excellent piece of advice ... though so far, *not much has happened*. It appears that most U.S. attorneys recognize public sentiment on cannabis and perceive that cracking down on the drug would be a form of political suicide ... not to mention they actually *do* have more important drug-related matters on their hands.

Indeed, though cannabis stocks fell sharply after news about the Cole rescission broke, they didn't stay down long. As Aaron Smith reported for *CNN Business*, "The leading marijuana index, which tracks 15 stocks, lost about 25 percent of its value Thursday." Canopy Growth—a Canadian company which is the world's largest marijuana stock by market cap—fell 17 percent. Aphria Inc. was down 19 percent, while Terra Tech plunged 35 percent. But by Friday's close, U.S. marijuana stocks had already recouped half their losses—and *Canadian* share prices closed that same day at record highs. This is a testament to the volatility of the industry—but also to the speed at which indexes bounce back.

The *big* question behind the Cole reversal concerns the relationship between cannabusinesses and banks. After all, Cole was precisely the reason those 3 percent of banks felt they *could* serve the cannabis industry without coming into conflict with federal statutes; that justification for providing services has now been retracted. *In theory*, these banks could fall victim to charges of money laundering under FinCEN's Bank Secrecy Act again. Indeed, as news of the rescission broke in January, these were the kinds of predictions I was reading:

"Today's news undoubtedly changes the risk profile associated with offering financial services to the marijuana industry, and financial institutions may now be even more hesitant to do so" (*Bank Law Monitor*); "This reversal will throw further doubt into the financial sector, potentially leading to an increase in violent crime as cash transactions will once again be the norm" (*Forbes*); "There will, however, likely be a ripple effect from this news. Namely, current access to banking, any tax reform progress, and investment are going to feel the chill of uncertainty and the threat of federal enforcement" (*Canna Law Blog*); "Banks are incredibly conservative and taking down the Cole Memo will almost certainly lead some banks to stop providing banking services to cannabis businesses" (*Canna Law Blog*).

I'm writing this in December of 2018, and we have yet to see how things will play out in consequence of this turn of events. Some of the bigger, more conservative banks certainly *have* stopped providing services to customers with relationships to cannabis— though it's hard to say if this is a response to Sessions' rescission, or if those banks would have done so either way.

This past summer, for example, Wells Fargo—the fourth largest bank in the United States—closed the account of a candidate running for a seat on Florida's agricultural commission. The reason? Wells Fargo discovered that Nikki Fried had accepted donations from lobbyists from the medical marijuana industry. Michael H. Gray, an Assistant Vice President for Corporate Communications, explained: "It is Wells Fargo's policy not to knowingly bank or provide services to marijuana businesses or for activities related to those businesses, based on federal laws under which the sale and use of marijuana is illegal even if state laws differ." As Tom Angell writes in an article on the rescission for *Forbes*, "Wells Fargo's move appears to be the first time a financial institution has denied banking services to a candidate for public office as a result of donations from the cannabis industry."

If this is, indeed, Wells Fargo's (new?) company-wide policy, it could have ramifications for *other* politicians who accept campaign contributions from marijuana lobbyists—not to mention for nonprofit groups and campaign committees advocating for policy change.

That said, it appears that other banks—including community banks and credit unions—who already serve clients with relationships to cannabis plan on staying in the market, unless (or until) they start seeing prosecutorial activity from their respective U.S. attorneys. In fact, here's Tom Angell again, on why Sessions' rescission may hardly be a cause for lost hope:

> The number of banks that are willing to work with marijuana businesses is steadily climbing, even after the Department of Justice revoked protections for state cannabis laws, new federal data shows. By the end of March, 411 banks and credit unions in the U.S. were 'actively' operating accounts for marijuana businesses, according to a report from the Treasury Department's Financial Crimes Enforcement Network (FinCEN). That's up more than 20 percent from when President Trump took office early last year. While the number of financial institutions servicing cannabis growers, processors, retailers and related businesses dipped slightly in the two months immediately following U.S. Attorney General Jeff Sessions' decision this January ... the total has since started to climb again.

As I mentioned, so far attorneys aren't exercising their "discretion" to the detriment of the cannabis industry. The DoJ certainly lacks both the manpower and the money to go back to the kind of consistent, high-level federal enforcement we saw in the 60s. (Even *then*, enforcement at that level was untenable.) As James Cole—the author of the memo—remarked after the rescission: "It's well-known that you can't prosecute every violation of a criminal statute in the US Attorney's office. There just aren't the resources to do that."

And in *this* historical moment, with the country riding a powerful wave of legalization (and states seeing financial windfalls), citizens and politicians are responding to Sessions' rescission much differently than they responded to Nixon just decades ago. It's worth noting that *literally hours* after Sessions rescinded Cole, the state house of Vermont voted to pass H.511, a bill that legalized adult possession of one ounce of cannabis and allows individuals to cultivate two plants for personal use.

Here are some of my favorite responses to Sessions' rescission. Washington State Governor Jay Inslee issued a statement that read: "Make no mistake: As we have told the Department of Justice ever since I-502 was passed in 2012, we will vigorously defend our state's laws against undue federal infringement." Colorado Governor John Hickenlooper said: "Colorado has created a comprehensive regulatory system committed to supporting the will of our voters … Today's decision does not alter the strength of our resolve in those areas, nor does it change my constitutional responsibilities."

Oregon Governor Kate Brown's statement in response to the rescission reads: "States are the laboratories of democracy, where progressive policies are developed and implemented for the benefit of their people. Voters in Oregon were clear when they chose for Oregon to legalize the sale of marijuana and the federal government should not stand in the way of the will of Oregonians. My staff and state agencies … will fight to continue Oregon's commitment to a safe and prosperous recreational marijuana market." Seattle Mayor Jenny Durkan—who is, herself, a former U.S. attorney—said: "Let's be clear: Our Seattle Police Department will not participate in any enforcement action related to legal businesses or small personal possession of marijuana by adults. Federal law enforcement will find no partner with Seattle to enforce the rollback of these provisions."

Even the Koch brothers—who have tended to back conservative think tanks and fund members of the Republican Party—had harsh words for Sessions ... or at least, they "had harsh words" through the Senior Vice President of Koch Industries, Mark Holden, who "share[d] the Koch perspective": "That Attorney General Jeff Sessions, a Republican appointee in a Republican administration, is undoing a Democratic appointee's work from a Democratic administration is irrelevant. Republicans and Democrats alike have criticized the decision, and for good reason: It does little to improve the lives of people in our communities."

The Koch statement ends with a call for reversal: "The year is new, and there is still time to reverse course. Rather than grow the size and scale of the federal government and encroach upon the freedom of individual states and citizens, the Justice Department can reconsider their decision. They can choose to be on the side of individual liberty and states' rights. They can choose to be on the side of the millions of Americans who have made their voices heard loud and clear."

All this is to say that, on the whole so far, Sessions' decision—and the DoJ's current stance—hasn't had much of an impact on the cannabis industry. It certainly hasn't stopped companies such as Tilray—a Canadian company that touches the plant directly—from recently becoming the first marijuana producer to conduct an initial public offering (IPO) on Wall Street. In its first day of trading on the Nasdaq, Tilray's stock climbed 32 percent.

James Cole *himself* has said that the chances of a future impact from the rescission are "remote and unlikely." "What I've seen from a prosecutorial standpoint so far … is not much" Cole said last summer in a keynote address he delivered at the National Cannabis Industry Association's 2018 Summit & Expo. "I don't expect [U.S. attorneys] to do much, because th[e] political reality is going to be a natural barrier to them taking an aggressive approach and really defying the will of the voters."

Indeed, the silver lining of the Cole rescission might very well be the backlash from both sides of the aisle. Bipartisan reforms have already been proposed. One significant piece of legislation—introduced on June 7 of last year and currently supported by 11 senators and 30 members of the House of Representatives—is the Strengthening the Tenth Amendment Through Entrusting States (STATES) Act (S.3032). The bill was introduced by Senators Cory Gardner (R-CO) and Elizabeth Warren (D-MA). It hinges on conservative arguments about state sovereignty and would effectively replace the Cole Memo, turning decisions about cannabis legalization over to individual states, and ending Justice Department persecution of cannabis businesses.

And "ending" is the key word there. If it passes, the STATES Act will be stronger than the Cole Memo, insofar as it will *codify* what the Cole Memo only *recommended*. Under the bill, the Controlled Substances Act would no longer apply to individuals and businesses acting in compliance with state or tribal laws—whether producing, manufacturing, distributing, dispensing, possessing, or administering the delivery of cannabis. What's more, STATES would legalize industrial hemp, removing it entirely from the CSA. As Rebecca L. Haffajee, et al. write: "This solution [STATES] would be more permanent than attorney-general guidance or agreements between states and the attorney general regarding enforcement, which shift with the political winds, and would therefore promote stability for medical users and suppliers."

But there's more. According to a description of the bill in a fact sheet available on Elizabeth Warren's website: "To address financial issues caused by federal prohibition, the bill clearly states that compliant transactions are not trafficking and do not result in proceeds of an unlawful transaction."

You'll notice the important "T" word there. If the production or sale of cannabis in a legal state will, under the STATES Act, no longer constitute "trafficking," that means the STATES Act would effectively cancel the impact of IRC §280E on those businesses. And because the bill would effectively amend the CSA to create exemptions for state-legal cannabis activity, banks dealing with cannabusinesses would be protected.

When Sessions rescinded Cole, Cory Gardner tweeted that "the Justice Department has trampled on the will of the voters in CO and other states," and vowed to block President Trump's Department of Justice nominees until he received a commitment from the president that his state's rights would not be infringed upon. The Colorado senator was doubly angered by the fact that Sessions' decision "directly contradict[ed]" what Sessions had *told* Gardner just before Gardner voted to confirm him to Attorney General in 2017. "I am prepared to take all steps necessary, including holding DOJ nominees, until the Attorney General lives up to the commitment he made to me prior to his confirmation," Gardner said (also in a tweet).

Gardner did, indeed, hold up Trump's nominees for three months, refusing to approve any new judicial nominations. But after emerging from a sit-down meeting with Trump last April, the senator said the president agreed with him that leaving marijuana laws in states' hands was "the right thing to do and that we're not going back." In a press release issued April 13, 2018, Gardner wrote:

> Late Wednesday, I received a commitment from the President that the Department of Justice's rescission of the Cole memo will not impact Colorado's legal marijuana industry. Furthermore, President Trump has assured me that he will support a federalism-based legislative solution to fix this states' rights issue once and for all. Because of these commitments, I have informed the Administration that I will be lifting my remaining holds on Department of Justice nominees. My colleagues and I are continuing to work diligently on a bipartisan legislative solution that can pass Congress and head to the President's desk to deliver on his campaign position.

In June, when the STATES Act was introduced, Trump appeared to publicly confirm the pledge of support Gardner said he received from the president: "I support Senator Gardner. I know exactly what he's doing; we're looking at it. But I probably will end up supporting that, yes." Indeed, Trump had suggested on a number of occasions while on the campaign trail that he would support state sovereignty, if not federal legalization.

In a town hall event held in Wisconsin in March 2016, candidate Trump said: "I think that as far as drug legalization, we talk about marijuana, and in terms of medical, I think I am basically for that. I've heard some wonderful things in terms of medical. I'm watching Colorado very carefully to see what's happening out there." In October 2016, Trump told *The Washington Post*: "In terms of marijuana and legalization, I think that should be a state issue, state-by-state ... Marijuana is such a big thing. I think medical should happen—right? Don't we agree? I think so. And then I really believe we should leave it up to the states." Earlier that year (February 2), in a Fox News interview with Bill O'Reilly,

Trump responded to O'Reilly's statement that medical marijuana is a "ruse" by claiming: "But I know people that have serious problems and ... it really does help them."

We all know Trump's tendency to reverse course on a whim; but his verbal support for the STATES Act surely came as a blow to Sessions, whose relationship with the president began a downhill descent the moment he decided to recuse himself from Robert Mueller's Russia investigation. Now that Sessions is out of the position of Attorney General, it remains to be seen whether Trump will follow through on his commitment to Cory Gardner.

The grand irony for Sessions is that the STATES Act (a stronger, more robust version of the Cole Memorandum) likely wouldn't exist—and wouldn't have the kind of bipartisan backing it has— if it weren't for his *rescinding* of Cole. The Attorney General's aggressive stance toward marijuana was precisely the spur Gardner and Warren needed to bring the absurd conflict between the federal government and cannabis-legal states back into the spotlight.

In an interview with *Rolling Stone* in August, Warren said that the former Attorney General "moved both parties. Jeff Sessions has acted as a catalyst in getting people up off their rear ends and moving on this issue." She goes on: "We are in a moment when Jeff Sessions highlighted aggressive law enforcement on marijuana and a lot of folks here in Congress looked at each other and said, 'That's a bad idea.' What Cory and I have done is give them a place to channel that where we can make real change."

The STATES Act is one of a number of bills in the works that promise various degrees of cannabis decriminalization or legalization; I'll discuss some others at the end of this chapter. And even in the midst of congressional advocacy, *outside* groups are demanding further congressional action in supporting states and state-legal businesses in the face of the CSA. In August of last year, for example, the top financial regulators from thirteen states sent a letter to congressional leaders stating: "It is incumbent on Congress to resolve the conflict between state cannabis programs and federal statutes that effectively create unnecessary risk for banks seeking to operate in this space without the looming threat of civil actions, forfeiture of assets, reputational risk, and criminal penalties."

For the moment, because the bigger institutional players like Wells Fargo are steering clear of ties to cannabis, the current moment is an exciting—and potentially very profitable—one for smaller banks, financial institutions, and venture capitalists who are willing to take risks on cannabis businesses. Last year, the first cannabis-centered exchange-traded fund (ETF) in the U.S. opened trading. The fund, ETFMG Alternative Harvest, attracted about $400 million in its first six months, making it one of the fastest-growing ETFs of 2017. The fund makes buying into a range of cannabis companies easier on investors.

In a recent interview with *Business Insider*, Jon Trauben, a cannabis investor and partner at Altitude Investment Management, said that his New York firm—which manages around $25 million— "is taking advantage of that short 'window of opportunity' to invest in marijuana before prohibition recedes and the big institutional players jump into the sector." Of course, these early-stage investors—most of which are private funders—are taking their chances. "The lack of banking and lack of access to capital is creating a huge opportunity," the hedge funder Danny Moses said at the Cannabis World Congress and Business Expo last year in New York. "It's a goldmine, but it's also a minefield."

Micah Tapman, managing director at Canopy, a Colorado-based business focusing on early-stage cannabis investments, told *Business Insider*: "When there's complexity, when there's chaos, when there's uncertainty, that's when the people who are really good at doing what they are doing stand to make really strong gains."

My hope is that there are plenty of private investors out there who "are really good at doing what they are doing." Because there certainly *are* some aspects of the present industry that make it feel like the metaphorical "minefield" Moses mentioned. In part, this is to be expected: Hiccups of all sizes occur whenever an unregulated—or semi-regulated—industry becomes regulated. But in part, the cannabis industry's complexities are peculiar to itself: stemming less from a recent status change, and more from a history entailing a vague legal status and restricted access to the plant, which leaves much unknown about the product. And how do you fully regulate what's unknown?

"There's Confusion Out There": The Transition into Regulatory Frameworks for Cannabis Businesses

One of the predictions voiced after Sessions' rescission of Cole came from Arnaud Dumas de Rauly, CSO for The Blinc Group, a self-described "business incubator for brands that are changing the landscape of vapor and cannabis consumption technologies." De Rauly anticipated that "there might be one positive side-effect [of the rescission]: current businesses will be forced to be more rigorous with their operations, cash-flow, and compliance strategies." De Rauly seemed to suggest that the *more rigorous* businesses would be less likely to see enforcement of the CSA by the DoJ. But compliance is proving difficult even for those cannabusinesses doing their best to abide, as the industry comes to terms with what it means to move from an unregulated industry to a regulated one.

If the narratives of similar industries (think alcohol) are any indication of cannabis' future, these are just the necessary hiccups en route to a thriving, well-regulated industry. (In fact, I'll have more to say later about how the end of alcohol prohibition offers us a roadmap—at least in terms of tax strategies—that's worth taking notes on.) But since these hiccups are likely to last a few years, it benefits us to consider them at some length.

I'd like to take California as an example in this section. In part, that's because it's the state I live in; and so I know its complexities better than those of any other cannabis-legal state. In part it's because when California passed Proposition 64, fully legalizing marijuana after two decades of gray market existence, it became both the largest legal marijuana market in the United States *and* the largest cannabis economy of scale in the world. (At the time, California's marijuana marketplace was estimated to be worth around $7 billion.) What's more, Prop 64 marked California's transition from a statewide *medical* cannabis program to a fully regulated *recreational* market. So how it's handling—and how it will *continue* to handle—the rollout is worth paying attention to.

California voters approved Prop 64—the Control, Regulate, and Tax Adult Use of Marijuana Act (AUMA)—on November 8, 2016. In doing so, they made California the sixth state to roll out recreational sales: Adults can grow up to six marijuana plants at home and legally possess up to an ounce (up to 28.5 grams of marijuana and up to 8 grams of concentrated cannabis). In response to the ballot initiative, the California legislature passed its *own* Senate Bill, S.B. 94, which streamlined requirements for licensing and regulating both medicinal *and* recreational cannabis. (Until then, California cannabusinesses had been operating under the 1996 Medical Cannabis Regulation and Safety Act (MCRSA). S.B. 94 simultaneously repealed MCRSA *and* offered a framework that integrated the guidelines for both medicinal *and* adult use. This meant adding an "AU" (Adult Use) to the acronym: SB 94 is called the Medicinal and Adult-Use Cannabis Regulation and Safety Act (MAUCRSA).)

SB 94 laid out guidelines for cannabusinesses for registering for sellers' and tax permits, obtaining appropriate business licenses (and the conditions for such licensure), advertising, obtaining samples for laboratory testing, quality assurance, storage, packaging, transportation and delivery, excise taxes, identifying sources of water supply (for cannabis cultivators), and more. California's guidelines have been described as "notoriously complex." For instance, cultivators, distributors, and retailers all require specific and highly-specialized licenses.

SB 94 *also* laid out a number of regulations that substantially increased the duties of state and local agencies—in some cases, putting the onus on individual agencies to formulate the governing guidelines. In many cases, it recognized that these new regulations would take time to codify and put into place. "No later than January 1, 2021" is an oft-cited deadline: "The bill would require, no later than January 1, 2021, the department [of Food and Agriculture] to establish a program for cannabis comparable to the federal National Organic Program and the California Organic Food and Farming Act"; "The bill would require the department [of Food and Agriculture], no later than January 1, 2021, to establish a process by which licensed cultivators may establish appellations of standards, practices, and varietals applicable to cannabis grown in a certain geographical area in California."

Other departments weren't given that long at all:

> The bill would require, no later than January 1, 2018, the Secretary of Business, Consumer Services, and Housing Agency or the secretary's designee to initiate work with the Legislature, the Department of Consumer Affairs, the Department of Food and Agriculture, the State Department of Public Health and any other related departments to ensure that there is a safe and viable way to collect cash payments for taxes and fees related to the regulation of cannabis activity throughout the state.

SB 94 requires that the Department of Pesticide Regulation, in consultation with the State Water Resources Control Board, develop guidelines for the use of pesticides in cannabis cultivation and residual pesticides in harvested cannabis. It requires the Department of Food and Agriculture, in consultation with the bureau and the State Board of Equalization, to establish a track and trace program to report the movement of cannabis through the distribution chain by way of unique identifiers. It requires the California Highway Patrol to appoint a task force to develop recommendations for protocols, best practices, and proposed legislation addressing the issue of impaired driving.

In case you didn't know how many state departments and bureaus have to get involved in writing and implementing regulations for a new industry, this might give you a sense of the breadth of involvement. I'm writing this at the close of 2018; many of these departments still have over two years to establish processes and codify regulations. What's more, all of the pieces of the newly-regulated puzzle have to work together; and industry experts are currently concerned that the distribution system (which includes everyone from growers to testers to transporters to retailers) is simply not robust enough yet to support what promises to be an enormous emerging market. Lori Ajax—Chief of the Bureau of Cannabis Control and therefore the state's top marijuana regulator—wasn't kidding when she spoke what's become the title of this section: "There's confusion out there."

SB 94 also named Ajax's Bureau of Cannabis Control as the budding industry's governing body. As other departments began scrambling to create and put new regulations into place, the BCC—with help from the Department of Food and Agriculture and the Department of Public Health—published a set of "Transition Period Requirements" for licensees. During the six-month period (which has been described as both an "emergency period" and a "grace period"), growers, distributors, and dispensaries were allowed exceptions and eased regulations—in other words, time to make the transition and get their products and packaging under compliance. For example, during those six months, retailers could continue to sell untested products as long as the packaging explicitly told consumers that those products didn't meet state standards.

The new regulations went into effect on July 1. Effective that date, dispensaries and distributors who hadn't become fully compliant risked either hefty fines or loss of license. (You can imagine the kinds of frantic, last-minute fire sales that took place at the end of June: All cannabis products that didn't meet the new state standards come July 1, after all, had to be destroyed.) All licensed California cannabusinesses now must adhere to these rules governing the testing, packaging, and labelling of all cannabis products:

- Licensees can only sell cannabis goods that have been tested in a licensed or ISO accredited lab and (of course) passed all requirements. Labs are required to check for contaminants such as pesticides, microbial contaminants (fungus and molds), heavy metals, mycotoxins, terpenoids (the organic chemicals that give the plant its distinct aroma and taste), and residual solvents. They're also required to test cannabinoid levels—namely THC and CBD. Labs issue certificates of analysis based on batch and sample numbers; only *then* can products be transported from distributors to retailers. (Retailers are not allowed to send goods out for testing.)

- All packaging and labeling of cannabis goods must be performed according to regulatory standards *prior* to their being transported to a retailer. (Again, retailers cannot do this themselves.) Retailers who receive goods that aren't properly packaged or labeled cannot accept them.

Packaging must be child-resistant, tamper-evident, and must indicate that it contains a cannabis product, along with the date the product was made and a government warning statement. Labels must also include lab results, the amount of THC and CBD in the package, net weight or volume, manufacturer's name and contact information, ingredients, expiration date, instructions for use, and the unique ID or batch number. Packaging for edibles must be opaque and include the words "cannabis-infused." Nothing on the labeling can refer to the product as a "candy," include cartoons, be attractive to children, or make unproven health claims. Medicinal goods must be labeled "For Medical Use Only."

- The amount of allowable THC in each serving and package is limited. According to the BCC, "edible cannabis goods may not exceed 10 milligrams of THC per serving and may not exceed 100 milligrams of THC per package." (This applies to both medicinal and adult-use edibles.) On the other hand, "non-edible cannabis products shall not contain more than 1,000 milligrams of THC per package if intended for sale only in the adult-use market," and "non-edible cannabis products shall not contain more than 2,000 milligrams of THC per package if intended for sale only in the medicinal market."

Beyond these rules, California decided that rather than imposing *statewide* regulations, it would allow individual cities and counties to address remaining questions about how a marijuana agenda should ultimately be enforced ... including whether or not there should even *be* a "marijuana agenda." Naturally, jurisdictions don't work with a shared set of goals or values; and while some have embraced adult-use (leaving county officials scrambling to create regulations in a virtually unprecedented local industry), some continue to criminalize it—or at least, they've decided on a "wait and see" approach. Others have decided on a kind of "split permission" structure: Costa Mesa, for example, allows manufacturing, distribution, and testing labs; but it has banned cannabis *stores* of any kind.

Now keep in mind, there are 58 counties and 482 incorporated cities in the state of California, which means each of these now has its own specific set of governing rules and requirements around cannabis. This patchwork of region-specific regulations complicates things considerably for businesses, who have to get their local licenses before they can get their state licenses (California has a dual licensing requirement) ... which means navigating *two* murky sets of regulations—both still in formation—which may or may not agree with each other. As the writers at AllBud observe, "to call this a complex legal web is an understatement."

Perhaps most importantly, this complicates things for medical marijuana patients, whose lives are most impacted by these patchwork laws. Patients are burdened with finding the closest county to them where marijuana is legal (and therefore regulated and clean). If their *own* county has criminalized the drug, they have two options: Drive long distances to the closest dispensary to get the medical marijuana they need, or turn to the black market that surely exists in their jurisdiction. I'll discuss the black market shortly; but it's worth keeping in mind that black market marijuana doesn't meet state testing regulations. For healthy consumers, the effects may not be noticeable; but for patients with weakened immune systems (AIDS or cancer patients, for example), the pesticides, molds, or other toxins in black market marijuana could have harmful consequences.

As for the first option (driving long distances), many California jurisdictions that have decided to keep cannabis criminalized *also* ban deliveries of the drug to patients living in their jurisdiction—creating so-called "pot deserts" in the state. (Compare this to other adult-use products like alcohol and cigarettes, which can be ordered online and delivered anywhere in the state.) As *The Los Angeles Times* editorial board wrote in August of this year ("Marijuana is not really legal in California if residents don't have a reasonable way to buy it"), "Roughly half of Californians live in cities or counties that prohibit marijuana stores and delivery services from opening in their jurisdictions. An analysis by the Sacramento Bee earlier this year found residents in 40 percent of the state had to drive 60 miles or more to find a licensed dispensary to buy legal marijuana—medical or recreational."

California's Bureau of Cannabis Control has drafted regulations allowing cannabusinesses to deliver to private addresses in the state, regardless of local regulations, or whether brick-and-mortar shops are allowed in the jurisdiction of delivery—but as of this writing, these are still only drafts. (Naturally, there's plenty of opposition to these regulations from groups like the League of California Cities, who contend that the whole intent of Prop 64 was that local governments would have the authority to make their own determinations about cannabis in their jurisdictions.) So the practical effect remains that residents are either turning to readily-available black market products that are untested and unregulated, growing it themselves (which can be complex and costly), or not getting their medical marijuana *at all*.

Then there's the problem of testing. Because cannabis isn't a federally licit drug, the FDA hasn't established testing standards for products that contain it. The FDA and the DEA set the standards for source and quality of the raw materials, production, manufacture, characterization, labeling, packaging, delivery, and storage of *every* medicine in the U.S. to ensure that it's acceptable for use. This isn't so for cannabis. Nor does the *EPA* regulate pesticide use on state-legal cannabis, as it does for all other agricultural products.

This means that all of these processes fall to states to regulate. And because regulators at the state level aren't given any federal guidance from the very agencies that *set* health and safety standards—not only for medicine, but also for agriculture and food—they're having to figure it out on their own. As you can imagine, this involves a lot of trial and error; and standardization has been slow to evolve.

Let's take pesticide testing as an example. Pesticides on agricultural products have long been tested by the EPA. But because of decades of restricted access to the plant—and very limited federal funding for research—there's hardly any knowledge about *which* pesticides are safe for use on cannabis plants, or how cannabis tainted with certain toxins affects consumers. (I don't have to remind you that this problem would be solved by removing cannabis from Schedule 1 and permitting further study.) This becomes all the more important when you remember that concentrating cannabis (to create oils and tinctures, for example) may *also* concentrate pesticide residue. It's also not entirely clear which bacteria and fungi to test for. Some organisms that have been found on cannabis plants (like the fungus aspergillus, for example) can lead to infections in medical patients whose immune systems are already compromised.

California has chosen to err on the side of caution when it comes to aspergillus, and requires testing for the organism—which is great for medical patients. On the other hand, more tests means more expenses; and while the state hopes to head off any health crises before they occur, they're coming up against cannabusinesses' unwillingness to pay for testing that's both expensive *and* hasn't proven to improve safety—*yet*. (More tests *also* mean more laboratory time, and one of the complexities the industry ran into under new state regulations was the backlog: California simply didn't have enough testing facilities. Many dispensaries had empty shelves due to this backlog, and had to lay off staff and turn away customers.)

As the first month of new state safety requirements came to a close last July, 1 in 5 marijuana samples was failing laboratory testing according to the California Bureau of Cannabis Control. Nineteen percent of those failed tests were related to pesticides, and some of the pesticides found in those products were pesticides the cultivators never even *used*. According to *The Orange County Register*, "product from several growers who've taken over former vineyards, for example, failed initial tests because the soil was [already] contaminated, with stricter limits on pesticides allowed in marijuana than in wine." Indeed, state standards (developed by the California Department of Pesticide Regulation (CDPR)) are stricter for cannabis crops than they are for other agricultural products.

Xiaoyan Wang, a research scientist at United Chemical Technologies, has further described the complexities of testing for pesticides in cannabis: "Marijuana samples, including cannabis edibles, are complex matrices, containing lipids, organic acids, cannabinoids, sugars, food dyes, and natural pigments (such as chlorophylls and anthocynins) that can be coextracted with pesticides that interfere with the pesticide analysis. Another major issue commonly encountered is the extremely high concentration of the cannabinoids suppressing or masking the pesticide peaks, or both."

Sixty-eight percent of the failed tests, on the other hand, failed because of inaccurate claims on their labels. Many of those claims overstated the amount of THC in the product—and while that's hardly a safety hazard, it would mean consumers were overpaying for products that weren't as potent as the packaging suggested they were. Of course, as I've discussed, cannabis is complex plant, containing over 480 known components (well over 100 of which have been classified as cannabinoids—compounds that are unique to the plant); and this remarkable chemical diversity makes the plant difficult to test—not to mention that science is just beginning to characterize some of its compounds.

So while the FDA demands rigorous clinical testing of medicinal products that include documentation of how the body processes a drug and all the drug contains, it hasn't demanded that—indeed, it's *still not demanding, or funding, it*—when it comes to cannabis. We're talking something like 700 identified varieties of the plant; and the cannabinoid concentration can vary within a single strain as a factor of growing conditions and processing. That's why samples have what the Department of Health and Human Services calls "different safety, biological, pharmacological, and toxicological profiles." In addition to these genetic and environmental differences, a cannabis product's purity, potency, and overall quality is affected by whether the plant's flowers, leaves, and stems are included in the product itself.

Not only does this make precise chemical identity difficult to determine; it also means the mechanisms of action are indeterminate—which means doses are hard to quantify. (Doses vary based on mode of consumption and absorption rate. Smoking and vapor inhalation can't promise a consistent and reproducible dose. Neither can edibles, for that matter.) While many of these complexities are simply inherent to the plant, much more could certainly be brought to light with a federally-funded, scientifically-based framework by a governmental body with extensive experience in these matters—rather than forcing states to figure it out on their own.

In light of these complexities, California's trial-and-error testing standards surely seem frustrating to many cannabusinesses. This year, the state recalled three different products from dispensary and retail shelves because they didn't meet the new regulations. But as journalists at *The Orange County Register* note, "While that's concerning, in the short term, industry experts believe it's also a sign that California's cannabis industry is maturing and starting to look like other regulated markets, such as alcohol and food." Indeed, just three weeks after testing requirements were enforced and dispensaries experienced empty shelves due to laboratory backlogs, their shelves began filling up again with products considered safe for consumers. And one side effect of safety testing and accurate labeling is that consumers are now *demanding* products that meet those stricter regulations. So the industry is now in the position of working to meet shifting consumer demand.

Still, the shadowy half of the industry continues to thrive in California. Those rigorous testing standards—alongside the *cost* of that testing, the complexities of tax laws for cannabusinesses, and the obtuse nature of the licensing process—are helping ensure that an already-robust black market remains strong. Add to *that* the fact that some municipalities' sluggish approach to handing out licenses (either due to over-scrupulousness or backlog) means that many businesses continue to operate without legal permission.

In part, *too much* caution and an overzealous approach to regulation is undermining one of the primary objectives of legalization, which was to transform an uncontrolled black market into a legal, regulated one. The more rigorous the regulations—and the costlier the price point is to enter the legal market—the less likely underground businesses are to make the transition: There's little financial incentive to do so.

In Sacramento, for instance, first-year permit fees for commercial growers were as high as $28,910. (They were to be dropped to $26,630 in the second year). In Los Angeles, on the other hand, "The license application fee for sellers and others will be $1,000 annually, but there are additional license fees of $4,000 to $72,000 charged to retailers based on how much they sell," according to the *Times*. "Also, an additional fee for testing firms will range from $20,000 to $90,000, while an added charge for distribution licenses will go from $1,200 to $125,000 depending on the amount of product moved."

Of course, black market cannabusinesses aren't putting out cash for any of these things. While *licensed* California retailers shell out thousands for state *and* local permits, tax bills, and compliance with testing requirements, unlicensed retailers can undercut their product prices, because they've skipped those fees and aren't suddenly operating in the red. Add to this the fact that unlicensed businesses don't have to operate under restricted hours as licensed businesses do (the Bureau of Cannabis Control's mandated hours are 6 am to 10 pm for both medical and adult-use retailers), encouraging consumers to turn to the black market during hours of the day when intoxicant consumption tends to peak. (Alcohol retailers, on the other hand, can legally remain open until 2 am.) Nor do unlicensed businesses have limits on their product potency.

Given all this, you can imagine why business owners are complaining that they simply can't compete with the shops in the shadows.

Indeed, according Hezekiah Allen, executive director of the California Growers Association, "about half the state's 50,000 to 60,000 cannabis farms have been driven out of business by the new rules, and many are reverting to the black market." In the transition to tighter regulations and more oversight from local authorities, thousands of growers, manufacturers, and retailers lost their licenses. Growers that were already on parcels of land that weren't zoned by the state for growing, for example, may not have had the resources to pack up and relocate when regulations went into effect, and so carried on as they were—unlicensed. In many cases, the only possible response to the situation was to retreat from the open market into the shadows.

The result is that "the illicit market outnumbers us by five to one," according to Kenny Morrison, president of the California Cannabis Manufacturers Association. "You can go to a random city and find four legal stores and 20 illegal stores. What's worse, those four legal stores are charging two and three times the price of the illegal stores." According to New Frontier Data estimates, Morrison is nearly right: They estimate California's black market to be four times bigger than the legal industry.

From a consumer perspective, there's also the question of price—and not just product prices that are comparatively higher than black market prices, but also high *taxes*, which black market businesses don't have to charge at all. According to BDS Analytics, the sales tax on a gram of legal cannabis in San Jose is roughly 38 percent; and you might be able to imagine—or maybe you've experienced—the sticker shock that happens when a $9.12 gram suddenly costs $12.57 with tax. (In some places, taxes are as high as 45 percent.) When adult-use was first legalized, the Associated Press estimated that a batch of cannabis that went for $35 in California's medical market would cost between $50 and $60 in its medical market, amounting to a 70 percent increase. As Will Yakowicz notes, "Part of the price increase is because [of] a 15-percent state tax, plus an additional 7.5 percent city sales tax on each purchase."

Naturally, consumers frustrated by prices in legitimate cannabusinesses, along with their inability to access the product when they need it, results in them turning to the black market to meet their needs. According to a study from the cannabis startup and delivery platform Eaze, nearly 20 percent of Californians purchased cannabis from an unlicensed business over a three-month period 2018. What's more, 84 percent of those consumers are "highly likely" to continue buying from an unlicensed seller because "the illicit market ha[s] cheaper products and no tax."

California consumers' biggest frustrations with the legitimate market include high taxes (47 percent), lack of electronic payment methods (36 percent), "overpriced" products (32 percent), lack of delivery options (22 percent), and long dispensary lines (20 percent). You'll note that two of their three biggest frustrations concern cost. A February report by the California Growers Association rightly claims that "current cannabis tax policy is propping up the illicit market, preventing compliance from good-faith operations, and contributing to price increases for patients and consumers."

Much of this could be changed with a shift in regulatory practices. Or rather, my hope is that much of it *will be* changed when California's trial-and-error period is over. We saw something similar happen in Oregon. As Sophie Quinton reminds us, "initial rules rolled out [in Oregon] in October 2016 for marijuana testing and laboratory accreditation contributed to backlogs at laboratories and shortages of product on dispensary shelves. Regulators, seeking to ease the pressure on the market, issued new rules that December that reduced the number of times a harvest, or a batch of chocolates or candies, would have to be tested."

The reason for the new rules? According to Donald Morse, chairman of the Oregon Cannabis Business Council, it was an attempt to steer consumers away from the black market. After all, the more tests a cannabis product has to undergo, the higher its price point will be by the time it reaches consumers. "It would have been out of reach to most people," Morse said, "and they would end up going back to the black market."

Of course, Oregon is still learning its own lessons; but *this* is one that California will have to learn. The concern when the new regulations rolled out was that the black market would thrive during the *early* stages of the transition: For instance, a month after California began issuing licenses to cannabis cultivators (February 2018), fewer than 1 percent of the state's nearly 70,000 cultivators had been licensed, according to the California Growers Association. And illicit retailers and delivery services continued to have an abundance of (unregulated, potentially contaminated) products for sale while licensed retailers were destroying those of *their* products that didn't meet the new regulatory standards. Prices rose 20 percent on the licit products that remained due to the shortage.

During the first quarter of 2018, excise tax revenue for cannabis sales statewide was reported at $34 million, putting it on track to fall well below Governor Jerry Brown's projected $175 million for the first six months of legalization. In June, BDS cut its 2018 forecast for California's legal cannabis sales from $3.7 billion to $2.9 billion. Of course, $2.9 billion isn't exactly a number to despair over—Jack Kaskey at *Bloomberg* observes that "that's still higher than BDS estimates for the next biggest states: $1.5 billion in Colorado, $1 billion in Washington and $500 million in Oregon."

And I don't think anyone is scoffing at $500 million, either; the point is that *each* of these cannabis-legal states could be seeing higher revenues if its black market was extinguished. Will Yakowicz writes, "according to Erick Eschker, an economics professor at Humboldt State University, about $5.5 billion of California's $7.8 billion in pot sales is generated from unlicensed and unregulated growers, distributors, and dispensaries. (The remaining $2.3 billion in sales come from the medical market.)"

For the moment, that trend continues. In April alone, California state regulators sent out almost 1,000 cease-and-desist letters to cannabusinesses they believed were operating illegally. By August, they had sent out more than 2,500 total. Coordinated efforts to target the black market have resulted in *some* busts and shutdowns across the state, though the reality is that there isn't a workforce big enough to shut down 2,500 illicit operations. WeedMaps.com openly lists the black market dealers who'll deliver cannabis products anywhere in the state for consumers unwilling to pay high taxes, or who live in jurisdictions in which marijuana is illegal or licensure is slow.

And because Prop 64 downgraded nearly all marijuana-related crimes—including the possession of more than 28.5 grams—to a misdemeanor, this means that, while state authorities can seize both the cash and the cannabis of businesses caught operating in the shadows, those involved rarely face jail time, and they can reopen shop fairly quickly.

That the black market continues to bustle in the early days of legalization is hardly unexpected. Indeed, I've been talking about California all this time; but you can extrapolate these issues to every other state that's decided to legalize adult use and create a regulated market. Granted, each state has gone about things differently: States maintain different regulations on what the packaging of cannabis products has to include, or the amount of THC allowed in edibles. Testing standards vary by state (as well as *within* states): Some don't regulate testing at all; some test and regulate cannabis products according to pharmaceutical standards; some test and regulate them according to agricultural standards. *Sampling* for tests varies across states: In Alaska, for example, growers select their own samples and transport them to testing labs *themselves*; while in Oregon, labs choose the samples. Lab accreditation varies across states. Tax rates vary across states and municipalities. And so on.

As their separate industries endeavor to find their footing, each successive state has the benefit of looking at the *other* states who've put regulations in place before them. "Testing regulations are getting better over time as states learn from each other," said Jeff Raber, founder of the Werc Shop, a Southern California-based testing laboratory and research center. As Sophie Quinton notes, because of a lack of federal guidance, "The first states to regulate cannabis made their testing rules more or less on the fly, based on what scientists know makes people sick. For instance, foods generally need to be refrigerated and processed properly to avoid developing dangerous bacteria such as botulism. So Denver, one of the first cities to begin food safety inspections of pot products, requires dispensaries to refrigerate many edibles and hash oils at 41 degrees or less." These "on the fly" regulations will shift as intelligence grows; and states who legalize later will certainly have the benefit of working off of earlier states' failures.

Naturally, details are still being ironed out even in these "early" states: It's worth remembering that it's only been four years since Oregon–the first state to legalize recreational use—did so. Labs in Oregon, Washington, and Alaska continue to produce results that are inconsistent with each other. Standards, rules, and regulations are being rewritten to reflect new knowledge as it unfolds. In the meantime, the black market remains robust in these states, as well.

An assessment of Oregon's legal marketplace by the state police, for example, estimated that the legal market comprises only 30 percent of the state's total marijuana market. And in Colorado, surveys conducted by the Cannabis Consumers Coalition this year found that around 50 percent of respondents were not getting their marijuana products at legal dispensaries.

Of course, it probably doesn't help that cannabis is still illegal in every state *surrounding* Colorado: Black market organizations have even greater incentive to set up shop where the product can be smuggled and sold across state borders at a much greater profit margin. Indeed, Colorado has already seen lawsuits from attorneys general in Oklahoma and Nebraska, who complain that smugglers caught with Colorado cannabis are inundating their jails. And of course, states don't *have* to be contiguous for illicit interstate commerce to thrive. As Trevor Hughes writes, "A pound of marijuana might sell for about $2,000 in Colorado but could fetch three times as much in a large East Coast city."

You can perhaps imagine how much state revenue would increase if that other 70 percent of Oregon's marijuana market joined the legal industry, or if that 50 percent of consumers in Colorado started buying from the legal market.

Still, states in which adult-use has been legal for a few years *have* seen a decrease in black market activity and sales. John Hudak, deputy director at the Center for Effective Public Policy at the Brookings Institute, notes that there's "suggestive evidence in Colorado and Washington that the black market is decreasing." Francisco Gallardo, a former gang member and current program director for the Gang Rescue and Support Project in Denver, told journalists at *The Atlantic* that the black market in Denver is "neither as large nor as violent as it used to be." According to Green Wave Advisors, a cannabis research group and consulting firm, legal sales nationwide made up only 16 percent of total cannabis sales in 2016; but the firm predicts that, by 2020, legal sales will eclipse black market sales.

In part, the decline of the black market—albeit the *slow* decline—is a matter of what prices organically *do* in any new market. Oregon is a perfect example of this. Its market saw a disruption—and black market *organizations* saw a loophole to fit themselves into—in its initial shift to lab-tested and regulated recreational products. This included product shortages, spiked prices, and businesses going under.

But the trend started reversing after about five months. As Will Yakowicz wrote just days after adult-use became legal in California: "Prices in California's new recreational legal market are expected to initially inflate, just like they did in the early days of regulated markets in Colorado, Washington, and Oregon. The Associated Press calculated that a batch of cannabis that sold for $35 in the medical market could cost $50 to $60 in the recreational market ... [but] eventually, as the legal market matures and supply and demand increase, prices will drop." After all, "prices dropped in Washington's legal market from $50 to $15 for a gram of marijuana about 12 months after the first day of legal sales."

As more and more legal growers, dispensaries, and retailers enter the legal market, the market will do what it *does* when competition increases: It will adjust. This means prices will fall. It means the illicit market will correspondingly shrink. Since recreational cannabis became legal in Colorado, prices have gone down by 50 percent. In this sense, the *size* of California's black market is a temporary situation. Erick Eschker, professor of economics at Humboldt State, has predicted that about half of *California's* total black market sales will convert to sales in the legal, recreational market by next year. John Hudak believes the state's black market "should be substantially smaller in five years." The Chief of the Bureau of Cannabis Control, Lori Ajax, has noted that legalization isn't a "magic button" that will instantly dissolve California's black market. According to Yakowicz, "Ajax says it will take years of enforcement to reduce the size of California's underground cannabis economy."

So much for the market organically doing what it does. But there are two ways I can imagine *speeding up* the weakening of states' black markets.

The first is to begin educating consumers on the reasons it's so important to support the legal market. Granted, as cannabis legalization has spread, consumers' standards for the products they're ingesting have *already* increased. Molds and pesticides simply aren't tolerated anymore, as consumers recognize the degree to which testing procedures have already begun to mature. We want to know exactly what we're putting into our bodies ... and this is perhaps especially true for a product that can be both smoked *and* consumed as an edible. Indeed, according to the Eaze study I mentioned earlier, 90 percent of consumers in California claim to be using cannabis as a "wellness product." What this means, according to Peter Gigante—head of policy research at Eaze—is that California consumers are "looking for high quality products."

The more consumers recognize the value of high-quality, regulated, lab-tested products—and the more they *demand* that the marketplace offer *those* products—the more quickly the market will shift to the detriment of black market vendors. But in some cases, this requires educational campaigns. After all, many black market dispensaries and retailers operate in broad daylight. Consumers often don't *know* they're buying from illicit businesses unless it occurs to them during checkout that they aren't paying sales tax. As Josh Drayton, communication director for the California Cannabis Industry Association, told a journalist at *Merry Jane*, "We [currently] have tech platforms that are still advertising unregulated operators, so in some way, shape, or form, we need to create educational campaigns about why it's important for consumers to support regulated businesses, how it benefits their community, guarantees they're getting clean product, and tends to public safety and health."

I'm with him.

A second strategy for shrinking the black market—if you've not guessed it already—would entail lowering taxes on the products. I'd like to refer to Tom Jones at *The Atlantic* for this one. While he recognizes that it isn't a perfectly analogous industry, Jones offers a succinct summary of Luther E. Gregory's approach to taxing alcohol in Washington State as prohibition came to an end, and a legitimate market had to be strategized ("The Failed Promise of Legal Pot"). The bootleggers had become well-established during the years of prohibition, and lawmakers had to figure out how to force those illegal operations to enter the legal market. When

Gregory was tapped to head Washington's new Liquor Control Board, he did the unexpected: Among other things, he "arranged for alcohol taxes to be set as low as any in the nation, which allowed those willing to follow the law to keep a significant amount of their profits, and it made room for legal operators to compete with bootleggers' prices."

"Predictably," Jones writes, "this caused some turmoil in a legislature anxiously awaiting an infusion of cash from liquor sales, but the governor backed Gregory. Faced with a low cost of entry and legal profits, bootleggers and speakeasies around the state mostly turned legitimate. Meanwhile, the few remaining stragglers were quickly put out of business, and drinkers flocked to a competitive legal market." That's why, after three years, when Gregory suddenly raised alcohol taxes so much that Washington's were among the steepest taxes in the nation, consumers kept buying. After all, there were no alternative sources to turn to: The black market no longer existed.

Granted, legislatures in cannabis-legal states are unlikely to follow Gregory's lead and radically cut taxes. As Jones notes, both Washington and Colorado lowered cannabis taxes in 2015 *with the stated goal* of pressuring illicit businesses. But the cuts were too small to be very meaningful (from 44 percent to 43.5 percent in Washington, and from 27.9 percent to 25.9 percent in Colorado).

Consumers appear to want something slightly more drastic. The Eaze survey I've mentioned included a question that asked California residents how tax reductions would shift their willingness to buy from the legal market. Twenty-three percent of survey respondents said that a 5 percent decrease in California's cannabis tax rate would lead them to turn from unlicensed sellers to the legal market. And while a 5 percent tax cut might *feel like* a lot of lost revenue for the state, I imagine the 23 percent who returned to the licit market would make up for that lost revenue. After all, the same study found that 84 percent of Californians are "very satisfied" with the state's legal market. So those who transition are likely to stay.

While reducing the tax rate would be no *guarantee* of anything (consumers often say one thing on surveys and do another, so increased participation in the state's legal market is hardly a given), history has shown it to be a practical strategy. "Gregory's strategy can still be mined for shards of economic and social truth," Jones writes. His is an article California legislators—indeed, *all* state legislators—would benefit from reading.

Proponents of cannabis legalization have long argued that legalizing, regulating, and taxing the drug in the context of a legitimate marketplace would allow the government to rake in big money and either force underground operations into the light, or extinguish them altogether. Opponents of this line of thought have been quick to point out how wrong that logic was in light of cannabis-legal states' struggle with their transitions. But I think time will soon tell that those opponents jumped the gun in their criticisms.

Yes, profit margins may remain thin for cannabusinesses for a few years more. But this is also the natural turbulence that's stirred up whenever a gray market is fully legalized. And, as Brooke Staggs notes, "the producers that do survive are competing to see who will be the first Anheuser-Busch of cannabis." Those businesses that can manage to stay in the game through this transition will ultimately win brand loyalty from their markets. But we're talking marathon-not-sprint mentalities.

In the next chapter I'll talk at greater length about what businesses who want to be "the first Anheuser-Busch of cannabis" will have to focus on *now* if that's their end-goal. But first—after all those details that might make the industry seem like a less-than-ideal one to enter—I'd like to end this discussion with a bit of hope (not to mention excitement) for its future. After all, politicians on

Capitol Hill seem to be fighting for cannabis decriminalization in droves right now; and the results that states like Colorado have seen—even over the short term—have made for great economic success stories.

Cannabusinesses that figure out how to navigate these currently-choppy waters will not only ultimately find themselves in lucrative positions; they'll also ultimately help contribute to their communities: Infrastructure, education, law enforcement, transportation, and public health are among the many beneficiaries of Colorado's cannabis industry. In other words, *everyone* benefits.

Reason for Optimism: The Goings-On in Washington and Colorado

In April of last year (on the eve of 4/20 to be exact—a date that wasn't lost on marijuana enthusiasts), Senate Minority Leader Chuck Schumer (D-NY) announced in an interview on VICE News Tonight that he would be introducing legislation that would decriminalize cannabis at the federal level ("from one end of the country to the other" were his exact words). The bill, called the Marijuana Freedom and Opportunity Act, would deschedule cannabis, removing it from the DEA's Schedule I category under the 1970 Controlled Substances Act. Under Schumer's bill, states would continue to function as independent laboratories of democracy, determining how they'd implement and regulate cannabis and treat marijuana possession.

While federal authorities would still have the power to prevent marijuana trafficking from cannabis-legal states to cannabis-*il*legal states under Schumer's bill, they wouldn't be able to harass cannabis businesses working within states that have determined to legalize the drug. The bill would allow the Department of Treasury to continue to regulate marijuana advertising—just as it regulates tobacco advertising—to ensure that advertisers don't target children. According to the Senate Democratic Leadership website, it would also

> ... invest $500 million across five years for the Secretary of Health and Human Services to work in close coordination with the Director of National Institutes of Health (NIH) and the Commissioner of Food and Drug Administration (FDA) in order to better understand the impact of marijuana, including the effects of THC on the human brain and the efficacy of marijuana as a treatment for specific ailments.

In other words, the scientific studies that have been hindered by the drug's Schedule I status would not only be *unobstructed*; they'd also be *funded* in the name of public health.

What's more, the bill would assist communities that have been disproportionately hurt—both historically and currently—by marijuana laws by "establish[ing] dedicated funding streams to be administered by the Small Business Administration (SBA) for women and minority-owned marijuana businesses," essentially leveling the playing field. It would allot $250 million over a five-year period "to ensure federal agencies have the resources they need to assess the pitfalls of driving under the influence of THC and develop technology to reliably measure impairment." And it would encourage state and local governments, through grant programs ($100 million over a five-year period), to let individuals expunge records for marijuana possession convictions.

Schumer's proposed bill is co-sponsored by Bernie Sanders (I-VT), Tammy Duckworth (D-IL), and Tim Kaine (D-VA). As Douglas A. Berman observed earlier this year, "this is big news not only because it provides still further evidence that 'establishment Democrats' are now fully behind federal marijuana reform, but also because Senator Schumer is positioned to be the House majority leader if Democrats retake control of the Senate in either 2018 or 2020.

If that happens, Senator Schumer presumably would be most interesting in having his version of marijuana reform considered first among all the competing bills now floating about." Of course, we just watched the Democrats retake control of the *House* in November; and if the party keeps this momentum going, 2020 looks promising.

Yet it's not *just* "establishment Democrats" who are realizing they've got to keep up with the American public's progressing views on the issue. According to a recent Gallup poll, 64 percent of Americans support legalizing adult use marijuana. An April 2018 Quinnipiac poll shows that 94 percent of Americans support legalizing medical marijuana—including 41 percent of Republican respondents. Perhaps unsurprisingly, the age demographic with the staunchest support is millennials. As Alexandra Hutzler observes:

> In the long run, Republican lawmakers may support marijuana decriminalization for the simple fact that it may help them get elected as they play a catch-up game with young, nonwhite voters. An estimated 24 million people ages 18 to 29 cast votes in the 2016 election… Millennials are about to inherit the kingdom as the largest voting block in the country, and, according to one poll, over 80 percent believe the drug is safer than alcohol.

Earlier, I discussed the STATES Act, introduced in June by Cory Gardner (R-CO) and Elizabeth Warren (D-MA). Even in this particularly polarized administration, the bill's co-sponsorship shows an impressive bipartisanship. (It's currently cosponsored by 5 Republican senators, 6 Democratic senators, 15 house Republicans, and 15 house Democrats.) Gardner calls the bill a "federalism experiment," and has posed a challenge to Republicans: Voting against the bill would be fundamentally hypocritical. ("Republicans who have long been champions of states' rights can choose this as a moment to prove it.")

But there's more Republican support where *that* came from …
much more. Just over a week before Schumer announced his
Marijuana Freedom and Opportunity Act (on April 11), John
Boehner—former Ohio congressman and Speaker of the House—
announced on Twitter that he was joining the board of Acreage
Holdings, "one of the United States' largest vertically integrated U.S.
cannabis companies" according to *New Cannabis Ventures*. Boehner's
tweet read: "I'm joining the board of #AcreageHoldings because my
thinking on cannabis has evolved. I'm convinced descheduling the
drug is needed so we can do research, help our veterans, and reverse
the opioid epidemic ravaging our communities." Later last year, on
October 22—just days after Canada officially legalized adult use
marijuana across the country—none other than Fox News posted
that Boehner would be hosting a "marijuana investing seminar."

As Gene Demby observes, the move is a "startling about-face
for Boehner, who in 2011 said he was 'unalterably opposed' to
the legalization of marijuana. In 1999, he voted against legalizing
medical cannabis use in Washington D.C.; in 2015, Boehner wrote
to a constituent that he didn't want to reschedule, or reclassify,
cannabis … because he was 'concerned that legalization will result
in increased abuse of all varieties of drugs, including alcohol.'
At one point, NORML, one of country's leading marijuana
legalization lobbying groups, considered him enough of a hardliner
on legalization that it gave him a zero-percent approval rating for
his Congressional voting record."

Boehner's "evolved thinking" is just one of a string of Republican
pivots on Capitol Hill. Early last year, Senator Rand Paul (R-KY)
told a reporter that the "federal government has better things to
focus on" than enforcement of the CSA in cannabis-legal states: "I
continue to believe that this is a states' rights issue." And on April
19—the same day Schumer announced his Marijuana Freedom and
Opportunity Act—Senator Orrin G. Hatch (R-UT) published a

tweet rife with puns about a bipartisan attempt to stop Jeff Sessions from blocking medical marijuana research: "Tomorrow, purely coincidentally, we will be talking about marijuana. We'll get in the weeds to hash out some of the most potent arguments as to why it might be the budding answer doctors have long strained to find for countless chronic conditions."

It's worth pointing out that the letter Hatch co-write with Kamala Harris (D-CA) asking Sessions' DOJ to stop blocking research on medical marijuana included a long list of federal officials and departments advocating for further research on cannabis:

> Research on marijuana is necessary for evidence-based decision making, and expanded research has been called for by President Trump's Surgeon General, the Secretary of Veterans Affairs, the FDA, the CDC, the National Highway Safety Administration, the National Institute of Health, the National Cancer Institute, the National Academies of Sciences, and the National Institute on Drug Abuse.

We can add to this list the nearly 10,000 attendees of the 2018 Republican Party Convention—held in San Antonio last summer—who voted to revise the party platform concerning cannabis. As Alexandra Hutzler wrote ("Legal Weed: How Republicans Learned to Love Marijuana"): "The changes included supporting industrial hemp, decriminalizing small amounts of marijuana possession and urging the federal government to reclassify cannabis from a Schedule 1 to a Schedule 2 drug."

We can *also* add to that list Mitch McConnell, who introduced in March—indeed, fast-tracked through the Senate—the Hemp Farming Act of 2018. The legislation sought to remove hemp from the DEA's list of Schedule I substances, effectively divorcing it from its psychoactive cousin. (As I mentioned in the introduction, "hemp" and "marijuana" are both "cannabis," and both contain CBD.

The legal distinction between the two is a matter of *THC* content: Hemp is cannabis that contains less than 0.3 percent THC.) The provisions for McConnell's Hemp Farming Act were recently incorporated into the United States Farm Bill, which Trump signed into law this month (December 2018), as I was completing the final edits of this book.

Unsurprisingly, McConnell had good *personal* reasons for his Hemp Farming Act. Section 7606 of the Agricultural Act of 2014 (affectionately known as the "Farm Bill") created a pilot program that allowed both state departments of agriculture and universities, for the first time, to begin growing hemp for research purposes. It was an economy-strengthening strategy: At the time it was passed, Eric Steenstra, the president of the Washington, D.C.-based advocacy group Vote Hemp, said: "The market opportunities for hemp are incredibly promising—ranging from textiles and health foods to home construction and even automobile manufacturing. This is not just a boon to U.S. farmers, this is a boon to U.S. manufacturing industries as well." Mitch McConnell said of his home state: "We are laying the groundwork for a new commodity market for Kentucky farmers."

As it turns out, Kentucky happens to be the second-biggest hemp producer under this program (the first is Colorado). As McConnell wrote in an opinion piece last April: "Last year alone, the hemp pilot program yielded more than $16 million for Kentucky farmers. We've already seen remarkable innovation in everything from home insulation to concrete and from health products to beer. These hemp products are just the beginning." The *difficulty* of the 2014 Farm Bill, McConnell noted, is that although it paved the way for hemp pilot programs, it still left farmers vulnerable to obstruction from federal agencies. As McConnell writes, "This bill will remove roadblocks and encourage the domestic growth and production of hemp."

As I discussed in the last chapter, hemp does, indeed, have a myriad of industrial and agricultural uses, from textiles to plastics to construction materials. But since CBD has entered the mainstream consciousness—and since, thanks to the 2014 Farm Act, cannabis farmers have begun breeding strains that are high in CBD but can be classified as "hemp" because of their low THC content—the hemp industry has exploded. (Or rather, the *CBD* industry has exploded. As Amanda Chicago Lewis writes, "Label everything as a hemp extract ... and the consumer will know you mean CBD." *You're* a consumer, reader; I'm sure you're seeing "hemp extract" everywhere these days.)

I've already spoken at some length about the remarkable range of potential health benefits CBD offers. The fact is that consumers are beginning to recognize what CBD is capable of— and the market appears to be giving them what they want. Skin creams; lotions; balms; CBD-infused mascara, sleep masks, and bath bombs; CBD ice cream, coffee and dog treats ... you name it, it's probably available—and marketed for everything from stress reduction, to pain relief, to beauty, wellness, and hygiene.

And in many cases, the big corporations are jumping fully into the CBD industry. Lagunitas (owned by Heineken) launched a drink last summer called "Hi-Fi Hops"—billed as "hoppy sparkling water"—that contains CBD (and THC) instead of alcohol. Coca-Cola, which is keeping a finger on the pulse of the industry, "is in talks with Canadian marijuana producer Aurora Cannabis to develop [CBD-infused] beverages," according to *Bloomberg News*. (Kent Landers, a Coca-Cola spokesman, confirmed that the company is "closely watching the growth of non-psychoactive CBD as an ingredient in functional wellness beverages around the world.") Target briefly sold CBD products before pulling them in 2017 (I bet they'll be back); Walmart continues to sell CBD-infused oils and creams ... though of course, you'll have to search for "hemp" rather than "CBD" in their online shop if you want to find them.

According to the data company Brightfield Group, hemp-derived CBD sales exceeded $170 million in 2016 and $190 million in 2017. Hemp-derived CBD is poised to become a $1 billion market by 2010. I should point out that that $1 billion prediction was made by the Brightfield Group in 2017, prior to federal approval of Epidiolex and the descheduling of CBD from Schedule I to Schedule V in FDA-approved products. Since then, the group has made a much longer-term prediction that the CBD market will hit $22 billion by 2022.

It appears that the CBD boom was, in some ways, an accidental byproduct of the 2014 Farm Bill; and McConnell wanted to keep seeing returns on it. Of course, McConnell refused to *say* "CBD"; in the op-ed I referred to above, he writes: "We've already seen remarkable innovation in everything from home insulation to concrete and from health products to beer."

But if you're wondering if McConnell's incentive was *really* about hemp's CBD component, and not something else in the plant, here's Amanda Chicago Lewis again:

> Though he's focused his hemp legalization rhetoric on helping farmers and bland-sounding industrial products, his true intentions became abundantly clear about two weeks ago, when Sen. Chuck Grassley (R-IA) proposed an amendment that would exclude CBD … from the definition of legal hemp. McConnell shot the proposal down, saying, 'I've declined to include suggestions that would undercut the essential premise of the bill, namely that hemp and its derivatives should be a legal agricultural commodity.' At no point did he refer directly to the 'derivative' that was up for discussion. But anyone paying close attention understood what he was talking about.

The 2018 Farm Bill Trump just signed—based on McConnell's Hemp Farming Act—deschedules all cannabis plants with maximum THC levels of 0.3 percent, making "hemp" a mainstream crop after years of prohibition. The plants will now be treated like any other agricultural crop, and will therefore be regulated by the Department of Agriculture, rather than the DoJ and DEA. A March press release from Senator McConnell's office, in which he discusses his Hemp Farming Act, reads: "This legislation … will also give hemp researchers the chance to apply for competitive federal grants from the U.S. Department of Agriculture—allowing them to continue their impressive work with the support of federal research dollars."

Let's hope that federal funding is, indeed, used to research cannabis.

And *that's* just Republicans, whose reassessments appear to be occurring at warp speed. Other federal activity includes Senator Cory Booker's (D-NJ) Marijuana Justice Act, proposed in August 2017, which would: 1) remove cannabis from the Controlled Substances Act, effectively legalizing it at the federal level; 2) withhold federal funding from states that continue to criminalize the plant, and—according to Tom Angell—"continue to have radically disproportionate arrest and incarceration rates for cannabis" (low-income and people of color); and 3) instruct federal courts to expunge previous marijuana convictions (use and possession), allowing those punished under the aforementioned disproportionate enforcement procedures to file lawsuits against their respective states.

Booker's bill is co-sponsored by Kirsten Gillibrand (D-NY), Bernie Sanders (I-VT), Kamala Harris (D-CA), Jeff Merkley (D-OR), Elizabeth Warren (D-MA), and Ron Wyden (D-OR).

Then there's Resolution HR 4779—dubbed "The R.E.F.E.R. Act"—introduced in the House by Representative Barbara Lee

(D-CA) in January of this year (2018). According to congress. gov, the bill would prohibit funding to any federal department or agency that sought to "restrict a state or local law that authorizes the use, distribution, possession, or cultivation of cannabis"; "detain, prosecute, sentence, or initiate civil proceedings against an individual, business, or property involved in cannabis-related activities in accordance with state or local law"; or "penalize a financial institution for providing financial services to a business engaged in cannabis-related activities in compliance with state or local law." In other words, it would restrict federal agencies from taking punitive action against cannabis businesses operating legitimately in cannabis-legal states.

Finally, there's Tulsi Gabbard's (D-HI) Marijuana Data Collection Act—introduced in the House in July—which "would direct the Department of Health and Human Services to partner with other federal and state government agencies to study 'the effects of State legalized marijuana programs on the economy, public health, criminal justice and employment,'" according to Tom Angell. If the bill passes, the National Academy of Sciences would conduct the research on state-legal cannabis programs and publish its initial findings within 18 months (succeeded by biannual follow-up reports)—on everything from revenue and state allocations, to substance use, to medicinal use, to marijuana's impacts on criminal justice and employment.

Perhaps unsurprisingly, the bill's supporters consist only of those who support cannabis law reform. My guess is that those politicians with anti-cannabis sentiments fear that the Marijuana Data Collection Act will make cannabis *look* as good as it *is*: from job creation, to overdose rates compared with opioids and other painkillers, to the ways marijuana tax dollars are being put to use in legal states. As Justin Strekal, political director for NORML, has noted:

> This is not a marijuana bill, it is an information bill. No member of Congress can intellectually justify opposition to this legislation. Our public policy needs to be based on sound data and science, not gut feelings or fear-mongering. Approving the Marijuana Data Collection Act would provide legislators with reliable and fact-based information to help them decide what direction is most beneficial to society when it comes to marijuana policy.

Of course, politicians against cannabis legalization are apparently uninterested in "sound data and science"; but with the tide turning in the favor of precisely these things, they may have little choice. The United States Conference of Mayors has called upon the federal government to remove cannabis from the CSA. This past summer, the 48-member Congressional Black Caucus called on the federal government to "decriminalize the use and possession of marijuana," arguing that "the states should be allowed to make their own decisions about how to regulate marijuana and the federal government should be out of the business of prohibition and related law enforcement of marijuana." What's more, the caucus wants an "automatic expungement for those convicted of misdemeanors for marijuana-related offenses." A recent policy at the Department of Veterans Affairs encourages doctors at the VA to *discuss* medical marijuana with veterans (though they can't directly recommend it).

The list goes on. The movement is afoot.

The legislation I discussed above isn't inclusive: These aren't the *only* cannabis-related pending bills, but hopefully they're enough to fill in the larger narrative of the shift that's occurring at the federal level. Indeed, according to the National Cannabis Industry

Association, in the 115th Congress (which will run through January 3, 2019) "there are more cannabis reform bills than ever before—dozens, as a matter of fact."

And now that there's actual *money* in the cannabis industry to work with, pro-cannabis special interest groups are beginning to flex their muscles, just as Big Pharma has been doing all along. As Alfonso Serrano notes, "pro-pot lobbyists in Denver now battle on equal footing with their counterparts in the pharmaceutical and alcohol industries." In Colorado, State Senator Pat Steadman has watched the marijuana lobby "become increasingly sophisticated." "They're investing more money in government relations, elections, marketing and public relations," he's said. Rick Schettino at the *Pot Network* writes:

> In the second quarter of [2018], spending by [pro-pot] lobbyists surged to almost half a billion dollars with Weedmaps. com being the biggest spender at $75,000. Between April and June Weedmaps contributed more than $150,000 to political campaigns including more than $50,000 on June 1st to the California Democratic Party. Cannabis delivery company Eaze Solutions spent nearly $66,000 lobbying.

Republicans, too, are starting to see the financial benefits of supporting the cannabis industry. Dana Rohrabacher—of the Rohrabacher-Farr Amendment—has received checks from organizations such as the National Cannabis Industry Association and cannabusinesses such as Scotts Miracle-Gro (a leader in the hydroponics industry) and WeedMaps. Prior to Rohrabacher's loss in November, Alexandra Hutzler wrote: "Rohrabacher, who is facing his toughest re-election campaign in three decades and is seen as one of the most vulnerable Republicans in the House, has been rewarded for his pro-weed stance … Since 2016, Rohrabacher has received more than $80,000 in marijuana industry money."

And of course it's not just individual candidates "seeing returns." California's own Prop 64 received funding to the tune of $31 million from PACs such as Californians for Responsible Marijuana Reform, the Marijuana Policy Project of California, Drug Policy Action, and the Fund for Policy Reform.

Finally, there's the money that's coming in as tax revenue to consider—because I think this is where the other half of the hope lies. (It's also the other half of the compassion aspect I keep returning to: Not just compassion for medical patients, but compassion for communities at large.)

Let's take our poster child, Colorado. In the first four years that marijuana was legal in Colorado, the state saw tax revenues of $67 million (2014), $130 million (2015), $193 million (2016), and $247 million (2017). (That's just tax revenue, by the way; *sales* reached $1.5 billion in 2017 alone.) Not to complicate things too much (they're already fairly complex), but the state has three cannabis taxes: 1) a 15 percent excise tax on recreational marijuana, paid by the retailer each time a product moves from a production facility to a dispensary; 2) a 15 percent "special" sales tax on recreational marijuana, paid by the consumer; and 3) a 2.9 percent sales tax on *medical* marijuana, paid by the consumer.

On top of that, all cannabis sales—whether recreational or adult-use—are also subject to local district taxes. For example, Michael Hancock, the mayor of Denver, has recently proposed raising the city's special sales tax from 3.5 percent to 5.5 percent to raise money for Denver's Affordable Housing Fund. (Denver cannabis consumers already pay an additional 1 percent tax to help fund the Regional Transportation District and the Scientific and Cultural Facilities District.) And Pueblo County used its local excise tax to give $420,000 worth of college scholarships to 210 students in 2017, and $624,000 to 563 students in 2018.

Of the 15 percent excise tax (the one paid when cannabis products are transferred from growers to retailers), the first $40 million or 90 percent (whichever number is greater) goes to Colorado's Building Excellent Schools Today (BEST) program, through which schools and school districts can apply for grants to build or renovate existing facilities. This means prioritizing health, safety, and security issues for Colorado's children: new roofs, asbestos removal, fixing building code violations and repairing failing infrastructure, improving indoor air quality, and more. The money in excess of that $40 million ($31.6 million in 2016-2017) goes to the Public School Permanent Fund, which supports K-12 education.

The 15 percent special tax (the tax on recreational marijuana) goes primarily to the state's general fund, though a portion of that is reserved for the Department of Education's State Public School Fund, and another portion for the Marijuana Tax Cash Fund (MTCF). The 2.9 percent tax on medical marijuana, on the other hand, goes *entirely* into the Marijuana Tax Cash Fund. The MTCF funds health care, health education, substance abuse prevention and treatment programs, law enforcement, and monitoring the health effects of marijuana. According to the Colorado Department of Education, money received from MTCF has allowed for "the School Health Professional Grant program to address behavioral health issues in schools; a grant program to help schools and districts set up initiatives to reduce the frequency of bullying incidents; grants to fund drop-out prevention programs"; and "early Literacy Competitive Grants to ensure reading is embedded into K-3 curriculum."

Marijuana tax revenue is also going to the Department of Agriculture, the Department of Transportation, and the Department of Human Services. Thanks to cannabis, after school programs are maintained, roads are being fixed, Coloradoans' mental health is being attended to (both outside and within the prison system), more affordable housing is being built, financial help is being generated for low-income residents, farming problems are being solved … and law enforcement is getting funded to combat the black market, so that more cannabusinesses turn legitimate, ultimately generating more tax revenue. In Fort Collins, Team Wellness & Prevention, a substance abuse non-profit for teens, has received grant money from the MTCF. In Aurora, tax money has been used to create The Aurora Day Resource Center, where homeless people can go during the day for meals, health services, showers, employment services, computer access, housing assistance, financial literacy, and more.

In other words—while the presence of the black market means the state may not (yet) boast of the revenue it anticipated seeing— the cannabis industry is proving to be a significant contributor to state and local economies. It's created an estimated 30,000+ jobs in the state—and Coloradoans at every level are benefitting. What's more, an article in the *Coloradoan* (*USA Today*) reminds us that the cannabis industry in Colorado is contributing to businesses, communities, and the economy in quieter ways. Most businesses get tax breaks for donations to charities. At this point in time it shouldn't surprise you to hear that those tax breaks don't apply to cannabusinesses… but many decide to donate anyway.

> Sometimes dispensaries choose to donate anonymously be- cause many people do not want to know they are benefitting from cannabis money," the article reads. It then quotes Aman- da Woods, Marketing Manager and Compliance Officer for Fort Collins-based Choice Organics, a dispensary and recre- ational shop: "[Dispensaries] don't get to write [donations] off. Anytime we donate, we're trying to be good community members and contribute back to benefit everybody. When we make those anonymous donations, people don't even know that they are benefitting from the cannabis community.

By all accounts, cannabis has done Colorado well. The same can be said of every state that has decided to decriminalize and legalize the drug. As Congressman Tim Ryan (D-OH) wrote last summer in an op-ed:

> As co-chair of the House Addiction, Treatment, and Recovery Caucus, I've been hesitant to support legalizing marijuana in the past. But after meeting with countless Ohio families and youth whose lives have been irreparably harmed by a marijuana arrest, I find the social and economic injustices of our marijuana policy too big to ignore. . . . I am calling for an end to marijuana being used as an excuse to lock up our fellow Americans. Marijuana should be legal in all 50 states. Studies have shown that marijuana legalization could save $7.7 billion in averted enforcement costs and add $6 billion in additional tax revenue—a $13.7 billion net savings. Not to mention the reported 782,000 jobs it could create on day one. Think of what our country could do with that money: rebuild our highways, bridges, and railroads; provide our communities with the resources they need to respond effectively to substance abuse and the opioid epidemic; and create jobs.

I, *too*, think a lot about "what our country could do with that money" . . . and I'd add to Ryan's list all the lives it could save. We're talking about one of the fastest-growing industries in the United States—*whether or not* Big Pharma or Big Alcohol wants to acknowledge that. It's an unstoppable force at this point, with projections as high as $22.6 billion in sales in the North American market by 2021, and $75 billion by 2030. (After all, Canada legalized recreational country-wide as I was drafting this book.) But regardless of whose data you're choosing to believe, there's not a single data company out there that isn't predicting major—if not explosive—growth for the industry.

4

Industry Forecasts and Success Factors

*How to Thrive in the Cannabis Industry
in 2019 and Beyond*

I could continue to give predictions about sales and revenue here: An international market expected to hit $31.4 billion by 2021, according to the Brightfield Group. A "$21+ billion market in California *alone*" by that same year, according to Zachary Venegas, quoting industry analysts. More conservatively, ArcView projects $21.6 billion in sales *across* North America by that year, while New Frontier Data predicts $6.5 billion in California in 2025. A $63.5 billion-dollar *global* market by 2024, according to Statista. (ArcView's global projection is $47.3 billion by 2027.) Long before that—indeed, by 2020, predicts New Frontier Data—the cannabis industry will be creating more jobs than the manufacturing industry. I've heard numbers around 300,000 by 2020.

While some estimates are certainly more "conservative" than others—and while analysts continue to modify their numbers as the industry matures and its story unfolds—I've not yet heard a single analyst or industry insider predict that growth will slow anytime soon. Add to this the fact that the majority of marijuana sales are still transacted on the black market (an estimated 87 percent of sales, or $46 billion, in 2017); and as the market matures and the black market dwindles, the legal industry will see *that* money coming in, as well.

It certainly doesn't hurt that Canada just legalized recreational marijuana nationwide (October 2018), or that Mexico legalized medical marijuana in June of 2017. And the most remarkable thing about the explosive growth in this industry is that it has *nothing to do* with a discovery or a technological innovation. The plant is *still the plant*; all that's occurred is a shift in public perception. Cannabis is winning converts among small-town politicians and skeptical cops as marijuana tax dollars fund schools, scholarships, infrastructure, and drug treatment programs. Public opinion grows by the year. Ninety-three percent of Americans now support the legal use of marijuana for medical purposes if it's been prescribed by a doctor. Fifty-nine percent say marijuana should be legal nationwide.

I can't think of another industry *anywhere* that's experiencing this kind of growth and this kind of potential. And so the sales and revenue predictions are accompanied by others. The principal one is an informed consensus that cannabis will be rescheduled and have federal approval by 2024. As Arnaud Dumas de Rauly, CEO of The Blinc Group, says, "the majority of the industry doesn't think this will happen within the current administration but we believe it will happen sooner than later." Regardless of whether cannabis is *re*scheduled or *de*scheduled, the change will mean at least two important things: 1) a single, national approach to compliance involving well-funded federal organizations like the FDA; and 2) the fracturing of the cannabis industry into three primary sectors: recreational/wellness, medical, and industrial.

Of course it will also mean—finally—a national destigmatizing, and a tremendous shift in the socio-cultural narrative that has surrounded the plant for nearly a century. Tax and banking laws (say goodbye to IRC 280E) will change to reflect the newly-legal drug. The recreational sector will continue to outgrow the medical sector as more studies confirm the wellness value of CBD and the industry as a whole promotes cannabis as compatible with—indeed, as *indispensable* to—a long and healthy life. Oils and concentrates will outsell flower (smokeables). "Pot," "weed," and "marijuana" as terms will fall out of style and the new nomenclature will simply be "cannabis," as it was from the beginning.

More studies—thanks to access to a descheduled drug—will also mean a better, more sophisticated understanding of the still-mysterious compounds and properties of the plant. That new knowledge will enable doctors, physicians, and health-and-wellness experts to more specifically target symptoms and conditions. (After all, we're *already* beginning to see CBD as the new natural alternative to a multitude of ailments.) I'm talking product personalization, hyper-personalized administration methods, and creative consumption methods. Cannabis will be the new exit drug—rather than the gateway drug it's been unjustifiably feared to be—and will evolve into an essential household item, kept in bathroom drawers and kitchen cupboards because of its wide range of applications.

From the *consumer* side of things, this looks incredibly optimistic (*assuming*, that is, big businesses don't completely take over the industry—though more on that shortly). But what about smaller cannabusinesses? While the *numbers* look promising, history has shown that industries with exponential growth attract big entrants who want a piece of the market—and it's already begun in this industry. If you're a small business, the reports and projections may be exciting and invigorating to read. But what you're likely *experiencing* is an oversaturated market that's lucrative for a select few ... and there's a good chance you're not among them.

Of course, after all the blood, sweat, toil, and activism that small business owners and cannabis pioneers have put into growing this industry and making it legitimate, *no one* (even the most exhausted of you) wants to see big businesses entirely take over. There are a thousand good reasons to want to see small businesses thrive. But if the market splits as it's expected to, Big Pharma will naturally have interests in the medical sector, while Big Alcohol and Big Tobacco will have interests in the recreational sector. And history is a good indicator of the fierceness with which they'll enter those sectors. On the production side, a few large factory growers producing on an industrial scale will dominate. On the retail side, the Costcos and Walmarts of the world will sell packaged cannabis and CBD in concentrate, smokeable, and edible forms.

So how will you withstand the imminent storm of this increasingly-cutthroat industry, outpacing smaller competitors and fending off big business? If you want to remain—and *flourish* in—your dedicated niche as a boutique retailer or an artisanal grower for a specific target market, how do you strategize? What if you want an exit strategy? What if, on the other hand, you hope to *grow* your business in the face of this fierce competition—perhaps even eventually becoming one of the acquirers?

In this chapter, my goal is to speak to each of those aspirations. First, though, let's take a look at what's happening with mergers and acquisitions (M&A), new entrants, and the general reshuffling of the industry *now*. If you're *in* it, you probably feel the effects of it; but may not know the details. If you're *outside* of it, you don't have the empirical experience of the industry's many pain points. Either way, you can't move forward without a clear idea of the industry landscape … in *this* moment.

Mergers, Acquisitions, and the Current Cannabis Landscape

Even before recreational marijuana became legal in Canada a few months back, rapid consolidation had begun. Indeed, if you were paying attention to the market in the months before legalization, you know that deals among Canadian cannabis companies dominated the news. In May, Aurora Cannabis made industry history when it signed a deal to acquire its rival producer

MedReleaf for $3.2 billion Canadian ($2.5 billion U.S.). Aurora officially acquired MedReleaf at the end of July. The acquisition was the biggest deal to date in the cannabis industry, and it created one of the largest cannabis companies in the world—capable, Nick Kovacevich writes for *Forbes*, "of producing 570,000 kilograms of high-quality cannabis per year at a cost of below $1 per kilogram."

While it was the *largest*, Aurora's MedReleaf acquisition wasn't the first: Over the course of two years it acquired more than nine companies. In fact, in the months leading up to the MedReleaf purchase, Aurora had acquired CanniMed Therapeutics for $1.23 billion ($1 billion U.S.); which until *that* point had been the largest deal to date. Last year the company estimated that, once all of its acquired growing facilities reach full capacity, it will be producing at least 70 percent of Canada's cannabis. In the meantime, the top *eight* growers in Canada—which rapidly bought up independent growers and distributors in the face of imminent legalization—are set to collectively own that 70 percent. Combined, they produce around 1.8 million kilograms of cannabis per year—1.3 million of which are produced by the top *three* growers: Aurora Cannabis, Canopy Growth Corp., and Aphria.

Of course, cannabis has traditionally been produced by small farmers, so this is no small transition. And while it *could be*—and *has been*—argued that consolidating production in the hands of a few growers is precisely what has the potential to make the industry successful ("economies of scale" being the buzzword), that consolidation doesn't benefit small businesses. What's more, it only benefits *consumers* if the proportionate savings in costs are long-term—in other words, if big businesses don't suddenly hike up prices once they've forced out the competition. Even the U.S. Federal Trade Commission warns of this possibility (though let's call it the likelihood it is) on its website: "Many mergers benefit competition and consumers by allowing firms to operate more efficiently. But some mergers change market dynamics in ways that can then lead to higher prices, fewer or low-quality goods or services, or less innovation."

The word they mean to use there is "monopolies."

Of course, that's typically what happens, and there's really no reason to expect the cannabis industry to be any different. This is the oldest trick in the business book for gaining a stronghold: When big businesses see an opportunity in a new industry, they flood the new market with mass-produced product, *regardless* of demand. This oversupply drives down prices according to the basic logic of supply and demand. Of course, *because* they're mass-producing they can slash prices on each individual unit (or in this case, each gram) ... and because they sell such large volumes of product, they make up for that loss over the long term. What's more, because they reach so many consumers early on, they win customer engagement and brand loyalty early on in the game. (If you want a perfect example of how this works, think WalMart.)

While this might sound great for consumers, the euphoria is short-term. In the meantime, *all* businesses find themselves hurting financially: the small ones because they're not seeing sales; the big ones because profit margins are so small. The difference is that big businesses—with their big pockets and access to cash and capital—can hold out without seeing financial returns for much longer. Of course, in *any* industry where this occurs, small businesses typically don't have access to crucial lines of credit. This is *doubly* an issue in the cannabis industry, given the complexities—and restrictions—around banking I've discussed. Mom-and-pop shops have to keep making money in order to survive; they can't stay in the red. Big businesses, on the other hand, can continue to operate without profits for a long time.

Once the smaller businesses who simply can't sustain at those profit margins have exited the industry, the big businesses who are still standing can pare back on supply and raise their prices as high as they'd like to regain that margin and recoup their losses. (Of course, the prices *stay* up even after those losses have been recouped.) Consumers then have no choice but to buy at these inflated prices, since there's no one else in the market to turn to.

If you think the cannabis industry isn't already seeing this strategy, think again. Earlier, I discussed the radical drops in cannabis prices in both Washington and Colorado; this big business strategy is one of the reasons it's happening. And while it might *feel*, right now, like a consumer's market—one in which prices may continue to fall for the next few years—once the remaining businesses drive their prices up, taking advantage of their large market share and economies of scale, it'll be a good market for investors … but not for consumers.

In Washington State, both wholesale and retail cannabis prices plunged from 2014—when legal sales first commenced—and onward. Early on, wholesalers were getting up to $8 per gram; but by September 2017, that same gram was going for $2.53. The average *retail* price per gram in Washington's first month of sales was $32.48 (considerably higher than medical market prices). And while that price went up briefly the following month ($35.67), according to Top Shelf Data, prices saw a steady decline from that point on. Lester Black writes, "Within six months, the average retail price had dropped to $21.07 a gram; a year later, after a change in state taxes, pot was averaging just $12.32 a gram; and by September of this year [2017], the average retail price for a gram was $7.45, or 77 percent cheaper than when the legal market first began."

Growing has gotten cheaper *in part* because, in these recently-state-legal industries, cannabis farmers no longer spend time and energy evading law enforcement. But the *bigger* reason for the decline in prices is, of course, that big farmers have moved in with their industrial engineers and industrial techniques, built state-of-the-art, super-efficient facilities, and are producing at mass scale with low production costs. (Think Aurora Cannabis ... except in the U.S.)

Some of this could be blamed on state regulators' thinking as they initially planned out the legal market. As Black notes, "they created three tiers of pot producers based on the square footage of each farm. License different sizes of farms, the thinking went, and the market will support a range of small, medium and large producers." But "fast-forward three years, and it appears this thinking was flawed." At the time Black was writing (December 2017), the 10 largest pot farms in Washington State were harvesting 16.79 percent of the state's dry-weight cannabis—more than that produced by the smallest *500* farms combined (13.12 percent).

Part of the problem, it seems, is that while state regulators capped the *size* of grow farms (first at 30,000 square feet, then at 90,000), they *didn't* cap the number of cultivation licenses a given business could apply for and receive—so businesses with the money to do so can acquire 90,000 square-foot grow farms to their hearts' content. Or take Colorado, which issued a moratorium on issuing new marijuana licenses in May of 2016. The consequence of the moratorium was that big businesses hastily purchased most of the available licenses, and were then "protected" by the state from smaller businesses who *also* wanted to get in the game. The big cultivators who got those licenses were given no restrictions on the number of plants they could grow.

The wholesale price for a pound of cannabis in Colorado dropped from nearly $3,500 at the start of legalization, to $2,000 in January 2015, to $1,300 in December 2017, to $1,012 in April 2018, as reported by the Colorado Department of Revenue.

The Economist attributed the drop in Colorado's wholesale prices to an increase in supply, which makes perfect sense. Susan Gunelius writes, "this oversupply, led by an oligopoly of big businesses, increased supply and pushed prices down."

In California, small growers had been promised a five-year moratorium on licenses for large growers who wanted to enter the market (a provision was supposed to prohibit farms larger than an acre—43,560 square feet—from getting licensed until 2023), giving smaller businesses time to adapt to the new industry. The state also restricted "medium" cultivation licenses (for up to 22,000 square footage of planting) to one per business. However, those protective measures were effectively revoked through a loophole that looked a lot like Washington's: Regulators didn't place restrictions on the *number* of "small" cultivation licenses (for up to 10,000 square footage) a business could buy up ... which served as a green light for mega farms.

Monica Senter, executive board member of the Nevada County Cannabis Alliance, told *Rolling Stone*: "It's a continued form of prohibition. The NorCal cannabis brand is born on the backs of these farmers [and] now large corporate farmers are coming in and capitalizing on it. And Prop 64 allows that to happen."

By February of this year [2018], according to the *Sacramento Business Journal*, just 10 California companies held 30 percent of the state's growing licenses. By July, 1,501 businesses owned 3,245 active cultivation licenses—but that ownership is hardly split evenly. One company in particular stands out. According to *Cannabiz Media*,

> Central Coast Farmer's Market Management, LLC holds over 175 cultivation licenses. That means one company holds 5 percent of all marijuana cultivation licenses in California. Based on the state's reported license fees, Central Coast Farmer's Market Management, LLC would have to pay

well over $1.3 million in application and license fees for its cultivation licenses. That's an expense small and mid-size businesses can't afford, and it's a key way big businesses force small businesses out of the marijuana market.

The California Growers Association is currently suing the state because of the loophole. And while small businesses in California and Washington are dealing with the repercussions of regulators who lacked the foresight to limit the number of cultivation licenses a business could buy up, small businesses in *other* states are suffering from the opposite problem: artificially limited competition due to restricted licenses. According to Kris Krane at *Forbes*, "Pennsylvania, with nearly 13 million people, only granted 13 licenses; Florida, with a population over 20 million, granted 7; while Ohio, with more than 11 million people, granted 12; and New York, with a population of nearly 20 million people, granted only 5 before recently expanding to 10. For context," Krane adds, "Colorado has roughly 1,400 licensed cultivators for a population of just 5.5 million people."

In states with such a limited number of permits issued, competition is naturally fierce. The companies who are lucky enough to obtain one see enormous values attributed to the licenses before the business even begins operations. Krane notes that a cultivation and dispensary license in Florida sold for $40 million before the company had seen a single dollar in revenue. In New York, a license sold for $26 million—*also* before the business saw any revenue.

We know what kinds of businesses can swallow these costs. And for those businesses who *score* such licenses in states with limited distribution, it's nothing but ascension from there on out: The return on investment (ROI) is virtually immediate.

So if you're hearing stories about businesses building larger and larger farms—50,000 pounds of cannabis flower cultivated in greenhouses as big as 250,000 square feet—it's because their respective states have either artificially limited competition (meaning small cultivators are excluded from the beginning), or failed to restrict the number of permits a business can buy up (meaning small cultivators won't be able to compete for long). Small businesses can't compete with big businesses at the level of scale *or* at the level of technology: state-of-the-art warehouses, automated processes, and cleanroom environments that look more like pharmaceutical manufacturing facilities than commercial agricultural grows.

It's quite possible that these mega cultivators are aiming for quick growth so *they* can keep the larger competition at bay when it comes around. Remember those top three Canadian growers I mentioned (Aurora Cannabis, Canopy Growth Corp., and Aphria), who are presently jockeying to create the biggest economy of scale? When cannabis becomes federally legal in the United States, interstate commerce opens up, and cannabusinesses can work with banks without risking legal repercussions, it's going to make sense for those mega-companies to make acquisitions *here*.

Take it from Harrison Phillips, Vice President at the New York-based Viridian Capital Advisors, which tracks M&A activity in the cannabis industry. "The U.S. is the end game for many operators because of the size of the market potential," Harrison told *Marijuana Business Magazine*. "The U.S. is still relatively untapped, and we're far from the scale and magnitude that this industry could be operating at."

And *all that's* just on the cultivation side of things. According to Viridian Capital Advisors, more than 145 mergers and acquisitions—to the tune of $4 billion—were announced in the first half of 2018. That's nearly double the activity during the same timeframe in the previous year (when 79 mergers and acquisitions were announced, totaling $1.3 billion). Lisa Bernard-Kuhn writes: "Top acquisition targets include cultivation and retail operators, as well as infused product and extract firms—and that's on top of the consolidation of cannabis investment firms." In other words, just about every sector of the industry. We just happen to be seeing it most *explicitly*, right now, in cultivation.

Last June, MedMen, which operates medical cannabis facilities in New York, California, and Nevada, added Florida to its list when it acquired Treadwell Simpson Partnership for $53 million—a deal that included permissions to open 25 dispensaries in the state. Treadwell was one of only 13 licensed medical marijuana operators in the state, which means MedMen is now a powerhouse in that arena. In May—on the ancillary side—Kush Bottles (California) signed off on an acquisition of Los Angeles-based CMP Wellness, which distributes vaporizers, cartridges, and other cannabis accessories. The deal cost Kush $1.5 million—though a month prior to that, Kush closed a deal to buy Colorado-based Summit Innovations for more than $3.2 million. Summit produces the hydrocarbon gas used in cannabis extraction.

In May of last year, four top cannabis companies announced a merger and joined forces to create TILT Holdings, "the first fully-integrated, multi-national cannabis company" that "maintain[s] competencies across the entire spectrum of the industry," according to *PR Newswire*. TILT builds cultivation facilities, offers software and financial support to cultivators and retailers, and more. And back on the retail side, Zachary Venegas notes that "just five years into Colorado's adult-use program more than 33 percent of dispensaries operate as part of a chain. Independent retailers are being forced to sell or go out of business largely due to the downward pricing pressures inherent in the commodity business that is the core of legal cannabis." The top five concentrates brands in the state have already captured 49 percent of the market share.

These are just a few *non*-cultivation examples of a much larger trend of consolidation, cross-industry, and cross-border investments. And of course we can't forget the alcohol and tobacco industries, which are more than primed to move in on U.S. cannabis companies. This past August [2018], Constellation Brands—which owns, markets, and distributes over 100 beer, wine, and spirits brands, including Modelo and Corona—announced a $3.8 billion ($5 billion Canadian) investment in one of Canada's "big three": Canopy Growth. (Canopy Growth had previously made notable acquisitions of Mettrum—in 2017 for $430 million—and Hiku Brands—in 2018 for $269.2 million.) To date, Constellation's move marks the largest corporate investment in a cannabis cultivator.

But perhaps the more noteworthy thing about Constellation's investment were the Wall Street giants *behind* it: Goldman Sachs advised Constellation; Bank of America Merrill Lynch provided the financing. It's a reminder that Wall Street is knocking—if not banging—on the door already.

Of course, given the ways the cannabis industry has spelled losses for Big Alcohol and Big Tobacco, Constellation isn't—and won't be—the only such company moving into an industry that would otherwise be its death knell. (These movements are probably as much for vertical growth as they are to preempt losses.) In 2017, the global tobacco company Imperial Brands appointed the chairman of PharmaCielo—a Canadian supplier of medicinal-grade cannabis oil extracts—to its board of directors. In 2018, tobacco leaf distributor Alliance One International acquired—according to its website—"a 75 percent equity position in Canada's Island Garden Inc ... and an 80 percent stake in Goldleaf Pharm Inc." Both companies produce and distribute medical cannabis.

Molson Coors is partnering with the Canadian cannabis producer Hydropothecary, according to a press release from the alcohol giant, to "pursue opportunities to develop non-alcoholic, cannabis-infused beverages for the Canadian market following legalization." Constellation Brands and Heineken have *also* invested substantial financial resources into creating cannabis-infused beverages—a sector that, according to Mike Adams at *Forbes*, "is predicted to bring $15 billion annually to the Canadian cannabis market alone." Naturally, Big Alcohol is looking to capitalize on this.

In 2016, Bob Morgan, a cannabis industry consultant and attorney, told *Marijuana Venture*: "There have already been substantial acquisitions on the ancillary side, such as vaporizers, cannabis consulting and management companies, and edible brands. But the mergers and acquisitions on the grow and retail side have just begun." Although we're *in* "phase 2" of the consolidation curve (more on this in a moment), that remains true. Much has yet to happen in the realm of mergers and acquisitions—among licensed cultivators, retail operators, and ancillary companies alike.

The Consolidation Curve

As I've mentioned, the consolidations in cannabis aren't unique to this industry. It's a pattern typical of nearly all new industries, which begin fragmented (whether through initial formation or deregulation) and consolidate as they mature. Graeme K. Deans, Fritz Kroeger, and Stefan Zeisel described the "consolidation curve" in a 2002 issue of the *Harvard Business Review*. I'll summarize here; but the article is a good resource for readers new to business. Deans, Kroeger, and Zeisel studied and analyzed 1,345 large global mergers over the course of 13 years, and "concluded that, once an industry forms or is deregulated, it will move through four stages of consolidation." Every business within that industry will either move through those four stages *with* it, or disappear from the industry entirely.

Sixteen years ago, the authors predicted that industries would take, on average, 25 years to move through all four stages—though they believed that future industries would progress even more quickly through them. *Today*, analysts predict that an industry will move through those stages in 20 years; but I believe that the cannabis industry will accelerate through these stages in only 8-10 years. What's more, I expect a 10 percent survival rate: By 2028, I predict, 90 percent of entrants into the industry will have bowed out. (I often think of the cannabis industry as a bit like the dotcom bubble, which shared a similar "hype" ... and which reached its endgame in 9 years.)

In other words, the window is closing. So regardless of what your long-term plan *is* (from becoming a target for acquisition, to becoming the *acquirer*, to holding your own through the transition as a boutique business that caters to a very specific niche), you'll need to know where in the cycle the industry is—and where your *business* stands in that stage—if you want to plan wisely.

Stage 1 is the "opening" (or "birth," or "conception") stage. This stage commences either with a single startup trailblazing into the unknown territory of a new industry of its own making, or with a recently deregulated or privatized industry. Companies who have first-mover advantage in this stage have to be strategic in defending that advantage; over the course of this stage, the combined market share of the industry's three largest companies drops precipitously (to between 10 percent and 30 percent) as competitors flood the new space. Any industry is bound to be highly fragmented in this stage; typically, revenues are low and *all* participants are unprofitable.

If this characterization sounds at all familiar, it's because cannabis has rapidly moved through stage 1. In 2016, according to *PR Newswire*, consumers walking into a typical dispensary were confronted with 94 different varieties of branded cannabis products. By 2017, that number had grown to 118; and by January of 2018, the average dispensary carried more than 150 different branded products. While that product diversity may be terrific (if overwhelming) for consumers from a power-of-choice perspective, the increasingly overcrowded nature of the market can feel suffocating for every business trying to stay afloat in the ocean of largely-indistinguishable brands. (Don't worry; I'll get to the part where you distinguish yourself shortly.) But as the cannabis industry rapidly matures, barreling through stage 1 into stage 2, we'll start to see those numbers take a downward turn.

Deans, Kroeger, and Zeisel recommend that:

> Companies in stage 1 industries … aggressively defend their first-mover advantage by building scale, creating a global footprint, and establishing barriers to entry by protecting proprietary technology or ideas. Stage 1 companies should focus more on revenue than profit, working to amass market share. And they should begin perfecting their acquisition skills, as these will be key to success in the next two stages of consolidation.

I'd add the importance of consumer education: Consumers at this stage need to be taught about the industry, its product, and its role in their lives, *as well as* the positioning of individual businesses within the industry and what each provides in relation to the others. Product differentiation is crucial at this early stage. And businesses who best educate their consumer base, demonstrating themselves as authorities at this stage, are more likely to win brand loyalty over the long run.

Stage 2 of the consolidation curve is the "scale" (or "growth") stage. A handful of major players begin to distinguish themselves in this stage, acquiring their competitors and assembling large domains for themselves. At this stage, consumers have begun to fully grasp the value of the offering, and demand grows correspondent to this understanding. Profits aren't yet a (or *the*) priority, since the companies who hope to survive have to devote themselves to research and development (R&D) and marketing—meaning improved processes and products throughout this stage. This includes a continued focus on product differentiation.

Once the offering has been deemed viable, companies in adjacent industries (alcohol and tobacco, anyone?) start jockeying to enter the market. The top 3 of the industry's major players will come to collectively own up to 45 percent of their market share by the time stage 2 is over. And here's what we're beginning to see in cannabis. Indeed, even as the number of *products* on retailers' shelves grows, research at the Brightfield Group suggests that dips in *brand* numbers mean the "scaling" has already begun. Already "by 2017," William Honaker writes, "the increase in competition [had] forced out many smaller brands, as evidenced by a slight decline in the number of brands available, despite continual increases in the number of dispensaries and products available."

Deans, Kroeger, and Zeisel write:

> Because of the large number of acquisitions occurring in this stage, companies must hone their merger-integration skills. These include learning how to carefully protect their core culture as they absorb new companies and focusing on retaining the best employees of acquired companies. Building a scalable IT platform is also crucial to the rapid integration of acquired firms. Companies jockeying to reach stage 3 must be among the first players in the industry to capture their

major competitors in the most important markets and should
expand their global reach.

I'd add that—for companies hoping to *exit* at this stage—the
best thing they can do is research how the emerging major players
evaluate candidates for acquisition. (More on that below.)

Of course, unlike most deregulated markets, full-scale
consolidation in the cannabis industry is hindered by patchwork
regulations across states and countries (not to mention state-imposed
limitations on vertical integration or scale), making geographic
expansion tricky. Given this, M&A and consolidation in this
industry will necessarily be patchy until federal decriminalization.

Stage 3 is the "focus" stage. (*Investopedia* calls it the "maturity"
phase.) Now that the voracious consolidations of stage 2 are
complete, the companies who are still standing can start focusing
on core business expansion, core capabilities, expense reduction,
price competition, cash flow, and achieving economies of scale to
win market share and outgrow their remaining competition.

This is the stage of mega-deals and *large-scale* M&A; those who
emerge from this stage will be the multinational powerhouses.
Deans, Kroeger, and Zeisel note that "the top three industry
players will now control between 35 percent and 70 percent of
the market. By this time, there are still generally five to 12 major
players." (The example they use is GM's strategic acquisition of
stakes in Subaru, Isuzu, Saab, Fiat, and Daewoo.) Barriers to entry
are heightened at this stage because those major players know how
to recognize startup competitors quickly and either squelch them
or acquire them. From both an internal perspective and a *consumer*
perspective, the competitive landscape comes more clearly into
focus.

Stage 4 is the "balance and alliance" stage. "Here the titans of
industry reign," say Deans, Kroger, and Zeisel,

... from tobacco to soft drinks to defense. The industry concentration rate plateaus and can even dip a bit as, at this stage, the top three companies claim as much as 70 percent to 90 percent of the market. Large companies may form alliances with their peers because growth is now more challenging. Companies don't move through stage 4; they stay in it. Thus, firms in these industries must defend their leading positions. They must find new ways to grow their core business in a mature industry and create a new wave of growth by spinning off new businesses into industries in early stages of consolidation. They must be alert to the potential for industry regulation and the danger of being lulled into complacency by their own dominance.

If you focus on its stage in the timeline, it may seem that the cannabis industry has quite a ways to go before it reaches the "endgame" ... but as I said, *it will move through these stages in the next ten years.* Over the next 2–4 years, there will be a flurry of acquisitions, during which 50 percent of entrants will be subsumed. In 4–8 years, we'll be in that "focus stage" with its large-scale acquisitions; I predict 70 percent consolidation by the end of it. We'll enter that final stage ("balance and alliance") in 8–10 years, at the end of which we'll see 90 percent consolidation.

Success at the endgame—or even in the middle—of the consolidation curve can look like a few things: 1) Becoming one of the remaining "titans"; 2) Becoming an impressive target for acquisition in stage 2 or 3 and exiting the market on a financially-rewarding buyout; 3) Becoming an impressive target for a *merger* in stage 2 or 3 and getting a deep pocket investment from one of those big businesses; or 4) Finding your niche and maintaining status quo throughout these stages as a boutique or artisan brand. Remember, at stage four, according to Deans, Kroger, and Zeisel, "the top three companies claim as much as 70 percent to 90 percent of the market." My guess is that, in this industry, it will be closer to 90 percent. That leaves a 10 percent market share for other businesses to gain ground in.

Below, I'll be speaking primarily to those businesses who are aiming for success in that fourth category—boutique or artisanal brands who'd like to weather the consolidation storm by catering to a very specific niche. There are a couple of reasons for this. In the first place, the big businesses who'll be the standing titans will have their own M&A teams—potentially with dozens of members—who will collectively see those deals through, from initial screening, to legal structuring, to integration. I spent years guiding corporations on precisely this process; but it isn't the realm of this book. In the second place, industry insiders largely agree that at the end of this frenetic period of mergers, acquisitions, and consolidations, there *will* be a strong handful of craft or artisanal producers who survive. And they'll be the ones who played their cards right.

Bruce Linton, founder, chairman, and CEO of Canopy Growth Corp, told Ernst & Young: "over the long term, I see an industry with two or three major, relevant players and a bunch of craft producers." Eugenio Garcia, CEO and publisher of *Cannabis Now* magazine, told *Forbes*: "you're going to see more of this smaller business model. Much like in the agricultural, farm-to-table movement around the U.S people will start producing cannabis legally for their immediate geographic locations. You go to any city in the U.S. and you're going to find a microbrewer that is only putting out enough quantity to support a couple thousand people in their neighborhood. People love that. And that's going to be very similar, I believe, with cannabis."

Garcia calls them "micro-players": the small businesses who have no interest in becoming the next Canopy or MedMen; who are in the game for the love of the plant, its healing properties, and the philanthropic and compassionate components that have remained so deeply rooted in its DNA. Claire Kelloway, too, expects that many "consumers will invariably [continue to] demand some quality cannabis from independent growers"; as the consumer market grows to include health-conscious, ethically aware, and affluent consumers, this will more and more be the case. So while consolidation will surely shift a vast majority of the industry to a few large corporations, if small and medium businesses can play the game *well*, the opportunities are there for *all* sizes of business to flourish.

"That's what I see at [cannabis] trade shows," Garcia told *Forbes*. "I see companies that are getting involved—worth billions—that will help with the science and growth of the cannabis plant. I also see the micro players becoming more powerful in their geographic location. And they're very happy with that."

It's an optimistic vision, and I'd like to hold it with Garcia. So as the flurry of activity accelerates and the industry becomes more cutthroat—and *you're* an early pioneer or recent entrant who's in it for the love and wants to stay in the game—how do you grow or maintain your market share?

Thing one is not to ignore the reality: that large-scale production and corporate takeover are inevitable. This would be the case in *any* industry that promises the kind of ROI cannabis promises; but a look at regulations that preempt equal competition in cannabis-legal states suggest this industry is particularly big business-friendly. With each new successful reform vote, more deep-pocketed entities will enter the space, and entry will virtually explode when prohibition comes to an end. *No* small business is going to survive the endgame by ignoring this fact.

We're at a stage in the industry's evolution where there's still hope for the small dogs. Businesses who are willing to professionalize, specialize, develop a strong brand position, predict a medical-grade regulatory framework, and form strategic partnerships are infinitely more likely to survive than their counterparts who hold firmly to the 1960's counterculture and its anti-institutional mindset. You're formally in the game with the big dogs now, which means evaluating each operational and strategic move as it relates to your vision of where you want to be in the endgame. Let's dig into the details of what this will need to look like.

Maintaining a Competitive Advantage in the Cannabis Game: Advice for Entrepreneurs and SMBs

"Imagine a big fence with wolves on the other side," Mike Straumietis ("BigMike"), founder and CEO of Advanced Nutrients—the largest hydroponics nutrient company for cannabis in the world—has said. "Right now you've got a few rogue wolves jumping the fence ... [but] the really big ones that are on the other side, the Big Pharma, Big Ag, they're waiting for the federal government to make [cannabis] legal. When that happens and the gate opens up and those 800-pound wolves come, you'd better be prepared."

It seems like an apt metaphor to me. Granted, *some* consolidation in a market that's currently this fragmented isn't necessarily bad news: It's a natural and necessary stage in any emerging industry. But the entrance of big business into the cannabis space could mean a few disagreeable things. It could (and likely *will*) mean lower-quality products. It could mean eventual price-gouging for consumers—even if they appear to be "scoring deals" over the next few years. In the meantime, the low prices that come with big business infiltration could hurt local governments who've banked on total sales to generate revenue. It could mean shifting revenues away from the very mom-and-pop businesses who use it to support local communities, and putting it in the hands of out-of-state corporations. Finally, it could mean the development of monopolies and oligopolies. Indeed, that latter threat is very real.

If you've been in the game since cannabis was a cottage industry, you have a few things that those wolves on the other side of the legalization fence *don't* have: the wisdom that can only be derived from years in the industry; the requisite knowledge about rules, regulations, relationships, and transactions that are *unique* to the industry; a deep understanding of the values the cannabis community has always stood for and rallied around; an experiential history with helping destigmatize the plant; a *company* history of legal risk, defiance, and community activism; and a quality product born of trial and error. Oh, and a strong customer base ... *because of* all of the above.

But all these things are up against brands backed by big investors with money to spend on research and development, new technologies, branding strategies, advertising, and more. According to Bethany Gomez at The Brightfield Group, already "in many states, the top ten brands make up at least 60 percent for edibles and 30 percent for concentrates." That said, I've spoken to quite a few cannabusiness owners who *don't* feel intimidated by the imminent consolidations. But those unintimidated owners are the ones being radically proactive and forward-thinking about how their day-to-day operations will impact their future in this space. In moment, I'll tell you what they're doing.

Many of these strategies are things that *any* small business in *any* industry should do to keep their heads above water ... and, ultimately, thrive. From giving campaigns to a business plan that allows for agility to consumer education to rewards programs to strategic partnerships, there are plenty of ways to position yourself, build community, and win brand loyalty. (All of these things will bring consumers to you from the *black market* as well.)

I'd be remiss if I didn't mention, though, that alongside everything I discuss below, *all* cannabusinesses should be fighting for rules and regulations that are as favorable to small companies as they are to the big dogs. Regardless of whether you'll ultimately be an acquirer, a target, or a business that hopes to maintain status quo as the industry matures and settles, getting political is a part of the role you really ought to play in this narrative.

As I mentioned earlier, my prediction is that by 2028, only 10 percent of entrants into the industry will survive. It will be consumers who ultimately separate the wheat from the chaff; so while it's important to fight at the political level, you have agency over relationships with your customer base that you simply *won't* have when it comes to legislation. (Keep fighting, though!) Here's how to elevate and protect your brand as M&A activity escalates:

Predict a Regulatory Framework

I'm beginning with this one because, as far as I'm concerned, it's the most indispensable activity of the lot. In my years as a C-Suite Executive with enterprise businesses, we called these "*de facto* standards": business usages or conventions that become so *widely* used that they attain dominant positions by virtue of general acceptance. I worked for Hewlett-Packard; so the first example that always comes to mind is HP's Printer Command Language (PCL), which was developed in the '80s for inkjet printers, but became the *de facto* industry standard for *all* printer companies, whether they were manufacturing thermal, matrix, or laser printers. The point is that something becomes a *de facto* standard through *emulation* ... and I'll say more about what I mean by that below.

In the last chapter, I used California as a case study to consider the kinds of chaos cannabusinesses experienced when the state legalized adult use and scrambled to put new regulations in place (in many cases, putting the onus on individual agencies with no experience in cannabis whatsoever to formulate the governing guidelines). Thousands of small businesses in California had to either shut their doors or turn to the black market because they couldn't afford licenses, or their products weren't passing the new mandatory testing requirements, or they couldn't afford to move to parcels of land that were zoned by the state for growing.

As a cannabis business in *today's* iteration of the industry, it's one thing to be wholly and flawlessly adhering to the new regulatory structures put in place by your individual state. Really; I applaud you; it is no small thing to have adhered in the midst of a complex and chaotic burgeoning framework. But *any* cannabusiness who hopes to survive will have to predict—and preempt—the regulatory framework that will inevitably be put in place in the months after cannabis becomes federally legal.

Because when *that* happens, you'll suddenly have a brand new set of regulations to be working under. And those businesses who've anticipated a framework in advance—and moreover, who've begun to "comply" with it, though it doesn't yet exist—will *already* be ahead as every other business scrambles to conform ... just as they did under new state regulations. Arnaud Dumas de Rauly predicts that federal legalization "will lead to a more mainstream approach to compliance and the involvement of organizations like the FDA ... Then will come a regulatory framework and we'll be confronted with inconsistencies regarding state-level and federal regulations. What this means is that each cannabis company must brace for increased scrutiny, both on the financial and operational side of things."

As far as I'm concerned, what this imminent "increased scrutiny" means is that *every business has to be thinking medical-grade* ... *even* if they're doing business strictly in the recreational sector.

While none of us can say what federal regulations will ultimately look like, better to prepare for the most stringent scenario. Study the testing requirements and procedures across states and prepare yourself to have to comply with the most rigorous of them. Read up on the standard operating procedures for manufacturing— again, even the procedures that don't apply to your state—and start adapting your business to the ones that are most exacting.

Develop your *own* internal list of processes and procedures, based on research and a "medical grade" mindset that would meet FDA-quality standards, to pre-empt whatever FDA mandates *are* handed down as a consequence of nationwide legalization. These *will become* the *de facto* standards, after all ... and it's better they do so because other businesses started emulating *your* procedures than because the iron fist of the FDA finally came down on *all* of you at once.

Tim Cullen, CEO of Colorado Harvest Company, is an outstanding example of this kind of preemption. When Thomas Mitchell at *Westword* asked him, "How do you ensure a profitable, quality plant without mold, pests or pesticide use taking over?" Cullen answered:

> I was a high school biology teacher for ten years before I started in this business as a grower. Science has always been a primary interest of mine. By studying, experimenting and applying the best production methods and clean growing practices, I knew we would never be tempted to use, let alone need, pesticides. I consulted with the Colorado Department of Agriculture and offered my expertise so that other growers could benefit from these methods. We measured energy and water use, and continuously strive to conserve.

I love, first of all, Cullen's willingness to offer his expertise to competitors. But I want to emphasize his decision to communicate with the ultimate authority on the matter—the state's Department of Agriculture—to ensure the best practices he was implementing were legitimate (even though they weren't necessary!).

This means using the cleanest possible CO_2 from a safe source if you're a grower. It means—like Cullens—applying clean growing practices so you won't *have* to use fungicides or pesticides. (Remember, you're thinking "medical grade"; and residual toxins in the product can be catastrophic for patients with weakened immune systems.) It means *not* using low-grade alcohols in your distillation processes. In short, it means abandoning anything non-organic or carcinogenic, and using the cleanest, highest-grade ingredients possible in whatever process you're involved in. Aim for absolute product purity.

Constantly ask yourself if your current operating procedures entail the best possible practices. Constantly ask yourself if you can fully stand behind what you're making as a product. Remember, we're talking a smokeable, edible product. Would you give it to *your* kids? *Your* nieces or nephews? *Your* grandparents? We're really back to the question of integrity here. If you're unclear about what this means for *your* place in the seed-to-sale supply chain, do your research! Talk to as many people as possible. Reach out to scientists (professors at your local college or university may be more than happy to advise you), authorities such as state or local departments, and other cannabusinesses you know that are doing what they can to anticipate significant regulatory changes and stay ahead of the curve.

Cannabusiness who *don't* do their research and develop a list of solid internal procedures and best practices will ultimately be forced out by necessity. After all, its health-and-wellness and medicinal properties are what will give the drug staying power. Thinking medical grade will legitimize *both* the recreational and medical segments, and will lead to improved health and safety for *all* consumers as a result.

Outsource Your Non-Core Competencies

Two primary types of "struggling entrepreneur" are entering the cannabis space these days: Those who are coming from the black or grey market and are struggling due to a lack of business acumen; and those who are coming from the business world who have no experience with the cannabis community, and are struggling to connect with their target market.

The brands that survive will be able to do *both*, blending business acumen with a keen familiarity with cannabis culture. The last thing you want is to be overtaken by a company that has no familiarity with the plant you love and have spent your life promoting, but that happens to have more business experience than you do. So win the contest for talent on both ends. And know that *you're not the one who has to possess all the talent*—but you *do* have to be wise enough to know where your core competencies are and where they *aren't* ... and where to go looking to fill those gaps.

Knowing all you can about cannabis is a given; so I won't linger on that here. From the *business* side of things, this ultimately means dispensing with your anti-establishment roots and wholly embracing the educational process of becoming-a-businessperson. Here's the advice BigMike gave to Zoe Wilder at *Merry Jane*. His advice is keen, and the warning is real:

> As we enter into a legal environment, there are very smart people getting involved. People with grow ops have Harvard MBAs. They know business. They know finance. They know the intricacies of what a strong management team should look like, how they should act, and what they should be doing. If you don't understand that, these multinationals will eat you alive. If you have a company, you may want to consider selling part of your business to someone who knows what they are doing, someone who can assist you.

"Selling part of your business" is, of course, an option; but so is hiring the most talented, experienced employees—or shared services—you can find. This means a strong management team and a strong back office. (I can't stress this part enough: *You want an experienced management team behind the wheel.* This will likely mean outsourcing another company to manage your back office.) It means hiring people who have the knowledge and ability to help you raise capital. It means having the right attorneys, accountants, and operational experts at the wheel. It means hiring employees for your retail shop with deep insights and intuition about the sales process, prospect pain points, and best approaches to educating customers.

In an article in *Green Entrepreneur,* Maryam Mirnateghi describes her experience of visiting cannabis retailers in Seattle and discovering that the majority of employees apparently weren't interested in learning as much about her needs as possible so they could personalize her purchase:

> Recently I visited several Seattle pot shops and found one major commonality amongst all of them—the first products the budtender suggested were the cheapest items they had in whichever product category I had asked for. I did not ask for the cheapest options or even for a good deal. Yet, three out of the four budtenders who helped me never asked me more than one question about my wants and needs ... Addressing [customers'] unique needs requires budtenders who are well-educated on the myriad nuances involved with cannabis and CBD products. Big mistakes here not only hurt your brand, they could also hurt your customer and lead to a lawsuit.

This really comes down to knowing your own skill set: Be honest and humble here! Different areas of the cannabis business demand different skills; and it's virtually impossible to be good at everything. No one's expecting an expert botanist or master grower to be brilliant with finances, or a brilliant salesperson to know about scaling infrastructure, or a master distiller to know how to best market their company. Be clear about where *you* excel, and then take stock of your team (assuming you already have one in place).

Be absolutely clear about where each of your employees excels, and what knowledge or skill sets you still need to fill with experienced bodies. And then? Outsource and offload your non-core competencies. (This is sometimes referred to as "horizontal integration," though I'll say more about that below.) *Don't* push your current employees into key decision-making roles just because they already conveniently happen to be there. How to handle complex legal and financial questions is *not* something one learns "on the job." Your employees will naturally thrive best where they're qualified, and not stretched for answers or solutions to the things they simply don't know.

Your business plans will ultimately only be as good as the people you can bring on to help execute them. Industry reports have suggested that it's easier to find and recruit talent in a marketplace in the midst of M&A activity and consolidation than in a market that's thriving. In other words, the moment is opportune. For all these reasons, winning the talent contest should be among your highest priorities.

Be in It for the Right Reason

This is the underlying theme. Textile, superfood, nutritional supplement, life-saving medicine, biofuel. However you think of cannabis, you *must* have a personal passion for what the plant is capable of if you hope to survive in the industry. Many of the cannabusiness owners I've worked with over the years got into the game precisely *because* they personally watched family members, friends, and colleagues recover, heal, and thrive by using it. Indeed, many of them virtually *worship* the plant; and it's this reverence that drives their business ambition. They understand it not only as a vehicle for healing, but also as a vehicle for broader global transformation (all the socio-economic benefits Colorado is seeing, for example). And they see it as their life's calling—an imperative— to provide their communities and the world at large with the means to access the drug for the variety of reasons they'd need it.

So *thing one* is to enter the cannabis space from a place of reverence, integrity, and positive intention. Without that reverence, you simply won't find it in yourself to endure the labor, the industry climate, the uncertainties and shifting terrains that cannabis entrepreneurship entails. Industry veterans—who've been running on passion for years—will view you with skepticism, making networking and industry relationships difficult to navigate. As I'll discuss below, this is an industry in which community and collaboration will be imperative for those who hope to survive. Your competitors and collaborators will smell insincerity from a mile away. And because your competitors will be driven by a higher purpose, they'll out-hustle you at every turn.

So if you're going to get into—or *stay* in—this industry, do it out of love for the plant and a fierce set of convictions about what it's capable of. This is as true for entrepreneurs looking to get into ancillary or "non-touch" businesses (security, nutrients, grow lights, packaging, legal services, etc.) as it is for those looking to get into businesses that directly touch the plant. If the plant *itself* is the lifeblood of your business, you're off to a solid start.

Raise More Capital than You Think You'll Need

I haven't yet met a cannabis entrepreneur who *wasn't* surprised by the amount of funding they needed to keep their heads above water. Of course, many of them took the time to meticulously plan out the kind of funding they'd need; but they didn't consider the wild, unpredictable ride that is the industry. Regulatory changes, pricing shifts, investors backing out at the eleventh hour, fierce incoming competition, so much hinging on whatever administration is in power at the moment … if you've been in the industry long enough, you know that changes and reversals can happen at the drop of a dime. And *all* of them will affect your finances.

So keep an eye on the big picture—the reality of *this* industry— rather than the smaller picture that's the "bare-bones-*plus-a-little-padding*" strategy for financing a business. Take into consideration every possible cost variable related to hiring workers, obtaining operational space, distributing or wholesaling your product, complying with possible regulatory changes (this takes some conjecturing—so conjecture for the most expensive outcomes), and more. And even after *that*, know that *whatever* costs you're currently estimating for your business are almost certainly too low. Indeed, I'd make sure you have *double* what you estimate you'll need in the bank. Chances are, you'll need it.

Jonathan Barlow, a senior partner at the Detroit-based consulting firm Cannabis Practice Group, has given *Forbes* some numbers that seem accurate ("2 Cannabis Entrepreneurs Share their Secrets for Success"):

> The minimum investment range for a startup canna-business is from $750,000 for retrofitting an existing retail store into a provisioning center to $12.5 million for a newly constructed cultivation facility. This includes licensing, permits, facility compliance, staffing, technology, security systems, HR systems, legal, tax and general operational compliance. You need the mandatory capital to provide an opportunity for success and meet the compliance and regulatory standards of your operating state.

The key word in that excerpt is "minimum." I probably don't have to remind you about the number of companies that had to go out of business when testing became a requirement in California because they couldn't afford to build the new mandatory procedures into their operations. These are the storms of regulatory change you'll have to be financially prepared to weather.

Capitalization will *also* be important to those entrepreneurs hoping to position their companies for a merger or an acquisition. Potential acquirers will naturally be looking for targets that are well-capitalized. *No* company is going to acquire a target that is only going to serve as a financial drain.

Of course, some *types* of businesses in the industry (concentrates, for example, which eliminate trimming, manicuring, and curing process costs) will naturally entail lower production costs and higher profits than others; so if you're just now looking to get into the industry, I'd suggest you do the legwork of ascertaining costs across a variety of cannabusiness types: indoor versus outdoor cultivation, oils versus raw flower, and so on.

That said, I've spoken at great length about the fact that both banks and the majority of investors are wary of putting their money into cannabis businesses. If you're looking for funding, there *are* some private investors out there who are excited about the industry and its growth potential … *and* who have a deep passion for the plant (see my point above). Both *Ganjapreneur* and *New Cannabis Ventures* offer directories of marijuana investment groups (see the resources list at the end of this book) who can bring both experience and expertise to the table … along, of course, with their money.

Either way, you'll want financial guidance from industry professionals who have a long, clear view of the industry landscape. So make sure you have an experienced team that can support you in the process of raising capital (you'll likely be raising it in phases) and help you prepare for whatever financial issues you're likely to face.

Develop a Brand Ethos

I'll say more about the "brand" part below; for the moment, let's focus on the ethos. The *Oxford English Dictionary* offers two beautiful definitions of the word: "the characteristic spirit of a people, community, culture, or era as manifested in its attitudes and aspirations; the prevailing character of an institution or system"; and "the character of an individual as represented by his or her values and beliefs; the moral or practical code by which a person lives."

You want this for your cannabusiness. You're a consumer, reader; so I don't have to tell you that consumers don't always choose the businesses they buy from and the brands the associate themselves with *entirely* because of the products those businesses offer. They choose them because they share a set of values, an ethos, a worldview. So you'll want to make sure yours are fully developed and clearly communicated to your target market. Essentially, this means hitting the pause button on answering the "what" of your business, and beginning to answer the "why." Why have you chosen to offer your market *this* cannabis product or service? Why do you believe in it? What about it gets you out of bed and back to work every morning?

As the cannabis industry grows and then consolidates, so much of this will boil down to integrity. As Eugenia Garcia told *Forbes*:

> There will be people who have no problem walking into a liquor store type of dispensary and grabbing a pack of pre-rolled cannabis cigarettes, and that's what they want. But there's going to be equal, if not more consumers that will want to know where the cannabis came from. They will want to know that it's organic. They will want to know the grower. They will want to know where the genetics are from. And they want to consume it in a more ritualistic way than a party, liquor kind of expression.

As cannabis consumers mature (fewer and fewer are simply looking to get high; more and more are making cannabis an integral part of a health-and-wellness lifestyle), things like brand transparency, accountability, and responsibility to your target market are no longer negotiable. *Not* accepting feedback from employees, customers, and your community, for example, is not an option. But beyond these broad, fundamental components of integrity, you need to choose a *particular set* of values that make up your company ethos.

And here's why: When the mergers, acquisitions, and consolidations finally begin to slow, the smaller brands that will still be standing will be the artisanal brands—just as the small brewers still standing in the alcohol industry are the craft brewers that produce more exclusive, and more expensive, products. Of course, consumers are willing to by those products not only because of company integrity, but because of a particular ethos that the brand has taken up and lived by.

Atlanta-based Sweetwater Brewing Company is a great example of an ethos that goes beyond integrity. The company has chosen environmental sustainability as their keyword. And remember the definition of ethos—"the moral or practical code by which a person [or company] lives"? "Sustainability" isn't just key to Sweetwater's brewing processes; it's a value upheld in the company culture, more broadly speaking. "Sustainability ain't just a buzzword round these parts," their website reads. "Whether it's using electric hand dryers instead of paper towels in our bathrooms or utilizing natural skylights throughout the building, we're committed to keeping things green wherever and whenever we can." The brewing company is currently hosting a "Save Our Water" campaign, with plans to donate $100,000 to a number of organizations dedicated to clean water initiatives.

So it's time to think beyond organic ingredients and overall product quality. These are givens at this point: Cannabusinesses who can't uphold these now-fundamental features are quickly closing their doors. As a business, you'll have to convince *me* that we share an ethos. In a market of quality products, I'll consume Sweetwater if my priority is environmental sustainability. I'll consume *your* product if your ethos or your brand story resonates for me. I want to appreciate what I'm paying for *not* just because of the product I'm getting, but because of what it suggests about me, my values, and my worldview. In the end, great brands don't actually *sell* products; they sell an ethos.

So choose your "value keyword": whether it's community, customer storytelling, socio-economic equality, or one of hundreds of other ways to live out an ethos, choose *something*. And once you've chosen it, live it and breathe it—with *every* internal decision you make and *every* marketing message you put out there. Make it part of your story and the stories of your team members. (Think CLIF Bar, which survived the consolidation of the energy bar market with its dramatic story about "The Epiphany Ride": a 175-mile bike ride during which "an exhausted and hungry Gary Erickson realize[d] he [couldn't] choke down another unappetizing energy bar." The brand goes beyond organic ingredients, differentiating itself by making what *they* call "food we'd like to eat.") Your customers will be steadfastly loyal to you for your fidelity to this set of values.

Know Your Customer (and Educate Them)

… and by the way, "all marijuana consumers over the age of 21" is *not* a target market. You've *got* to narrow it down if you want your customer segment to feel seen, heard, and spoken to. Your customer persona—the semi-fictional person you'll have in mind for all your messaging—will have specific demographic characteristics (age, gender, education, ethnicity, income) and specific psychographic characteristics (attitudes, values, opinions, beliefs, and personality).

Think environmentally-conscious millennials coping with chronic pain. Or Gen-X men who are starting to think about skincare in ways they didn't need to a decade ago. Or young mothers trying to finally get some sleep ... *without* having to resort to Ambien. Or even senior citizens. (As Alex Halperin notes, "today, seniors are the fastest-growing group of marijuana users in the US.") You get the picture: The point is to go beyond the traditional core stoner demographic of young, white, middle-class men. While it may seem counter-intuitive, the more targeted your customer persona is, the better. Cannabusinesses—indeed, *any* businesses—who try to sell to *everyone* will only end up creating vague marketing messages that don't speak to *anyone.*

What are your customers' biggest pain points? What problems are they trying to solve? What *else* are they interested in? Where do they get their media? What do they value? What language do they use to describe these things? *How*, exactly, does your cannabis product offer a solution? What other products do they use? Where, how, and how often? And so on.

Ask every possible question you can about your primary customer segment. There are a world of resources out there to get these answers from: what your customers are talking about on social media, what they're saying on review sites, what they're asking on Q&A websites (such as Quora), what they're telling you explicitly in the surveys you send out to them. (Note: If you're a grower or manufacturer, this means you'll want close ties with your retailers who are on the consumer-facing end.) This intelligence will give you a sense of who your customers are what they want, so you can better provide for them.

The more thoroughly you know your consumer base—that is, *who* exactly is likely to be interested in your product or service—the better you'll be able to market to them based on their wants, needs, frustrations, desires ... and buying behavior. Take it from Bethany Gomez, director of research for the cannabis-focused market research firm Brightfield Group. Gomez told Zoe Biehl at *Bplans*:

> When starting a cannabis business, two things are crucial: understanding the unique challenges of this industry and understanding your consumer base and the unmet need you are filling for them ... The legal cannabis space is becoming crowded and targeted consumer segmentation is increasingly important, so it's key to understand who your core consumers are and what they want from their products.

While I'm at it, you should be doing as much research on your *competition* as you are on your target market. After all, your cannabusiness doesn't exist in a vacuum; and you'd do well to position yourself in relation to *their* positioning. If you're just entering the market, take a look at whom your primary competitors are marketing to. What's their customer base and how are they talking to that base? What are they offering them? Is there a customer persona who is being overlooked or underserved? Your competition might be your greatest asset in determining your (unique) ideal customer. Leverage the segments they're overlooking, or failing to cater to.

Once you're clear who your target market is, it's time to educate them. Not only will this set you apart from the competition (consumers, after all, will recognize you as an authority on the product, the plant, and/or the industry); it will also demonstrate a level of transparency that consumers simply don't *get* when doing business on the black market. This means more consumers eventually converting to the legitimate space.

Teach your target market about the differences in effects that various strains create. Describe the medicinal benefits of various terpenes and break down extraction and infusion processes so they understand what your product entails. Educate them about safe consumption, concentrate dosing, and the differences between consumption methods. Summarize your state's testing processes in a brochure for your brick-and-mortar customers; write a blog post about the difference between tinctures, oils, and extracts. And so on.

Above all, educate prospects and customers about the health factors of cannabis—because *this*, I believe, is where the industry is set to take off. George Blankenship—former executive for Tesla, Apple, and Gap—perhaps said it best when he told Kristen Nichols at *Marijuana Business Magazine*: "I do think that somewhere down the way someone is going to nail how to communicate in a professional way the truly medical benefits that can be derived from cannabis. And we'll get over this stigma. And that's when we'll see this industry take off. Somebody is going to figure out how to do that."

Take up George Blankenship's challenge. After all, the modern consumer's first priority *is* health, so you've got a ready audience. They've quit their coffee for tea; they eat local and organic, practice yoga, and use fitness apps to track their daily workouts. They're less likely to "smoke weed" than they are to use concentrates. Indeed, as Eric Sandy and Melissa Schiller wrote just a few months ago (September 2018):

> A new report from BDS Analytics and Arcview Market Research confirms that cannabis concentrates sales far outpace both flower and edibles in legal U.S. markets. This market segment shows no signs of slowing down. Retail concentrate sales are projected to hit the $8 billion mark by 2022 ... Concentrates have become the fastest growing of the three major segments of the legal cannabis market (flower, concentrates and edibles), largely due to consumer appeal ... [since] concentrates are a healthier option for cannabis inhalation.

Bring these patterns of buying behavior into your business strategy. We all "know" that cannabis fits organically (pun intended) into any lifestyle that revolves around health and wellness; but we're also constantly learning more about its health benefits. Keep your target market up-to-date on these new insights. Not only will it make you look like an authority, it will also make your product look all the better.

Finally, educate consumers on the importance of buying from a *legitimate* market. While cannabis has been part of the national conversation for quite some time now, that "conversation" has tended to revolve around stoked fears and uninformed opinions. You might be surprised to discover how little consumers actually *know* about the plant. Educate them on the superior quality of smaller-batch craft cannabis compared to the mass-produced corporate cannabis they'll soon have access to. Educate them on the significance of a socially-conscious industry comprised of smaller businesses who will promote the compassionate values that the movement was spurred by. Educate them on the health benefits of buying from dispensaries that support cannabis farmers who uphold best practices. (As Hezekiah Allen, executive director of the California Growers Association, says: "Know your retailer, know your farmer ... I don't like to be negative, but don't buy 'Walmart Weed,' yo.")

Consumers simply won't know the difference unless you educate them yourself: There's simply too much information out there for many of them to be willing to wade through on their own. So describe for them the benefits they're missing out on (health, social, communal, ethical) when they purchase cannabis from mass-producing big businesses. Once consumers know the true value of locally-produced products, and the care that smaller businesses put into growing, curing, and processing, they'll likely go small-and-local for life. As Scott Michael Foster writes, "the best cannabis is grown from the people who care about the future of this industry, and not only the increase they see in their profit margins." Let your target market know this.

Innovate, Differentiate, and Specialize

The cannabis products that are currently taking the industry by storm—and that will ultimately thrive in this space—won't look anything like the pot you smoked in high school. (The industry term is "flower": the nuggets you may have packed into bongs and rolled into joints). Remember that, when cannabis is finally descheduled at the federal level—a development that informed industry consensus suggests will happen by 2024—the industry will branch off into three predominant sectors: industrial, medical/pharmaceutical, and recreational/wellness. And each of these sectors will contain a wide variety of sub-sectors, thanks to cannabis' radically wide breadth of applications. So you have plenty of potential spaces in which to play.

In the recreational/wellness category *alone*, producers are getting more and more creative with the mediums through which they deliver cannabis to their customers—from topical rubs to cannabis-infused mineral water to CBD mascaras. As Lester Black writes, "Washington's weed data shows that consumers have clearly developed a taste for these processed products"; and of course, Washington's consumers aren't the only consumers for whom this is true. Trends in Colorado and other states with regulated cannabis markets are showing the same shifts in market share. Here's Black with some data:

> When legal weed stores first opened in Washington in July 2014, flower … made up 94.80 percent of the market, but a year later, flower accounted for only 72.62 percent of sales. That share had further dropped to 54.50 percent by September of this year [2017] … Other forms of

pot—like concentrates, vapes and edibles—take up the rest
of the market. Concentrates, highly potent products *that can
be consumed in a variety of ways*, made up just 5.2 percent
of all sales in July 2014 but accounted for 17.96 percent
in September of this year. Vape cartridges ... accounted for
7.67 percent in September, while edibles made up 8.46
percent of sales.

The italics there are mine so you can see which way the market
is moving: in the direction of diversification, differentiation, and
ingenuity. "Innovation" and "diversification" mean—first and
foremost—recognizing that flower is simply not at the center of the
cannabis ecosystem anymore. Consumers are looking for healthier,
more convenient options and different forms of high. Many *more*
are wanting to experience the benefits of cannabis without the side-
effects of getting stoned: Hence the current explosion in the CBD
market. Given that non-flower cannabis products make up the
fastest-growing segments of the market, the question will become
how to find a niche with high growth and market share potential in
which you can innovate on creative consumption methods.

Of course, diversification is virtually inevitable in an industry
such as cannabis because the elemental product—the flower—is
relatively inexpensive to produce. This means that cannabusinesses
can only command a price premium by processing that flower into
a more refined or complex product: edibles, concentrates, vape
pens, pre-rolls, beverages, tinctures, sublingual sprays, topicals,
capsules, and so on. Granted, diversifying beyond flower *does* mean
greater production costs: The equipment necessary to process
and produce concentrates and edibles can demand a massive
investment. But if *that's* where the demand is, the investment will
be well worth your while.

This summer, Cy Scott wrote for *Ganjapreneur*: "The products
that continue to show high growth rates are niche ones like

tinctures, topical, and capsules. Companies looking to break into the market later in the game would do well to look outside of the flower category. For producers with a long history in flower, like Humboldt's big medical growers, thinking early on about other ways to use that flower is wise." Those were growth rates in June of 2018; but as consumers become more informed about their consumption options (thanks, no doubt, to your educational efforts), those market shares may shift.

That's why doing market research—*really* digging in and looking at the data before entering the market or determining the next product you'll launch—will be invaluable. And yet that statement is too gentle: Your company *simply won't survive* without market research. If the top eight brands for CBD gummies already own 70 percent of the market share in your state, launching your own gummy product won't necessarily be an impossible endeavor; but it'll certainly be an uphill battle. Rather, focus on a product that fewer businesses are offering: The opportunities for differentiation will be greater this way. Data on brand shares, category market sizes, and market forecasts should guide you. Identify underrepresented segments and less concentrated markets, and ask questions of veterans *in* the industry.

Remember, your unique product, process, or niche—regardless of the *currently-unmet* need it fills—doesn't have to be in a business that touches the plant. Grow operations and dispensaries may not be where your core competency lies—and thank goodness, because the industry is much vaster than this. Consider the "bud and breakfast" industry, which offers "cannabis-friendly lodging" with an infrastructure similar to Airbnb's. Fertilizer, hydroponics, consulting, media and publishing, legal services, security, education and training, staffing and payroll, extraction equipment, packaging, lab testing … the list is endless; and I bet you could come up with a hundred other services over the course of a week's worth of research.

The point is that you shouldn't *only* ask how you can aid cannabis *consumers* (this is called a B2C business model); you should also be asking how you might aid the industry *as a whole* (B2B). If you're considering a B2B model, visit grow farms, testing labs, and dispensaries, and ask about their unsolved pain points. Then develop processes and products that are working solutions to these problems.

That said, "differentiating" doesn't necessarily have to revolve around the product—indeed, it's *more than* a quality product. It's about providing a singular customer experience apart from the cannabis itself. Consider value-add components such as customer loyalty programs or monthly subscriptions (like wine clubs do) that not only incentivize customers to choose your business, but also build brand loyalty over the long run. Offer product discounts to customers who subscribe to your email newsletters ... and include juicy educational information in each of those emails, perhaps along with further discounts. Helen Cho, Director of Integrated Strategy for the Hawaii-based Aloha Green Apothecary, told Joseph Peña at *Marijuana Business Daily* that her dispensary sees up to 25 percent increases in sales on the days communications are sent out to patients.

Or maybe you'll determine that, for *you*, "differentiating" means *customizing*. CannaCraft, a California-based and vertically-integrated medical cannabis producer and distributor, has differentiated its brand this way. As Joseph Peña writes, CannaCraft produces "AbsoluteXtracts, a brand that offers 19 strain-specific vape cartridges that allow consumers to find a strain with the taste and effects that meet their needs"; and "Care By Design, a CBD-rich line that's available in five ratios of CBD to THC and in eight applications—vape cartridges, softgel capsules, concentrated oils, sublingual sprays and droppers, chocolates, dissolvable strips and pain creams. Such options allow MMJ patients to decide the level of treatment and mode of consumption that works best for them."

None of these differentiation strategies may ultimately be for you; but you get the picture … and there *is* a perfect strategy out there for you. Remember that you're in an industry with no beaten path (*every* road is the road less traveled), which means that the opportunities for "innovation"—however you want to define it—are everywhere. What's more, you have the advantage of a target market that is, broadly speaking, more open-minded and creatively-inclined than the markets for other consumer products. The creative risk-takers—the ones who are willing to experiment, make mistakes, fail, and begin again—are very likely to be the ultimate trend-setters in the industry. And of course, the better you know the intricacies of the industry and the desires of its market, the more clearly those creative opportunities will jump out at you. So keep a finger on its pulse, at all times.

Finally—even if you decide that your differentiator will be "variety"—you've *got* to specialize. This means that if your company is vertically integrated, you *must* have specialists at *every step*, from seed to sale. If any of those steps is not your core competency, put it in the hands of someone whose core competency it *is*. BigMike said it well: "I'm a fertilizer guy. That's my niche. I was in the equipment industry for a while and I decided to get out of it because it was taking too much time and resources away from my core competency. Consider one aspect of this industry. You may be an inch wide but a mile deep. That works extremely well. Manage your energy. It's a resource and you only have so much bandwidth."

You simply can't dominate in *any* area if you're trying to have hands in *all* of them. The great thing about specialization is that it forces you to focus on quality—which ultimately means better user experiences for your target market. Boutique growers and retailers that carve out unique niches for themselves will discover a group of loyal customers who remain with them for the long haul precisely *because* they trust their specialized knowledge.

My advice to entrepreneurs looking to enter the market now is to seriously look at what happened in the alcohol industry in the decades after legalization and regulation—*specifically* the craft beer sector of the industry. The craft cannabusinesses who hope to survive will need to take tips from their counterparts who *managed* to. Familiarity with craft beer's battle to weaken the stigma, its negotiations of the many layers of bureaucracy, and the business decisions of those that moved ahead in the midst of fierce competition will be invaluable for any startup.

Kayvan Khalatbari, an early cannabis activist who now runs the industry advocacy firm Denver Relief Consulting, also refers to the alcohol industry as a model of what's to come in cannabis: "You're always going to have Coors and Miller and InBev and … the consolidation in liquor, I think, is a great example of where the cannabis industry is probably headed," he told Rachel Estabrook at Colorado Public Radio News. "But you're also seeing this movement of 'craft;' small batch. Something that is higher quality. I'll be very honest and say that I don't buy cannabis from dispensaries in Colorado anymore because I don't believe that you can find the kind of quality that I've become accustomed to."

There *will* be a place in the market for the small-batch, differentiated, highly-specialized, and connoisseur-quality products. The target market that Kayvan Khalatbari belongs to, after all, is growing by the day.

Form Strategic Partnerships

I'll let BigMike lead this one. "One of the challenges our industry faces," he recently told *Merry Jane*,

… is that we're so busy fighting each other. We need to come together as a unified voice, and stay together. Focus on the big picture now, and the minutia later. If we stay divided, we're going to get conquered … Our community has a huge advantage in that we understand this marketplace better than anyone else. Other companies think they can run roughshod over us, and think we're going to be an easy target. But the fact is, when they do that, they're not respecting our community. They're getting it wrong and their sales [will] suffer. Now, these big corporations are not stupid. They're going to figure it out, so we have a three to five year advantage over them right now. I would hate to see us as a community throw that opportunity away.

And when Charles Wu asked Jennifer Sanders—founder of both the private equity firm CNS Equity Partners and the country's first holistic health and cannabis herbal retailer, The Green Heart—how she stays relevant in the industry with so many new players jumping in, she simply answered, "I don't believe in competition; I believe in collaboration."

Collaboration might seem like a counter-intuitive suggestion in light of all I've said about the fierce competition in the industry right now; but if you've *been* in the business, you know that there's a long-established undercurrent of community values just below the surface that industry players are simply going to have to dig for and use to their best advantage. One place to start might be Adam M Brandenburger's and Barry J. Nalebuff's *Co-Opetition: A Revolution Mindset that Combines Competition and Cooperation*. While the book isn't specific to the cannabis industry, it argues for a strategy of combining the advantages of *both* competition and cooperation in *any* difficult business climate.

Whether bulk purchasing with your competitors (which means receiving discounts and lowering the cost per unit for *all* parties involved) or co-sponsoring an environmental initiative (which benefits the brand image of all parties involved), consider the ways that you can leverage "co-opetition" in your best interests. There are so many creative opportunities to mutually support each other; it's simply a matter of refocusing your lens and redefining your relationship to "the *other* guy."

You may even need to go beyond collaboration and form strategic *partnerships*—indeed, the time may come when this is a make-or-break decision for your business. (Knowing *when*, of course, will be a matter of keeping your finger on the pulse of the industry.) Maybe your business is *already* considering partnering with other businesses to ensure you *all* can remain competitive when the adult-use market becomes federally legal. This isn't a point of pride. It's a complex and fiercely competitive industry; and the truth is you probably *can't* build a stand-alone operation that will survive on your own. Focus on your core competency … and if you find you need something beyond that, look for the cannabusinesses who share your values and who would make strong allies.

Structure Wisely

I discussed corporate structuring at some length when I discussed IRC 280E, so I won't go into it again here. Just know that it's very much worth considering segregating your business into separate operations—one that "touches" the plant and one that *doesn't*—for taxing purposes. What's more, if you're looking to be a target for acquisition in the long run, this is a corporate structure you'll want to have. Acquirers may be interested in the "non-touch" portion of your business but *not* the "touch" portion (this is still the case with many investors, who are more comfortable putting their money into the former); and you'll be in a much better position for acquisition if your two businesses can be operationally and legally separated.

More broadly speaking, make sure you have a plan for how different areas of your business will be siloed. Will your growing operations be handled by the same company that distributes the final product? Or is it wiser to handle them separately, ultimately allowing for easier compliance and regulatory adherence in all areas of your business? (Much of this will depend on regulatory conditions in the state you're doing business in. Some states require different licenses for different aspects of the business—cultivation, processing, retail—as they're considered distinct business operations.) Hire an experienced marijuana lawyer and tax professional who can help you set up a corporate structure that won't put you in a bind at the end of the year ... and that will allow your business to run most optimally *every day* in between.

Brand and Professionalize

Of course, much of what I've discussed so far falls under the umbrella of "professionalizing": differentiating your product, demonstrating credibility by educating your target market, using high-quality and organic ingredients, offering stellar customer service, and developing a strong company infrastructure with proficient staff are all prerequisites to running a cannabusiness that will thrive over the long term. This is a no-shortcut industry; shortcutting will only perpetuate the stigmas and stereotypes of the drug that we've just begun to shake off. Adhering to the list I've offered so far not only gives your *business* a good reputation; it also gives *cannabis* a good reputation.

"Running a professional operation" entails dispensing with the terms "ganga," "weed," "marijuana," "pot," "getting stoned," and "getting high." Use the word "cannabis," talk about "doses" rather than "hits" and "flowers" rather than "buds." Today's cannabis consumers are looking for refinement and sophistication; so drop the old-school stoner slang and speak to the higher conversation your market is already engaged in.

That also means dropping the rasta flags, bright green color schemes, and smiley faces. Widen your appeal to reflect the reality of the market. One of my favorite examples is Leafs by Snoop, the cannabis line the rapper and music producer Snoop Dogg owns. Snoop's product packaging lends his products a classy, fashionable, and super-clean appearance, akin to the kinds of products you'd see on a shelf at a high-scale grocery store or a luxury spa. Think what you'd see in a gift basket alongside fine soaps and expensive nuts. Think Apple's packaging. Or just get on Google Images and take a look for yourself.

What this really comes down to is a question of branding. The reality is that your cannabis product is probably like a lot of other cannabis products out there. And no matter *how* high-quality it is, customers will often only register the difference between you and your competitors through your aesthetic—which is one aspect of your branding. This means quality advertising, package design, and labeling with a consistent aesthetic and message. (That consistency will signal trust for your consumers.) Skimping on elements like packaging will make consumers wonder if you've skimped on the quality of the product as well. So no more shrink wrap on those edibles!

This also extends to the in-store experience. Peter Hogarth, CEO of Green Growth Brands, said it well in an op-ed in *The GrowthOp*:

> The future of cannabis retail is simple, with everything from store design and layout to the salesperson's banter (if/when engaged), geared towards subtle increases in understanding. Strains sorted into three price points, for example, to give customers a clear view of the high-end shelf, mid-range choices, and budget offerings. On one side are pure sativas, on the other straight indica, and inbetween [sic] are hybrids.

In other words, it's not just your packaging that needs to be clean and sophisticated; it's the entirety of the consumer's experience with your brand.

As far as advertising goes, use as much lifestyle content as possible. Lifestyle content includes the images and videos you see of consumers using or engaging with a product—while hiking, on road trips with friends, or laughing around a fireplace at a house party. Beyond simply *displaying* your product, lifestyle content demonstrates how your product will *help define* your customer, ultimately contributing to their way of life. It will also encourage them to envision *using* and *benefitting* from what you've got to offer ... and envisioning is a crucial step toward purchase. Most importantly, lifestyle content will help your target market connect with your brand. It'll make your business seem less like a *business* and more like a human character that they can relate to. And *that's* where the emotional connection lies.

Of course, a strong branding strategy entails much more than these things. It includes social media management. I know ... the social platforms out there—Facebook and Instagram in particular—have taken an anti-cannabis stance that makes offering a clear description of your business difficult. But that doesn't mean you can't have a strong social *presence*. Find a professional who knows how to navigate social platforms without being suspended or banned. Consistently update, keep your feeds dynamic, and interact with your customers there.

Another way to professionalize, get attention, and build trust as a brand is a clear content marketing strategy on your company blog. (In case I forgot to mention this: *Have a professional website!*) I discussed the importance of educating consumers above; content marketing is your strongest tool for that. If the term is new to you, "content marketing" is a marketing strategy that entails the creation and distribution of valuable information to your target market, *none of which* expressly promotes your product. Instead, this type of marketing positions you as an authority on a particular topic (one that meets a consumer need by solving problems or answering questions), and stimulates interest in your brand *by virtue of* the authority you prove. Maybe your blog provides the most up-to-date industry news. Maybe it provides health tips concerning cannabis products. Maybe it offers interviews with other authorities in the cannabis industry. The point is to offer consumers information— and an ongoing demonstration of your credibility.

Think about search engine optimization (SEO) when writing your blog posts—indeed, when writing the copy for your entire website. And if you don't know what SEO is, hire someone to think about it *for* you. Collaborate with media outlets (this will require a proactive approach) to help shape the public's understanding of your business and the value you're out to provide to your target market. You want as much positive media coverage as possible to raise your profile among your prospects, distinguish you from your competitors, and continue shifting public perception of the plant. Hire a PR rep to help you find "earned" or "free" media (editorial coverage, whether in newspapers, magazines, websites, or your local news). Hire a publicist—one who's as passionate about cannabis and its industry as you are—to help strategically market your product. Get your face and name out there by participating in expos and industry events.

All these things will be in service of building both your brand and your reputation. You can find other strategies—the basic building blocks of *any* marketing plan in *any* industry, really—by turning to some of the classic marketing texts: Geoffrey Moore's *Crossing the Chasm* and Al Ries and Jack Trout's *Positioning* are the first that come to mind. Remember, cannabis now needs to be thought of as a commodity like *any other* commodity, and its target customer like the target customer for any other product. Treat it as such and you'll shed the last of the long-standing negative perceptions of the industry. By professionalizing, you'll more quickly force out those businesses who refuse to do so—which means a bigger market share for *you*, and brand loyalty by the time M&A activity picks up with more ferocity.

Embrace Data

I've included this one in here because it's worth remembering what you'll be up against as the market consolidates: big businesses who almost certainly have a head start on you when it comes to using analytics technologies. But the thing about our historical moment is that analytics is becoming ever more democratized thanks to technology, and is now available to businesses large and small. I'm talking software that collects, organizes, and "reads" your electronic data *for* you. Even the smallest of companies might be surprised by the amount of data they begin collecting once that software is in place. As Abe Larsen writes, "even one-person startups generate data. Any business with a website, a social media presence, that accepts electronic payments of some form, etc., has data about customers, user experience, web traffic, and more. All that data is filled with potential if you can learn to access it and use it to improve your company."

If you've been in the cannabis space for some years now, your business decisions have probably been influenced by what you've "seen" or "heard" happening inside your company, what you've read in industry magazines, or simply what gut instinct has told you. Each of these things has likely been a useful indicator, and there are ways that they'll continue to serve you as this industry settles. But they're not enough anymore—*especially* in an industry undergoing M&A and consolidations. It's only through data—and *not* intuition, experience, or guesswork—that you can see the objective facts of the current moment, and ultimately make more informed decisions about every aspect of your business.

That includes real-time intelligence—in actual numbers—about company performance. If you're a retailer, for example, you can track the number of transactions per budtender per week, alongside the number of items sold per transaction and the total *price* of that transaction, discovering who your most outstanding salespeople are. Data analytics will tell you the most practical way to restock your inventory, or what elements could have been stronger in your last marketing campaign, or who your website visitors are, or what your customers' purchasing trends are right now, or what consumer sentiment about your brand is. Each of these data points is a little roadmap for your next step toward a more optimized, more productive business.

The editorial team at *CannabisTech* writes:

> As for cultivators and manufacturers, the ability to track inventory and inventory trends is essential to success. Not only are inventory trends readily available at the click of a button, but so is the entire competitive landscape. Knowing inventory trends is crucial for several reasons, such as the ability to make an educated decision, based on facts and not guessing, when dictating grow cycles and production schedules. It also gives insight into other aspects of the business, such as packaging needs, staffing and product rollouts. Market intelligence allows cultivators and manufacturers to stay informed and ahead of national trends, which allows for easier navigation of the market.

There are hundreds of examples I could give of the kinds of intelligence data can offer your business. Whether you're a cultivator, a processor, running an extraction facility, a seed genome lab, or a dispensary, data can help you make your most informed business decisions. Of course, you'll have your work cut out for you when it comes to determining which platform (or, more likely, *platforms*) is best for your business: Much will depend upon your digital presence, your company's infrastructure, your processes, and your customer base. But the research will have been worth it. The predictive intelligence that data affords will ultimately make you nimbler than your competition. You'll see market shifts coming and adapt more quickly than they will. And the speed at which you move in response to the problems and opportunities data identifies *for* you will directly impact the success of your business.

Stay Endlessly Curious

"The best thing in cannabis hasn't even happened yet." That's what Meg Sanders, CEO of Mindful, one of Colorado's first dispensaries, told Michael Zaytsev at *Forbes*. Of course, if you want to be a professional in this industry—no matter *how* late in the game you enter—you've got to possess the historical knowledge *as if* you've been around from the beginning. That's why I've included the introduction and the first chapter in this book.

You *must* know about the plant's scientific and medicinal properties, what its mechanisms are in the body, the long history of its medical use, the history of prohibition, and the names of its biggest champions who put their livelihoods on the line in the early days of cannabis activism. You also have to know the basics about growth, extraction, and infusion; safe consumption methods; and quality standards. You have to keep up on the changing regulatory frameworks and the shifts in the political, technological, and cultural landscape. As the culture of the cannabis community grows and transforms—as new language comes into the lexicon—you have to know about it. In short, study should be one element of your daily business routine.

The cannabis industry is a cutting-edge sector whose central product—the plant—remains a mystery in many ways. Given the nature of uncertainty—and I mean both the shifting landscape and all we have yet to learn about the plant—you've *got* to put yourself in a position of perpetual studentship if you plan on staying in the industry for the long term. Be the dumbest person in the room as often as possible. Go to business expos where you know the most successful businesspeople in the industry—or in *any* industry— will be. (Looking to other industries can yield some great insights). Show up at trade shows and seek out cannabusiness owners who have been proponents of the plant from the beginning. Be humble and curious. Ask every question people are willing to answer. Listen carefully. Take notes. You may be surprised by how willing people are to share what they know.

Read books and industry publications. Subscribe to the top cannabis blogs. Attend conferences. Go to seminars. Attend mastermind groups. Enroll in courses at THC University. Talk to expert growers. Find coaches and mentors. Talk to the folks at your local NORML chapter. Other resources include *Ganjapreneur* the National Cannabis Industry Association (NCIA), both of which post industry events and conferences on their websites. The Association of Cannabis Professionals (ACP) offers legal, financial, policy, scientific, and technological expertise—expert panels discussing the latest cannabis technology, for example. There's really no "minimum" amount of knowledge you need to succeed in this industry. Education should be an all-consuming endeavor. After all, as your knowledge about cannabis grows, so does your ability to add value to the industry.

Exercise Philanthropy (The Compassion Component)

Here we are, back to where we began. As I near the end of this final chapter, I'm no less convinced that *this*—compassion—is the driving force that will keep this industry thriving. Compassion is the plant's point of origin; it's the current that's carried it through this long history; it's the quiet power behind the industry's current explosion. And it will ultimately be the reason that *your* company thrives in the midst of this consolidating market.

Of course, philanthropy has its roots in a commitment to community—the fundamental notion of a living-togetherness that requires we have *everyone's* best interests at heart if we're all going to (collectively) thrive. And if you've been following along with me, you're *already* thinking about community in some way because you can't think about branding without contemplating what it means to cultivate an emotional connection with your target market. Consumers need to know the humans—and the humanity—behind your business.

But now it's time to put your giving hat on.

As I've discussed at length, philanthropy has been an integral part of cannabis subculture from its inception. Granted, it's been called "compassion," and it hasn't necessarily been proffered in the form of money. But if there's one value that the plant has imbued in us over time, it's generosity. Remember that the medical marijuana movement began with "giveaways." Individuals like Dennis Peron, who organized San Francisco's Proposition P—the medical marijuana initiative—in 1991, were fueled by a selfless desire to ensure all members of the community had access to a life- and health-giving drug. Mary Jane Rathburn ("Brownie Mary") helped Peron lobby for medical legalization; Rathburn earned her nickname for the cannabis brownies she illegally baked and gave away to AIDS patients at San Francisco General Hospital, where she volunteered.

These individuals dedicated their lives—and put their freedoms on the line—for the cause; such acts of "civil disobedience" eventually led to the voter-approved Compassionate Use Act of 1996. Since the '90s, cannabusinesses and non-profit organizations have delivered free medical marijuana to terminally ill patients, donated money to community groups, offered free holistic services to their local communities, and more. Compassion, philanthropy ... call it what you want; it's baked into the DNA of the plant, its proponents, and its industry.

Again, it's worth remembering what you'll be up against. Big businesses who'll be entering the space looking to acquire as much market share as they can will have "Corporate Social Responsibility" (CSR) baked into *their* DNA. CSR originated from the view that a company *ought to be* socially involved with the community its presence affects in other ways. It's largely associated with big businesses who have to work against the forces of corporate distrust (both in the wake of the 2008 economic crisis and in the face of our currently-looming financial crisis), political polarization (consumers simply don't *want* to do business with political fence-sitters), and competition (*no* business wants to be seen as out-of-touch or ethically inferior to its counterparts).

In other words, CSR is driven by a "business case": While these enterprises *are* engaging in non-profit causes, integrating social or environmental concerns into their brand strategies and corporate "philanthropy" into their marketing plans, their efforts are often ultimately undertaken to attract high-profile media attention and protect their reputations—*both* with consumers and with their stakeholders. While "voluntary," there's an obligatory force to them: CSR, after all, is in the long-term financial interests of the business.

You can see, then, why I put the word "philanthropy" in scare quotes above. Though these activities might *look like* philanthropy from a consumer perspective, they're carried by an ulterior motive. True philanthropy isn't motivated by the long-term economic interests of the business engaged in the philanthropic act. It simply wants to be a good neighbor ... because it realizes that what's at stake is our humanity.

So your "community involvement" will have to entail more than the relationships you build as part of your branding strategy. It could entail cannabis donations, monetary contributions, participation in social justice movements, and more. And I'd stress the activism aspect here. This industry was *born* of a social justice movement. It exists as such today thanks to decades of community organizing, political engagement, civil disobedience, and civic participation. Honoring those roots by continuing to engage in activism is a mandatory element of *any* cannabusiness in today's industry.

Fundraisers, community service, and volunteer projects are all up for grabs here. Pay attention to what *your* community is most interested in. Restorative justice? Expunging the records of those arrested for non-criminal drug offenses? Bringing attention to the ongoing racial disparity in incarcerations for drug possession and use? Ongoing care for veterans, AIDS patients, or the disabled? Ensuring the groups who took risks and suffered most in "the War on Drugs" can now enjoy the profits of legalization? How do these things actually fit into your business model? In other words, compassion is a business activity you need to write into your financial plan—see above ("Raise More Capital than You Think You'll Need").

Of course, I realize as I'm writing this that some states have— inadvertently or not—found ways to "regulate" compassion. In California, for example, Proposition 64 included licensing and distribution laws that restricted non-profits from sharing commercial cannabis. Retailers had to remit to the state the *equivalent* of the full retail sales tax on any products they marked down to $0 to give away, which meant more paperwork and, ultimately, a bigger tax bill—businesses essentially paid double for their generosity. Last winter, San Francisco Supervisor Jeff Sheehy amended city laws to allow for compassion programs. But cannabis providers still struggle to continue their "compassion programs" amid the steep taxes and costs of compliance I discussed earlier.

But even if you're doing business in a state in which compassion is taxed or generosity is curbed—or even if the money you'd initially allocated to compassion is now being eaten up by compliance—you *don't* have to invest hundreds of thousands of dollars to do some social good. Activism can be inexpensive. A "giving ethos" doesn't *require* cash. There are a thousand and more ways to create value for others. If you make this a business practice as conventional entrants (enterprises) enter the market, consumers will soon perceive the difference between big businesses looking for their payouts and *your* business, which is engaged in philanthropy simply because it's the value you've been taught by the plant that you love. No ulterior motive. Just a belief in the value of all life.

Know There's More to It than This

I haven't covered everything here: I don't know enough about *your* particular place in the industry to do so. Of course, there will be *other* best practices depending upon where you fall in the seed-to-sale trajectory. For example, one of the smartest moves *cultivators* can make right now is preempting future costs by addressing production efficiency—*today*. (I know; this may very well mean making significant, and expensive, changes in your facility design, equipment, and processes. But if you want to maintain your competitive edge as the industry expands, you don't really have an alternative. As the industry continues to grow, so will the need for lower energy costs and overall improved efficiency.) Invest in greenhouse fans, multi-tiered aluminum benches, and the most efficient lighting possible. Research how to maximize your growing space. Talk to other cultivators. Remember what I wrote above: Ask questions. Stay humble. Research relentlessly. Partner and collaborate where you need to.

Whatever your role in the industry is, what you ultimately want to keep in mind is what the future of the market will look like in 5—or 10, or 25—years. Consider the inevitable changes that will come with national legalization. Consider what each of those changes will mean for every aspect your business. Consider the reality of the enterprises you'll soon be up against—their capacities, resources, and capabilities. Consider what you have to do to win market share *before* the entry of those 800-pound wolves in BigMike's (apt) metaphor… and all you'll have to do to combat those enterprises when that fence comes down. And then get working.

It's a lot, I know. But it will have been worth it when you're still standing after the dust has cleared.

Advice for Medical Cannabis Programs

Medical cannabis programs will have a particular set of questions they'll have to ask themselves in light of imminent consolidation if they want to position themselves to succeed. While medical cannabis is now legal in 33 states (as well as in Washington, D.C. and the US. territories of Guam and Puerto Rico), each state has its own set of regulations and restrictions when it comes to qualifying conditions, permissible products, and retail locations. At least for the moment, these limitations will continue to affect your market size and the financial viability of your business. If you're an entrepreneur who's looking to enter the medical market, this section's for you. If you're already *in* the market, I'd suggest taking a moment to read this section, too. You'll want to know your chances of survival in light of the location you've chosen. The answer to *that* will help you discern your best next steps.

Andrew Livingston at *Leafly* breaks the inquiry down into five basic questions. (This section owes much to his article "What Makes a Medical Cannabis Program Succeed?"):

1. "Does the [state] law allow for commercial sales?
2. Does the law permit cannabis products with full-strength THC?
3. Does the law include chronic pain as an independent qualifying condition?
4. Does the law allow for the sale of cannabis flower?
5. How many stores or distribution points will be available to patients?"

Entrepreneurs should begin their research by making lists of the qualifying conditions in every state. After all, *only* patients who meet one (or more) of these conditions are permitted to enroll in a state medical system—and thus, to become your customer. Some of the conditions for which patients can *typically* access the drug include glaucoma, wasting syndrome, Crohn's disease, PTSD, hepatitis C, Alzheimer's disease, chronic pain, and epilepsy ... but again, patients must live in states that recognize cannabis' action on *that* condition if they want to legally obtain it (rather than, say, turning to the black market). The *Leafly* staff has made it easy for you; they've put together a resource called "Qualifying Conditions for a Medical Marijuana Card State by State." Look for it online. As far as I know, they'll continue to update it.

As Livingston notes, chronic pain is the most important qualifying condition from a business perspective. A September 2018 report by the Centers for Disease Control and Prevention estimated that *50 million Americans* suffer from chronic pain. (That's more than 20 percent of the population, by the way.) What's more, about 20 million Americans have what the CDC characterizes as "high-impact chronic pain"—pain that's severe enough to frequently limit day-to-day work or life activities.

Of course, cannabis has proven again and again to be an effective treatment for pain relief. (I'll say no more about opioids; you know about the crisis, the death rate, and their relative ineffectiveness when compared to cannabis by now.) So you'll want to be sure that *whatever* state you set up your dispensary in lists chronic pain as a qualifying condition.

Skimming the first entries on *Leafly*'s list now, and going into those states' respective public health websites, I already see that Connecticut and Delaware are among the states that *don't* list chronic pain as a qualifying condition—though if you're looking at a state that lists something like "severe pain," do your research to determine exactly what that means. Delaware, for example, allows cannabis use for patients who've experienced "severe, debilitating pain *that has not responded to previously prescribed medication or surgical measure for more than three months*, or for which other treatment options produced serious side effects." In other words, medical patients in Delaware have time to get hooked on opioids before they're allowed to turn to cannabis.

As for the other, less common qualifying conditions, you'll want to assess the patient-to-population ratio (PPR) to have a sense of how big your market share might be in that particular state. The CDC is a great resource for this (though some of its data needs to be updated). I just looked up epilepsy—another condition that's proven to be treated effectively with cannabis—on its website. While the numbers are from 2015, I discovered that "1.2 percent of the US population had active epilepsy ... This is about

3.4 million people with epilepsy nationwide: 3 million adults and 470,000 children." The CDC's site also offers a map of "Active Epilepsy Prevalence, by State." I learned that Wyoming—for which "intractable epilepsy" is the state's *only* qualifying condition—has somewhere between 5,900 and 13,100 active epilepsy cases. Ohio, on the other hand, saw between 92,700 and 427,700 active cases in 2015.

You get where I'm going here. At least from the perspective of epilepsy, you'd do better to set up shop in Ohio than in Wyoming. Beyond the CDC, you should be able to get up-to-date data from state resources. Take the time to assess the number of registered qualified patients, the total number of cases per state for each condition (this will let you estimate the number of *un*registered qualified patients—those who could still enroll), and the patient-to-population ratio for each of the states in which medical cannabis is legal. *Somewhere* in there you'll discover the market's consumer base per state. As Livingston notes, "an unsuccessful market typically has a PPR of less than 0.5 percent, while successful markets typically boast PPRs of more than 1 percent."

While you're doing this research—*particularly* as you look at states with shorter lists of qualifying conditions—find out what the process is for adding new conditions. (Find out what the process is for adding new product *types,* as well ... though more on this in a moment.) While the addition of product *types* typically requires legislative action, it's often the case that new qualifying conditions can be added any time by an independent medical review committee.

Analyzing this intelligence will require you to put your prediction hat on. When cannabis *does* become federally legal, what does the data suggest the biggest overall medical market will be? Or when "that study" is finally published that shows how cannabis prompts an autophagic process in the body wherein malignant tumor cells consume themselves—scientifically demonstrating the mechanism through which cannabis works on cancer—what state has a population that will be most affected by this news? How quickly can cancer be added as qualifying condition? And so on. Livingston reminds us that when Minnesota added "intractable pain" to the list of qualifying conditions for its state medical cannabis program, patient enrollment rates tripled.

This is the kind of phenomena you'd want to be ready for.

Another set of data points to consider is those "unregistered qualified patients" I mentioned. You'll measure these against official enrollment. If you've been with me from the beginning, you'll recall the enormous black market that still exists—even in the wake of legalization. These businesses have their own reasons (most of them financial) for staying in the shadows; patients often *turn* to them for those same (financial) reasons. But black market cannabis isn't only cheaper; it's also less of a hassle: No drawn-out and frustrating search for a physician, no paperwork, no registration fees. So while patients run the risk of obtaining contaminated black market cannabis, the benefits of speed and lower cost can often outweigh the convenience.

All this is to say you want to set up shop in a state where the black market is a *less* compelling option for patients. What's the estimated ratio of patients who are getting their cannabis on the black market to those who are getting it on the legitimate market? How many dispensaries are in the state, and how many of them are accessible to rural patients? (Note: *Too few* dispensaries doesn't necessarily mean a bigger share of the market for you; it may simply mean a stagnant market.) Do they offer delivery services? If so, how far do they have to drive to those "pot deserts"—the remote regions of the state with no easy access to medication? Are the existing dispensaries offering high-quality options at prices that *compete* with options on the illicit market? Can patients easily find cannabis products on the black market that are *prohibited* by the state on the legal medical market? How *well* are those current dispensaries *doing*? These are all questions worth asking.

Finally, take into account methods of consumption. Many medical cannabis patients are used to—indeed, they *prefer*—smoking or vaping raw cannabis. But not all state medical marijuana programs allow dispensaries to sell flower. As of this writing, for example, Georgia only allows for low-THC oil (less than 5 percent THC); Mississippi only allows for CBD oil; Montana only allows oils, edibles, and concentrates, as does New York. (Again, these can change at any moment, so keep up.) Given the ongoing preference for smokeables—Livingston notes that "states that prohibit the sale of cannabis flower have the lowest patient-to-population ratios"—you'll absolutely want to ask if you can run a successful medical cannabis dispensary in states where patients may be less compelled to register due to product restrictions.

In short, do your market research. Ultimately, you're looking to set up shop in a state with a broad, inclusive set of qualifying conditions, no product restrictions, and in an area in which the currently-operating dispensaries (neither too few nor too many) are flourishing.

And you're already *in* the market, figure out what your findings mean for *you*.

For those who want an exit strategy

So far, I've been speaking to those of you who plan on fighting it out and hope to be among the last ones standing on the other side of market consolidation. Some of you, however, might be differently-motivated. Maybe you entered the industry with a plan to turn a quick profit and then cash in. Maybe you feel clear that you don't have the wherewithal to compete against the big dogs: You've got other priorities in life to attend to—family, your health, the next big venture. Maybe you're running out of capital and can't execute any of the strategies I detailed above, *let alone* your own business plan. Maybe, after years in the industry, you're simply burned out from taxes, compliance, regulations, etc. ("The most common theme I hear from operators is that they're just tired," Jason Thomas, CEO of Denver-based Avalon Realty Advisors told *Marijuana Business Daily*. "They're tired of the headaches, the regulations, the costs, the 18-hour days. They're eager to cash out.")

All of this is okay! Not everyone will have the time, patience, interest, stamina, or resources to stick around; and it's better to know this about yourself and your business sooner than later. But rather than closing your doors on what has probably been a labor of love for you and going out of business entirely, a better bet is to try to cash out at an attractive price. Indeed, this is the endgame many smaller businesses have been preparing for a few years now. Bob Morgan, an attorney and cannabis industry consultant at the Chicago-based law firm Much Shelist, tracks M&A activity in the cannabis industry. In 2016, he told David Hodes at *Marijuana Venture* that many of the early growers and dispensary owners were already in the initial stages of planning their industry exits. "The mergers and acquisitions on the grow and retail side," he said, "have just begun." Of course, this goes for sales as well.

If your ultimate goal is to sell at a profit, of course, you'll want to build as much value as you can in the meantime. Following as many of the best practices I outlined above as possible is a sure-fire way to do so. You'll also want a plan for *when* you'd like to exit, and *how*. Do you want to sell the *whole* of your current cannabusiness, or only part of it? Do you have a vague idea—even if this is ultimately out of your control—about the kind of business you'd like to sell to or be acquired *by*?

Remember, there may be parties who *are* only interested in buying up one part of your business; and you'll be in a much better position to undertake that transaction if those parts of your business can be—or already *are*—operationally and legally separated. This means segregating your plant touching and non-plant touching operations along business lines—something I've already discussed at length as being a shrewd business idea. If you're in business in a state that *doesn't* demand that cultivation, processing, and retail operations be distinct and operate under separate licenses, *make* them distinct operations anyway. Each operation will be perceived as having a different value for potential buyers; and you want to make it as easy as possible for one operation of your business to be bought.

You'll also want to make sure that your real estate and fixed assets are separated from your operations. As CPA Michael Harlow writes: "We have seen several operators face an unexpected C-Corporation level of tax when they sell the real estate under their existing garden or dispensary. Had the real estate been held by a separate tax partnership and then leased to the operating business, the C-Corporation income tax could have been properly avoided." I'm guessing you've already experienced your fair share of headaches when it comes to taxes; don't put yourself in a position to exit the industry with a migraine.

Finally, make sure your bookkeeping and 280E compliance is thorough and organized. *No* company with any business sense is going to purchase your business if they can't quantify their tax exposure on your filings from the prior year, or if they have no confidence in the overall state of your financial reporting.

If you're looking to get acquired rather than to sell your business outright—which is a way of "staying in the game"—these things are no less important. Companies want to acquire targets that will be true assets for them, both now and over the long term, so you'll want these business practices in place starting *now*. I'd add that it's also worth doing your research to learn exactly *how* companies assess candidates for acquisition. What criteria do they look for? What questions do they ask? A simple Google search for "screening and evaluating acquisition candidates" or "how to assess candidates for acquisition" will give you at least a *starting* idea for what acquiring companies traditionally look for. Then you can determine your best business strategies for meeting the criteria you're likely to eventually be evaluated on.

I mentioned a moment ago that it's worth considering what kind of business you'd like to sell or be acquired by. There are reasons why this is a particularly important question to ask when it comes to *acquisition*: After all, you'll continue operating under your acquirer; and so a shared worldview, adherence to a similar code of ethics, or complementary business practices will be invaluable here. Mark Daoust, a Minnesota-based broker, recommends that you "let potential acquirers know in advance that your business might be acquirable. In most strategic acquisitions that I've seen successfully completed," he goes on to say, "the company that is acquired had a previous relationship with the acquiring company and informed them that selling might be an option they would explore in the future. By letting your intentions be known early, you give potential acquirers the time and the ability to consider acquiring your business as a part of their strategic plans."

Daoust also recommends building your internal strengths to eventually address your acquirers' internal weaknesses. This is another reason why identifying potential acquirers early on is valuable; it gives you time to maximize and optimize with an eye to gaps you'll be filling after the acquisition.

I want to stress here that deciding upon an exit strategy is neither a failure nor a defeat. Acquisition in the midst of industry consolidation doesn't have to be a loser's position. Colby McKenzie at *Direct Cannabis Network* put it rather beautifully:

> Being acquired allows a company to capitalize on that company's value-add, whether that be a well-known brand, some useful technology or a well-established distribution channel or operational structure. If a company is not going to be a market leader or does not have the capital to be an active acquirer, one great option is to position itself during a time of active merger and acquisition as a target. A target company could merge with another company to give the combined company a chance at being a market leader or cash out and reward its investors through a sale at a hefty multiple of the company's earnings.

Eugenio Garcia, CEO of *Cannabis Now*, agrees. Mergers and acquisitions can "giv[e] a cannabis company access to hundreds of millions [or even billions] of dollars in working capital from which they can make light years faster expressions than any other competitors," he told Mike Adams at *Forbes*. These investments can ultimately allow for more rigorous and exhaustive research on the plant, allowing it to be "expressed in a way that it never could with mom and pop operations."

If you're in cannabusiness for the sake of the *plant*, this is a powerful argument for prioritizing *its* advancement.

Acquiring Strategically

On the flipside of that "target" coin is, of course, another motivator that drives consolidation: the eagerness to grow as big as possible to gain the competitive advantage in terms of market share. My *biggest* advice to companies looking to acquire is *not* to base your decisions solely on financials. I wrote this in a LinkedIn article last year ("Looking to Acquire? Forget Profitability"); and it's worth reiterating:

> A key goal of M&A should always be to fill strategic gaps in IP, technology, service, or product. And internal business teams are usually best positioned to identify these opportunities. However, many acquirers hand over the primary candidate screening to other teams who may base decisions mostly on financials. Working deep within a company *and* with corporate teams to combine strategic and financial assessments has produced the best performing acquisitions…

> Business groups are best positioned to assess whether an acquisition could satisfy a strategic need, such as filling geographic, skill, and product or capability gaps. The business team understands the internal gaps of the strategy, the external competitive landscape and the market disruptors. These opportunities may not clear the traditional screenings based on the financial approach … [but] allowing the business team to co-lead helps expand the universe of possible targets by including the acquisition of technologies and product lines, instead of entire companies and/or orphan divisions.

> Successful acquirers use a strategic business assessment and employ business and product teams rather than rely solely on a traditional financial approach for identifying and screening targets.

In doing so, they win.

Keep in mind that you're not *necessarily* limited (except by state law in some cases) to horizontal acquisition—also known as horizontal integration—the acquisition of other businesses that handle the same aspect of the production process. Vertical integration—acquiring a business that's engaged in a *different* aspect of production in the seed-to-sale process (cultivation → distillation/extraction → testing → distribution → retail/sales) can mean any *number* of things for your company. The ability to ship your products at lower costs, for instance (since you now own distribution), or to control the quality of the goods you sell (since you now own cultivation). Not to mention the possibility of new tax deductions available to you that may not have been available before—if you were strictly a retailer, for example.

So consider where you are in the supply chain and where your bottlenecks or frustrations are—whether "upstream" or "downstream" from your place in the chain. Controlling more than one stage might be the very thing that allows you to über-optimize (or lower costs, or customize products, or increase sales through expanded consumer touchpoints and enhanced knowledge of your market's tastes and preferences), and thus outclass your competitors. Keep in mind, however, that the tradeoff for these benefits includes a lack of specialization, a loss of focus, and a loss of flexibility. Take a distributor who acquires a manufacturer, for example. Once that acquisition is made, the distributor can no longer pivot or add product lines as consumer demands fluctuate. They're now beholden to the processes of the factories they've acquired.

As I mentioned briefly in a parenthetical above, vertical integration is geographically contingent—at least *for now*. Some states *permit* vertical integration, leaving it up to individual businesses to decide how much of the supply chain they want to control. Some states *require* vertical integration because it allows them to exercise tighter controls over fewer licensees. Others *prohibit* it. If you're *in* business in a state that requires or prohibits vertical integration, you already know this; but it's certainly something you should know *now* if you're planning an entry or considering participating in M&A in any way. My sense is that *mandatory* vertical integration will soon be obsolete; but in *this* iteration of the industry, you may have restrictions to work with in either direction.

All that said, Marc Goedhart, Tim Koller, and David Wessels have a useful article at McKinsey & Company ("The Six Types of Successful Acquisitions") worth reading. The authors describe six strategic rationales for acquisition that, in their experience, ultimately created value for both acquirers and targets. Those reasons are:

1. "[To] improve the target company's performance
2. [To] consolidate to remove excess capacity from industry
3. [To] accelerate market access for the target's (or buyer's) products
4. [To] get skills or technologies faster or at lower cost than they can be built
5. [To] exploit a business's industry-specific scalability
6. [To] pick winners early and help them develop their businesses"

Note that—as I argued should be the case above—none of these reasons has financials at its center point. *Whatever* your strategic reason for acquiring ends up being, you should be able to clearly articulate and specify *what kinds of value* that acquisition will create for both your business *and* your target ... and the values you articulate *shouldn't* revolve around money (though of course, that's the return you'll ultimately get).

Vague rationales ("filling a gap in our portfolio," "growth," "strategic positioning") simply aren't as likely to be successful. Translate your rationale into a tangible outcome. What gaps would your target fill in your business? What activities, skills, technologies, or complementary strengths would they be adding (or would you be offering *them*)? What ingenuity would they be supplying in a key area of operations? What percent of your company's revenue spent on internal innovation (R&D) would be cut by acquiring them? How might they help you drill down and sharpen your business focus? *How* would they improve your current performance (or how would you improve *theirs*), and in what areas? What would market access or market share look like after the acquisition (for example, accelerated sales or revenues for you *both* now that they have access to *your* global sales force)? If they're helping you diversify, to what end?

Cost-cutting is important; I'm certainly not arguing with that. But think beyond this and ask yourself about the real strategic benefits and value-add that *that* particular acquisition would offer your company (and vice-versa). And ensure you have a strong corporate strategy team to see the acquisition through. There are a hundred reasons to acquire, and as many strategies for doing so. I can only start you on the right track here.

Final Thoughts

If I've not made it clear enough yet, my advice is *not* to wait until cannabis is federally legal to jump into the industry—but *know* (and you have a sense of this now) what it will take to compete. Of course, there's still time to achieve a first-mover advantage (FMA), whether in certain states that might legalize before federal decriminalization, or in a new product or service you might innovate and bring to market. If you're the cautious type and want to wait on the sidelines a bit longer, I understand that, too. While I *may* advocate for you jumping in sooner than later, know that you don't necessarily have to be the first to market in this industry (or *any* industry, for that matter) to be successful.

Of course, there are plenty of pros to the first-mover advantage. It means—if you play your cards right—strong brand recognition and customer loyalty early on. It means that your company gets to set the market price. It means you'll have time to perfect your offering while other companies get their acts together to prepare to move into the space *you've* created. It means that—because you'll have "more time" than later entrants will—you'll have the most *likely* chance of establishing economies of scale. In other words, you'll have a head start ... with all its accompanying advantages.

But that head start doesn't make you *impassable*. Indeed, there are plenty of examples out there of late-to-the-game entrants who ultimately outgrow their competition. It's worth noting, in fact, that first movers are *historically* less profitable over the long run than later entrants to any industry. Because the market is so new, they often struggle to establish supply, distribution, and marketing channels. They also tend, over the long run, to spend much more on exploratory research—a consequence of the mindset that they *must* hold the lead in the industry of their own making. If their value proposition stresses innovation, they run the risk of becoming obsolete fairly quickly: New entrants inevitably come onto the market with improved versions of their technology. And so on.

That said, we're dealing with a market in which technological innovation is moving at a rather leisurely pace; it's the size of the *market* that's growing at high speeds. A solid defense of FMA in the cannabis industry demands a strong brand, and the resources to *maintain and grow* your market share at pace with the growth of the market, more than anything. Can you grow with your base? Do you have the internal structures in place to continue serve them through rapid expansion? It's an attractive market for consumers right now; and it's only going to become more attractive. So implement as many of the best practices I discussed above as possible ... but don't forget that a compelling brand will invite growth. You *must* be ready for that when it happens.

Regardless of which of these roles you take up—acquirer, target, niche business fighting to stay in the game—*all* the efforts you make will reflect upon the thing that matters most, which is the plant. As the industry grows, transforms, and settles, and as consumers keep entering, public health officials will become all the more invested in studying its health effects. This is exactly what happened in the alcohol and tobacco industries: New studies quickly began showing that cigarettes were bad for *everyone*, causing smoking rates to decline and prompting governments to tighten restrictions on advertising. Alcohol studies are certainly taking more time to get to the truth of the matter, as I've discussed. For now, Big Alcohol is able to continue positioning its product as one element of a happy, playful lifestyle; but I like to think—*especially* with cannabis now on the scene as an alternative to weigh it against—that won't last much longer.

I'll return us to the topic I covered at length in the introduction to this book: the endocannabinoid system. The fact that our bodies contain a system that's *uniquely equipped* to respond to the plant—that we're hard-wired for it, and therefore able to heal ourselves through it, *without* the toxic side-effects of Big Pharma's offerings—inevitably spells a favorable future for the plant if *you* play your cards right. In other words, if your branding, marketing, and overall business efforts are successful, public health officials will have no choice but to pay attention. And more attention means more research. And more research will undoubtedly continue to reveal the surprising ways in which cannabis beneficially affects our—*everyone's*—general health and well-being.

Companies who are not ready or willing to compete (or to prepare for acquisition) will go out of business; that's simply what happens when markets mature. The *good* companies will put themselves in a solid position to merge with, or be bought up by, the great companies. The *great* companies will grow, increase their brands, and help those *good* companies they merge with become great companies. Do I think all big businesses who end up market leaders in the endgame will be ethical and principled? No; I don't harbor those illusions. But if *your* business supports *other* businesses in remembering what the plant is ultimately about, big businesses may have no choice but to go along. The plant, after all, is at the center of this story.

Further Reading and Resources

Books

Beazley, Jonathan and Stephanie Field. *Cannabis on Campus: Changing the Dialogue in the Wake of Legalization.* Routledge, 2018.

Booth, Martin. *Cannabis: A History.* Picador, 2005.

Brandenburger, Adam M. and Barry J. Nalebuff. *Co-Opetition.* Currency Doubleday, 1997.

Conrad, Chris. *Hemp: Lifeline to the Future: The Unexpected Answer for Our Environmental and Economic Recovery.* Creative Xpressions Publications, 1993.

Deitch, Robert. *Hemp—American History Revisited: The Plant with a Divided History.* Algora Publishing, 2003.

Earleywine, Mitch. *Understanding Marijuana: A New Look at the Scientific Evidence.* Oxford University Press, 2005.

Green, Jonathon. *Cannabis: The Hip History of Hemp.* Chrysalis Books, 2002.

Grinspoon, Lester and James B. Bakalar. *Marihuana, the Forbidden Medicine.* Yale University Press, 1997.

Grinspoon, Lester. *Marihuana Reconsidered.* Harvard University Press, 1971.

Holland, Julie. *The Pot Book: A Complete Guide to Cannabis: Its Role in Medicine, Politics, Science, and Culture.* Park Street Press, 2010.

Hudak, John. *Marijuana: A Short History.* Brookings Institution Press, 2016.

Lambert, Didier M. *Cannabinoids in Nature and Medicine.* Wiley, 2009.

Lee, Martin A. *Smoke Signals: A Social History of Marijuana— Medical, Recreational, and Scientific.* Scribner, 2012.

Mack, Allison and Janet Joy. *Marijuana as Medicine: The Science Beyond the Controversy.* National Academies Press, 2000.

Mathre, Mary Lynn. *Cannabis in Medical Practice: A Legal, Historical and Pharmacological Overview of the Therapeutic Use of Marijuana.* McFarland, 2010.

Randall, Robert C. and Alice M. O'Leary. *Marijuana Rx: The Patients' Fight for Medicinal Pot.* Da Capo Lifelong Books, 1998.

Robinson, Rowan. *The Great Book of Hemp: The Complete Guide to the Environmental, Commercial, and Medicinal Uses of the World's Most Extraordinary Plant.* Park Street Press, 1995.

Rosenfeld, Irvin. *My Medicine: How I Convinced the U.S. Government To Provide My Marijuana and Helped Launch a National Movement.* Open Archive Press, 2010.

Russo, Ethan B. *Cannabis and Cannabinoids: Pharmacology, Toxicology, and Therapeutic Potential.* Routledge, 2002.

Sloman, Larry. *Reefer Madness: A History of Marijuana.* St. Martin's Griffin, 1998.

Online Articles

"33 Legal Medical Marijuana States and DC: Laws, Fees, and Possession Limits." *ProCon.org.*

Adams, Mike. "Cannabis Now CEO Says Beer and Marijuana Mergers are Good for Business." *Forbes.com.* 8/21/18.

Abel, Ernest L. *Marihuana, the First Twelve Thousand Years.* McGraw-Hill, 1982.

"Alcohol Facts and Statistics." *NIAAA.nih.gov.* Updated August 2108.

Angell, Tom. "Bernie Sanders Backs Bill To Punish States With Harsh Marijuana Laws." *Forbes.com.* 4/19/18.

Angell, Tom. "Congressional Black Caucus Calls For Major Marijuana Reforms." *MarijuanaMoment.net.* 6/8/18.

Angell, Tom. "Federal Report On Marijuana Legalization Required Under New Bill." *Forbes.com.* 7/24/18.

Angell, Tom. "Marijuana Won The Midterm Elections." *Forbes.com.* 11/7/18.

Angell, Tom. "Mayors From Across U.S. Call On Feds To Deschedule Marijuana." *MarijuanaMoment.net.* 6/11/18.

Angell, Tom. "More Banks Working With Marijuana Businesses, Despite Federal Moves." *Forbes.com.* 6/14/18.

Angell, Tom. "Wells Fargo Closes Florida Politician's Account Due To Marijuana Donations." *Forbes.com.* 8/20/18.

Anslinger, Harry. "Marijuana: Assassin of Youth" (July 1937). *RedHouseBooks.com.*

AntiqueCannabisBook.com.

Auerbach, Brad. "How Cannabis Entrepreneurs Feel about Sessions' Reversal of The Cole Memo." *Forbes.com.* 3/3/18.

Awad, Ann Marie. "Where Does All the Marijuana Money Go? Colorado's Pot Taxes, Explained." *CPR.org.* 10/22/18.

Bachhuber, Marcus A. et al. "Medical Cannabis Laws and Opioid Analgesic Overdose Mortality in the United States, 1999–2010." *JAMANetwork.com.* 10/14.

Balsamo, Michael. "Surge in Illegal California Pot Shops Undercuts Legal Market." *News-herald.com.* 7/5/18.

Barry, Rachel Ann, Heikki Hiilamo, and Stanton A. Glantz. "Waiting for the Opportune Moment: The Tobacco Industry and Marijuana Legalization." *NCBI.nlm.nih.gov.* 6/3/14.

Baum, Dan. "Legalize It All: How to Win the War on Drugs." *Harpers.org.* 12/29/18.

Begley, Sharon. "NIH Rejected a Study of Alcohol Advertising while Pursuing Industry Funding for Other Research." *StatNews.com.* 4/2/18.

Berke, Jeremy. "The CEO of the First Marijuana Company to IPO in the US Reveals Why This Was the Right Time to Go Public." *BusinessInsider.com.* 6/22/18.

Berke, Jeremy. "Coca-Cola is Reportedly Eyeing the Legal Marijuana Industry, and It could Soon Be a Bigger Market than Soda." *BusinessInsider.com.* 9/17/18.

Berke, Jeremy. "Federal Marijuana Prohibition has Opened a Short Window of Opportunity for Investors Willing to Stomach the Risk." *BusinessInsider.com.* 8/22/18.

Berke, Jeremy. "One of the Hedge Funders Behind 'The Big Short' Says Betting on Marijuana is 'The Big Long.'" *BusinessInsider.com.* 6/3/18.

Berman, Douglas A. "Defying Congress, Jeff Sessions Keeps Blocking Medical Marijuana Research." *LawProfessors.typepad.com.* 7/7/18.

Berman, Douglas A. "An Informed Accounting of those States 'Most Likely To Legalize Marijuana In 2019.'" *LawProfessors.typepad.com.* 12/26/18.

Berman, Russell. "Why Congress Gave In to Medical Marijuana." *TheAtlantic.com.* 12/17/14.

Bernard-Kuhn, Lisa. "Aurora Cannabis to Acquire Canadian Rival MedReleaf for CA$3.2B in Industry's Biggest Deal." *MJBizDaily.com.* 5/14/18.

Bernard-Kuhn, Lisa. "Cashing Out." *MJBizMagazine.com.* 10/18.

Bernard-Kuhn, Lisa. "Marijuana M&A Activity Spikes as Some Cannabis Pioneers Cash Out." *MJBizDaily.com.* 7/11/18.

Bess, Jeff. "Testing the Outer Limits of 280E: Californians Helping to Alleviate Medical Problems v. Commissioner." *CannaLawBlog.com.* 6/8/16.

Bianchi, Chris. "Koch Brothers Criticize Trump Administration Over Legal Pot." *Westword.com*. 2/19/18.

Biehl, Zoe. "So You Want to Start a Cannabis Business: Advice for the Absolute Beginner." *Bplans.com*. Undated. "The Big Data Boom." *CannabisTech.com*. 2/2/18.

Black, Lester. "Legal Weed Isn't the Boon Small Businesses Thought It Would Be." *FiveThirtyEight.com*. 12/29/17.

Bonn-Miller, Marcel O. et al. "Labeling Accuracy of Cannabidiol Extracts Sold Online." *JAMANetwork.com*. 11/7/17.

Borchardt, Debra. "Hemp Cannabis Product Sales Projected To Hit $1 Billion In 3 Years." *Forbes.com*. 8/23/17.

Borchardt, Debra. "Marijuana Industry Projected to Create More Jobs than Manufacturing by 2020." *Forbes.com*. 2/22/17.

Bornemann, Kalin and Danielle Hunt. "DOJ Rescinds the Cole Memo—What It Means for Your Financial Institution." *BankLawMonitor.com*. 1/4/18.

Bricken, Hilary. "Breaking News: Bye, Bye Cole Memo, Hello Uncertainty for Marijuana." *CannaLawBlog.com*. 1/4/18.

Brundin, Jenny. "Do Marijuana Taxes Go To Schools? Yes, But Probably Not In The Way You Think They Do." *CPR.org*. 10/22/18.

"BSA Expectations Regarding Marijuana-Related Businesses." *FinCen.gov*. 2/14/14.

"California Cannabis Confusion." *AllBud.com*. 6/15/14.

"California Proposition 64, Marijuana Legalization (2016)." *Ballotpedia.org*.

Campbell, Greg. "Farm Bill Clears the Way for Hemp Production." *DailyCaller.com*. 2/8/14.

"Cannabinoids as Antioxidants and Neuroprotectants." *patft.uspto.gov*. Patent filed 10/7/03.

"Cannabis Eradication." *DEA.gov*.

"Cannabis Industry has Become Significant Community Contributor." *Coloradoan.com.* 3/9/17.

Caplinger, Dan. "Is This Cigarette Giant Looking More Closely at Marijuana?" *Fool.com.* 6/16/17.

Carome, Michael. "Director of National Institute on Alcohol Abuse and Alcoholism Must Be Removed." *Citizen.org.* 4/5/18.

Carroll, Rick. "Aspen Marijuana Shops Sold $11.3 Million in 2017, Topping Liquor Stores for First Time." *AspenTimes.com.* 2/7/18.

Chong, Alberto. "Medical Marijuana Laws Reduced Alcohol Consumption." *GSU.edu.* 12/12/17.

Cohen, Michael. "How For-Profit Prisons Have Become the Biggest Lobby No One is Talking About." 4/28/15.

Colbert, Mitchell. "The Upcoming Epidiolex Ruling: What it Means for the Hemp CBD Market." *TheHempMag.com.* 6/21/18.

Cole, James. M. "Memorandum for all United States Attorneys." *Justice.gov.* 8/29/13.

Crozier, Elizabeth. "5 Important Facts About Patent 6630507." *Prohbtd.com.*

Daoust, Mark. "How to Position Your Business for a Strategic Acquisition." *Entrepreneur.com.* 5/28/18.

Davenport, Danielle. "Everyone Should Buy a Startup ..." *LinkedIn.com.* 9/9/17.

Davenport, Danielle. "Looking to Acquire? Forget Profitability." *LinkedIn.com.* 8/30/18.

Deans, Graeme K., Fritz Kroeger, and Stefan Zeisel. "The Consolidation Curve." *HBR.org.* 2002.

"Deaths from Marijuana vs. 17 FDA-Approved Drugs." *ProCon.org.* 7/8/09.

Demby, Gene. "What John Boehner's Pivot on Cannabis Tells Us About the Legal Weed Boom." *NPR.org.* 4/16/18.

DeSalvo, Karen B. Letter to the Honorable Chuck Rosenberg, June 5, 2015. *DEAdiversion.usdoj.gov.*

"Detailed Analysis of California SB 94 Changes." *TheLeafOnline. org.* Undated.

Devinsky, Orrin et al. "Trial of Cannabidiol for Drug-Resistant Seizures in the Dravet Syndrome." *NEJM.org.* 5/5/17.

Doblin, Rick. "The Medicinal Use Of Marijuana: A Progress Report On Dr. Donald Abrams' Pilot Study Comparing Smoked Marijuana And The Oral THC Capsule For The Promotion Of Weight Gain In Patients Suffering from the AIDS Wasting Syndrome." *Maps.org.* 1994.

Doyle, Kathryn. "Prescription Painkiller Deaths Fall in Medical Marijuana States." *Reuters.com.* 8/25/14.

Dumitrescu, R.G. and P.G. Shields. "The Etiology of Alcohol-Induced Breast Cancer." *NCBI.nlm.nih.gov.* 4/2005.

"Eaze Insights: The High Cost of Illegal Cannabis." *Eaze.com.* 8/6/18.

Eddy, Mark. "Medical Marijuana: Review and Analysis of Federal and State Policies." *ProCon.org.* 4/2/10.

"Edmondson v. Commissioner. Docket No. 4586-76." *Leagle.com.*

Estabrook, Rachel. "Where's Colorado Cannabis Headed? We Asked 3 Entrepreneurs For Their Predictions." *CPR.org.* 6/12/18.

"Fact Sheet: Drug Offenders in Prison." *MN.gov.* 8/17.

Fang, Lee. "Police and Prison Guard Groups Fight Marijuana Legalization in California." *TheIntercept.com.* 5/18/16.

Fang, Lee. "The Real Reason Pot Is Still Illegal." *TheNation.com.* 7/2/14.

Fassa, Paul. "Hypocrisy: Cannabis has 'No Medicinal Value,' but Big Pharma can Sell It with Approval." *NaturalSociety.com.* 5/26/14.

"FDA Approves First Drug Comprised of an Active Ingredient Derived from Marijuana to Treat Rare, Severe Forms of Epilepsy." *FDA.gov.* 6/25/18.

"FDA Briefing Document: Peripheral and Central Nervous System Drugs Advisory Committee Meeting." *FDA.gov.* 4/19/18.

Ferro, Shaunacy. "Why It's So Hard For Scientists To Study Medical Marijuana." *PopSci.com.* 4/18/13.

"FinCEN's Mandate From Congress: 31 U.S.C. 310." *FinCen.gov.*

"Forecast: Legal Cannabis Spending Worldwide from 2016 to 2024." *Statista.com.*

Foster, Scott Michael. "Will Big Business Takeover the Cannabis Industry?" *Potent.media.* 2017.

"Four Top Cannabis Companies Announce Merger, Forming One of the Most Comprehensive Industry Platforms." *PRNewswire. com.* 5/15/18.

Fox, MeiMei. "2 Cannabis Entrepreneurs Share Their Secrets For Success." *Forbes.com.* 4/20/18.

"Gardner Protects Colorado's Legal Marijuana Industry." *Gardner. senate.gov.* 4/13/18.

Gettman, Jon. "An In-Depth Look At Federal Cannabis Prisoners." *HighTimes.com.* 10/30/17.

Gieringer, Dale H. "The Origins of California's 1913 Cannabis Law." *canorml.org.*

Gieringer, Dale H. "The Origins of Cannabis Prohibition in California." *canorml.org.*

Gill, Molly M. "Correcting Course: Lessons from the 1970 Repeal of Mandatory Minimums." *ProCon.org.*

Goedhart, Marc, Tim Koller, and David Wessels. "The Six Types of Successful Acquisitions." *Mckinsey.com.* 5/17.

Gomez, Bethany. "Cannabis Market Data, Insights and Branding: How to Succeed in a Crowded Market." *BrightfieldGroup. com.* Undated.

"Governor Kate Brown's Statement on Reports A.G. Sessions Will Rescind Federal Marijuana Policy." *Oregon.gov.* 1/4/18. "That Gram of Kosher Kush in California Now Heavy With New Taxes." *BDSAnalytics.com.* 1/11/18.

Grinspoon, Lester. "History of Cannabis as a Medicine" (DEA statement, 2005). *MAPS.org.*

Gunelius, Susan. "Big Businesses Force Small Businesses out of the Marijuana Market." *Cannabiz.media.* 7/17/18.

Gunelius, Susan. "How to Succeed in the Cannabis Edibles Market." *CannabisBusinessExecutive.com.* 10/29/18.

Gupta, Sanjay. "Medical Marijuana and 'The Entourage Effect.'" *CNN.com.* 3/11/14.

Gupta, Sanjay. "Why I Changed My Mind on Weed." *CNN.com.* 8/8/13.

Gurman, Sadie. "Huff, Puff, Pass? AG's Pot Fury Not Echoed by Task Force." *APNews.com.* 8/4/17.

Haffajee, Rebecca L., Robert J. MacCoun, and Michelle M. Mello. "Behind Schedule—Reconciling Federal and State Marijuana Policy." *PublicHealthLawWatch.org.* 7/12/18.

Halperin, Alex. "Cannabis Capitalism: Who is Making Money in the Marijuana Industry?" *TheGuardian.com.* 10/3/18.

Harlow, Michael. "Planning For The Coming Consolidation In The Cannabis Industry." *NewFrontierData.com.* 3/25/18.

"Health and Safety Code—HSC. Division 10. Uniform Controlled Substances Act." *LegInfo.legislature.ca.gov.* 11/5/1996.

Hecht, Peter. "Sacramento City Council Finalizes Licensing Fees for Commercial Marijuana Growers." *SacBee.com.* 3/8/17.

Hermanns-Clausen, M. et al. "Acute Toxicity Due to the Confirmed Consumption of Synthetic Cannabinoids: Clinical and Laboratory Findings." *NCBI.nlm.nih.gov.* 3/13.

Hightower, Kamaria. "Seattle Mayor Jenny Durkan Condemns DOJ's Decision to Roll Back Cole Memo." *Durkan.seattle. gov.* 1/4/18.

Hodes, David. "Boutique Businesses—Can the Small Survive?" *MarijuanaVenture.com.* 7/29/16.

Holden, Dominic. "Trump's Endorsement Of A New Marijuana Bill Is A Real F-You To Jeff Sessions." *BuzzFeedNews.com.* 6/8/18.

Holden, Mark. "Keep Local Marijuana Laws from Going Up in Smoke." *KochInd.com.* 1/18/18.

Honaker, William. "Growing Competition in the Cannabis Space." *BrightfieldGroup.com.* 4/2/18.

Hosking, R.D. and J.P. Zajicek. "Therapeutic Potential of Cannabis in Pain Medicine." *NCBI.nlm.nih.gov.* 7/2008.

"How Do You Define Your Future in an Undefined Market? Insights and Perspectives from Canada's Cannabis Industry Leaders." *EY.com.* 2017.

Hughes, Trevor. "Marijuana's Legalization Fuels Black Market in Other States." *USAToday.com.* 7/31/17.

Hutzler, Alexandra. "Legal Weed: How Republicans Learned to Love Marijuana." *Newsweek.com.* 8/16/18. "Industry Lifecycle." *Investopedia.com.*

Ingraham, Christopher. "More People were Arrested Last Year over Pot than for Murder, Rape, Aggravated Assault and Robbery—Combined." *WashingtonPost.com.* 9/26/17.

Ingraham, Christopher. "One Striking Chart Shows Why Pharma Companies are Fighting Legal Marijuana." *WashingtonPost. com.* 7/13/16.

Ingraham, Christopher. "A Pharma Company that Just Spent $500,000 Trying to Keep Pot Illegal Just Got DEA Approval for Synthetic Marijuana." *WashingtonPost.com.* 3/24/17.

Isikoff, Michael. "HHS to Phase Out Marijuana Program." *WashingtonPost.com.* 6/22/1991. "Ivy League Doctor Gets 4 Years in Prison for Insys Opioid Kickbacks." *Fortune.com.* 3/10/18.

Jaeger, Kyle. "State Financial Regulators Push Congress to Fix Marijuana Banking Problems." *MarijuanaMoment.net.* 8/27/18.

James, Tom. "The Failed Promise of Legal Pot." *TheAtlantic.com.* 5/9/16.

Jenison, David. "The DEA Fails to Reschedule Cannabis." *Prohbtd. com.*

Jikomes, Nick. "What Is the Endocannabinoid System and What Is Its Role?" *Leafly.com.* 12/12/16.

Johnson, Jenna. "Trump Softens Position on Marijuana Legalization." *WashingtonPost.com.* 10/29/15.

"Joint Budget Committee Appropriations Report Fiscal Year 2017–2018." *Leg.colorado.gov.*

Kaplan, Jennifer. "U.S. Cannabis Sales Projected to Pass Soda by 2030." *BNNBloomberg.ca.* 4/4/18.

Kaskey, Jack. "California's Weed Black Market Ramps Back Up." *Bloomberg.com.* 6/28/18.

Kelloway, Claire. "Rapid Consolidation in Canada's Cannabis Market Raises Fears Among Small Growers—Both North and South of the Border." *FoodAndPower.net.* 5/24/18.

Keneally, Meghan. "Trump Administration's Stance on Marijuana Use Clouded in Mystery." *AbcNews.go.com.* 4/20/17.

Kennedy, Paul P. "NEARLY 500 SEIZED IN NARCOTICS RAIDS ACROSS THE NATION." *NYTimes.com.* 1/5/1952.

King, Tiffany. "The DEA Has Seized $3.2 Billion Worth Of Assets Without Arrest Or Conviction." *Herb.co.* 4/4/17.

Kovacevich, Nick. "With A Wave Of Consolidation, The Cannabis Industry Rises To The Next Level." *Forbes.com.* 8/29/18.

Krane, Kris. "Cannabis Cultivation Will Be a Race to the Bottom." *Forbes.com.* 4/25/18.

"Kush Bottles Acquires CMP Wellness, a Premier Distributor of Vaporizers, Cartridges and Accessories." *PRNewswire.com.* 5/4/17. "The La Guardia Committee Report: The Marihuana Problem in the City of New York" (1944). *DrugLibrary.org.*

LaCapria, Kim. "Drug Law Lobbying by Corrections Corporation of America." *Snopes.com.* 4/4/16.

Lamers, Matt. "Constellation Invests CA$5 Billion in Cannabis Giant Canopy in Deal Financed by BofA Merrill Lynch." *MJBizDaily.com.* 8/15/18.

Larsen, Abe. "Why is Data Important for Your Business?" *Grow.com.* 11/14/17.

Laslo, Matt. "Elizabeth Warren: Jeff Sessions Acted as 'Catalyst for Weed Legalization." *RollingStone.com.* 8/27/18.

Lassiter, Matthew D. "Impossible Criminals: The Suburban Imperatives of America's War on Drugs." *Academic.oup.com.* 1/6/15.

"Legal Cannabis Market is Growing More Competitive as Demand Grows." *PRNewswire.com.* 8/13/18.

"Legalization On The Ballot: Live Marijuana Election Results." *MarijuanaMoment.net.* 11/6/18.

Lewis, Amanda Chicago. "Mitch McConnell: Drug Warrior, CBD Champion?" *RollingStone.com.* 6/29/18.

Livingston, Andrew. "What Makes a Medical Cannabis Program Succeed?" *Leafly.com.* 10/18/17.

Lu, Hui-Chen and Ken Mackie. "An Introduction to the Endogenous Cannabinoid System." *NCBI.nlm.nih.gov.* 10/30/15.

Margolin, Madison. "How Legalization Is Already Hurting California's Small Pot Farmers." *RollingStone.com.* 1/8/18.

"Marihuana: A Signal of Misunderstanding." (The Report of the National Commission on Marihuana and Drug Abuse, 1972.) *DrugLibrary.org.*

"Marijuana is Not Really Legal in California if Residents Don't Have a Reasonable Way to Buy It." *LATimes.com.* 8/14/18.

"Marijuana Tax Data." *Colorado.gov.*

"Marinol vs. Marijuana: Politics, Science, and Popular Culture." *NaturallyHealingMD.com.*

Maurer, Matt and Whitney Abrams. "M&A in the Canadian Cannabis Industry." *FinancierWorldwide.com.* 5/18.

McCarthy, Justin. "Record-High Support for Legalizing Marijuana Use in U.S." *Gallup.com.* 10/25/17.

McConnell, Mitch. "Growing Kentucky's Economy with Hemp." *Mcconnell.senate.gov.* 4/20/18.

McConnell, Mitch. "Opinion: Let Kentucky Farmers Grow State Economy with Hemp." *Cincinnati.com.* 4/30/18.

McGreevy, Patrick. "New Rules with Hefty Fees Set for Growing and Selling Marijuana in California." *LATimes.com.* 11/16/17.

McKenzie, Colby. "Why Cannabis Industry Consolidation will Affect Your Business." *DirectCannabisNetwork.com.* 3/28/17.

McVay, Robert. "Feds Green Light Marijuana Banking." *CannaLawBlog.com.* 2/14/14.

McVey, Eli. "Chart: Marijuana Stocks Stumble, then Rebound after Sessions Announcement." *MJBizDaily.com.* 1/8/18.

"Medical Cannabis Poised to Cannibalize The Pharmaceutical Industry." *NewFrontierData.com.* 5/24/17.

"MedMen Inks $53 Million Acquisition of Florida Cannabis Cultivator, Dispensary Sites." *MJBizDaily.com.* 6/6/18.

Mercola, Joseph. "Big Pharma Tries to Monopolize CBD Oil Market." *Mercola.com.* 12/11/17.

Mercola, Joseph. "Medical Cannabis as an Underutilized and Vilified Therapeutic Option: A Special Interview with Margaret Gedde." *Mercola.com.* Undated. "Mergers." *FTC. gov.* Undated.

Mirnateghi, Maryam. "How to Not Get Squeezed Out by the Coming Cannabis Market Consolidation." *GreenEntrepreneur. com.* 10/26/18.

Miron, Jeffrey and Katherine Waldock. "The Budgetary Impact of Ending Drug Prohibition." *Cato.org.* 10/27/10.

Mitchell, Thomas. "Colorado Harvest's Tim Cullen on the State of Colorado Marijuana." *Westword.com.* 5/31/18.

Mitchell, Thomas. "Denver Could Raise Pot Sales Tax to Fund Affordable Housing." *Westword.com.* 4/17/18.

Mukherjee, Sy. "Feds Arrest 6 Former Insys Execs for Allegedly Bribing Doctors." *Fortune.com.* 12/8/16.

Müller, L. et al. "The Synthetic Cannabinoid WIN 55,212-2 Elicits Death in Human Cancer Cell Lines." *NCBI.nlm.nih. gov.* 11/17.

Nichols, Kristen. "Building Credibility to Succeed in the Long Term." *MJBizMagazine.com.* 1/18.

"NIH to End Funding for Moderate Alcohol and Cardiovascular Health Trial." *NIH.gov.* 6/15/18.

"'No-Touch' Approach Reduces Risk as Public Companies Tap Explosive Growth of Cannabis Industry." *NetworkNewswire. com.* 3/15/17.

Noonan, David. "Marijuana Treatment Reduces Severe Epileptic Seizures." *ScientificAmerican.com.* 5/25/17.

Novak, Matt. "Jeff Sessions, Anti-Weed Crusader, Was a Shill For Big Tobacco." *Gizmodo.com.* 3/1/17.

Paul, Jesse. "Cory Gardner Says AG Jeff Sessions' Decision to Rescind Marijuana Policy 'Has Trampled on the Will' of Colorado Voters." *DenverPost.com.* 1/4/18.

Pellechia, Thomas. "Legal Cannabis Industry Poised for Big Growth, in North America and Around the World." *Forbes. com.* 3/1/18.

Peña, Joey. "'Global Paradigm Shift': International Cannabis Business Opportunities Will Accelerate." *MJBizDaily.com.* 8/16/18.

Peña, Joseph. "How Marijuana Entrepreneurs Can Outsmart Black-Market Competitors." *MJBizDaily.com.* 3/20/18.

"Pharmaceutical Executives Charged in Racketeering Scheme." *Justice.gov.* 12/8/16.

Pickle, Katharine. "Big Pharma Takes On Marijuana Legalization: The Synthetic Marijuana vs. Botanical Marijuana Paradox." *Law.Emory.edu.* 2018.

Pizzorno, Lara. "New Developments in Cannabinoid-Based Medicine: An Interview with Dr. Raphael Mechoulam." *JeffreyDachMD.com.* Undated.

Porter, Nanette. "Three Different Cannabinoid-Based Medicines Approved by the FDA." *MedicalJane.com.* 5/1/17.

"The Price of Cannabis is Falling, Suggesting a Supply Glut." *Economist.com.* 11/16/17.

"Provision of Marijuana and Other Compounds For Scientific Research—Recommendations." *DrugAbuse.gov.* 1/1998.

"Pure Food and Drug Act (1906)." *ProCon.org.*

"Qualifying Conditions for a Medical Marijuana Card by State." *Leafly.com.*

Quinton, Sophie. "Testing for Tainted Marijuana Challenges States Regulators." *HuffingtonPost.com.* 12/21/17.

Rapier, Graham. "Marijuana Stocks are Getting Slammed after Reports that Jeff Sessions Plans to Roll Back Legal Pot Rules." *BusinessInsider.com.* 1/4/18.

Rappold, R. Scott. "Raising the Bar in Cannabis Growth." *CultureMagazine.com.* 12/1/16.

Rathge, Adam. "Pondering Pot: Marijuana's History and the Future of the War on Drugs." *OAH.org.*

Rauly, Arnaud Dumas de. "What Will the Cannabis Industry Look Like in Five Years?" *TheBlincGroup.com.* 8/8/18.

Re, Gregg. "John Boehner to host marijuana investing seminar." *FoxNews.com.* 10/22/18.

"Reasons for Escalating Enforcement Costs: California Drug and Marijuana Arrests, 1960–67." *DrugLibrary.org.*

Reichmann, Deborah et al. "State Medical Marijuana Laws: Understanding the Laws and Their Limitations." *Academia. edu.*

"Review of the Department's Oversight of Cash Seizure and Forfeiture Activities." *Justice.gov.* 3/17.

Roberts, Michael. "Here's Where Your Colorado Marijuana Tax Dollars Go." *Westword.com.* 4/18/18.

Ryan, Tim. "Rep. Tim Ryan: Marijuana Should be Legal in All 50 States." *CNN.com.* 7/20/18.

Ryan-Ibarra, S., M. Induni, and D. Ewing. "Prevalence of medical marijuana use in California, 2012." *NCBI.nlm.nih.gov.* 3/15.

Sandy, Eric and Melissa Schiller. "Cannabis Concentrate Sales are Growing, but Consolidation is Coming." *CannabisBusinessTimes.com.* 9/19/18.

"SB-94 Cannabis: Medicinal and Adult Use." *LegInfo.legislature. ca.gov.* 6/27/17.

"Schedules of Controlled Substances: Placement in Schedule V of Certain FDA-Approved Drugs Containing Cannabidiol; Corresponding Change to Permit Requirements." *FederalRegister. gov.* 9/28/18.

Schettino, Rick. "California's Cannabis Chief: 'There's Confusion Out There.'" *PotNetwork.com.* 8/21/18.

Schettino, Rick. "Department of Veteran Affairs Eases Up on MMJ." *PotNetwork.com.* 1/10/18.

Schettino, Rick. "Senator Schumer To Introduce Federal Cannabis Decriminalization Legislation." *PotNetwork.com.* 4/23/18.

"Schumer Introduces Marijuana Freedom and Opportunity Act— New Legislation Would Decriminalize Marijuana at Federal Level." *Democrats.senate.gov.* 6/27/18.

Schupska, Stephanie. "Not Blowing Smoke: Research Finds Medical Marijuana Lowers Prescription Drug Use." *UGA. edu.* 7/6/16.

Scott, Cy. "How to Survive in the Increasingly Competitive Cannabis Industry, According to Data." *Ganjapreneur.com.* 6/12/18.

Scott, Elsa. "Marinol: The Little Synthetic that Couldn't." *MarijuanaLibrary.org.* 7/1994.

"Senator McConnell and Commissioner Quarles Announce Hemp Legislation." *Mcconnell.senate.gov.* 3/26/18.

Serrano, Alfonso. "Inside Big Pharma's Fight to Block Recreational Marijuana." *TheGuardian.com.* 10/22/16.

Sharp, Richard. "Can Hemp Save the Economy?" TheHempNews. com. 7/15/09. "A Short History of Medicinal Cannabis." *ncsm.nl.*

Siff, Stephen. "The Illegalization of Marijuana: A Brief History." *OSU.edu.*

Skerritt, Jen. "It's High Times for Pot Deals in Canada Ahead of Legalization." *Bloomberg.com.* 1/24/18.

Sledge, Matt. "Marijuana Prohibition Now Costs the Government $20 Billion a Year: Economist." *HuffingtonPost. com.* 4/20/13.

Smalley, Craig W. "A Final Article on Cannabis and Section 280E." *CPAPracticeAdvisor.com.* 1/11/18.

Smith, Aaron. "Jeff Sessions is a Buzz Kill for Pot Stocks." *CNN. com.* 1/6/18.

Staggs, Brooke. "California Didn't Make as Much on Marijuana Taxes as Expected; Black Market Blamed." *OCRegister.com.* 5/10/18.

Staggs, Brooke. "First Tests are In, and 1 in 5 Marijuana Samples in California Isn't Making Grade." *OCRegister.com.* 7/26/18.

"State-by-State Medical Marijuana Laws." *ProCon.org.*

"Statement from Inslee regarding reports that USDOJ will rescind Cole Memo." Governor.wa.gov. 1/4/18. "The STATES Act." *Warren.senate.gov.*

Stewart, Briar. "Why Colorado's Black Market for Marijuana is Booming 4 Years After Legalization." *CBC.ca.* 5/28/18.

Sulak, Dustin. "Introduction to the Endocannabinoid System." *NORML.org.*

"Taxation of Marihuana" (House of Representatives Committee on Ways and Means, 5/4/1937). *ProCon.org. THCUniversity.org.*

Thiele, Elizabeth A. et al. "Cannabidiol in Patients with Seizures Associated with Lennox-Gastaut Syndrome: A Randomised, Double-Blind, Placebo-Controlled Phase 3 Trial." *TheLancet.com.* 1/24/18.

Thompson, Matt. "The Mysterious History of 'Marijuana.'" *NPR.org.* 7/22/13.

Tomoski, Miroslav. "Big Pharma Is Donating To Anti-Legalization To Gain A Head Start In The Weed Business." *Herb.co.* 10/19/17.

Touw, M. "The Religious and Medicinal Uses of Cannabis in China, India and Tibet." *NCBI.nlm.nih.gov.* 1981.

"Transition Period Requirements." *BCC.ca.gov.*

"Trends in Cannabis Analysis." *CannabisScienceTech.com.* 2/27/18.

"U.S. Cannabis Operator Acreage Holdings Details Plans to Go Public." *NewCannabisVentures.com.* 9/21/18.

"The U.S. Hemp Industry grows to $820mm in sales in 2017." *HempBizJournal.com.*

"U.S. Voters Believe Comey More Than Trump, Quinnipiac University National Poll Finds; Support For Marijuana Hits New High." *Poll.qu.edu.* 4/26/18.

Venegas, Zachary. "Cannabis Industry Slow Rollouts and Consolidations to Drive Ancillary Partnerships, M&A." *CannabisBusinessExecutive.com.* 11/5/18.

Wagner, Pete and Wendy Sawyer. "Mass Incarceration: The Whole Pie 2018." *PrisonPolicy.org.* 3/14/18.

Weixel, Nathaniel. "Senators Call for DOJ to Stop Blocking Medical Marijuana Research." *TheHill.com.* 4/12/18.

"What to Know About the New Bill: Marijuana Data Collection Act." *TheCannabisIndustry.org.* 7/24/18.

"Who Are the Patients Receiving Medical Marijuana through the Federal Government's Compassionate IND Program?" *ProCon.org.*

"Why California is the World's Largest Cannabis Market." *InvestingNews.com.* 1/24/18.

Wilder, Zoe. "Cannabis Industry CEO Offers Tips on How to Stay Ahead of the Competition." *MerryJane.com.* 3/8/17.

Williams, Sean. "Combined, Canada's Top 8 Pot Growers Could Yield 1.8 Million Kilograms Annually by 2020." *Fool.com.* 6/18/18.

Williams, Sean. "Big Business Is Taking Over California's Marijuana Industry." *Fool.com.* 6/23/18.

Williams, Sean. "Ready or Not, Big Business Is Taking Over the Marijuana Industry." *Fool.com.* 2/25/17.

Winkler, Natasha. "Blunt Talk: Big Green Myth." *YellowScene.com.* 6/1/18.

Wu, Charles. "5 Things You Need To Know In Order To Succeed In The Cannabis Industry With Jennifer Sanders." *Medium. com.* 8/28/18.

Yakowicz, Will. "Legal Cannabis Entrepreneurs in California Get a Rude Awakening: A Thriving Black Market." *Inc.com.* 1/4/18.

Yost, Pete. "Feds Let Banks and Marijuana Sellers Do Business." *NBCBayArea.com.* 2/14/14.

Young, Saundra. "Marijuana Stops Child's Severe Seizures." *CNN. com.* 8/7/13.

Zaytsev, Michael. "What Every Cannabis Entrepreneur And Investor Must Know To Succeed." *Forbes.com.* 8/18/2017.

Zhang, Mona. "The Global Marijuana Market Will Soon Hit $31.4 Billion But Investors Should Be Cautious." *Forbes.com.* 11/7/17.

Zhang, Mona. "Legal Marijuana Is A Boon To The Economy, Finds Study." *Forbes.com.* 3/13/18.

Zinko, Carolyne. "A New Strain of Philanthropy." *GreenState.com.* 2/12/18.

Zochodne, Geoff. "Molson Coors Partnering with Quebec Pot Producer Hydropothecary to Develop Cannabis Beverages." *FinancialPost.com.* 8/1/18.

Zuardi, Antonio Waldo. "History of Cannabis as a Medicine: A Review." *NCBI.nlm.nih.gov.* 6/2006.

Additional Online Resources

Association of Cannabis Professionals. *CannabisProfessionals.org.*

"Cannabis Industry Events and Conferences." *Ganjapreneur.com.*

"Cannabis Investors." *NewCannabisVentures.com.*

The National Organization for the Reform of Marijuana Laws. *NORML.org.*

National Cannabis Industry Association. *TheCannabisIndustry.org.*

"Marijuana Investment Groups." *Ganjapreneur.com.*

Made in the USA
Columbia, SC
14 April 2020